Contents

Preface   v
Acknowledgments   vii

PART 1 COMMUNICATION AND ORGANISATIONS
Chapter 1   Introduction to Communication   2
Chapter 2   Communication in Organisations   21
Chapter 3   Marketing Communication   39
Chapter 4   Electronic Communication   53

PART 2 RESEARCH AND WRITING SKILLS
Chapter 5   Finding Information   72
Chapter 6   Effective Writing (1): The Writing Process   90
Chapter 7   Effective Writing (2): Style   105

PART 3 BUSINESS WRITING
Chapter 8   Business Correspondence   120
Chapter 9   The Business Report   142
Chapter 10   Other Written Forms   163

PART 4 ORAL, VISUAL AND NONVERBAL COMMUNICATION
Chapter 11   Nonverbal Communication   186
Chapter 12   Oral and Aural Communication   201
Chapter 13   Giving Talks and Presentations   218
Chapter 14   Visual Communication   236

PART 5 COMMUNICATION AT WORK
Chapter 15   Groups and Teams   256
Chapter 16   Meetings   275
Chapter 17   The Employment Interview   302

Appendix I   Punctuation   327
Appendix II   Grammar   341
Appendix III   Reported Speech   350
Appendix IV   Useful Internet Addresses   352

Bibliography   354
Index   356

Support Material for

COMMUNICATION FOR BUSINESS
3RD ED

by Henry McClave

Dynamic and easy to use, online support material for this book provides **lecturers** with:

* PowerPoint presentation slides

  To access lecturer support material on our secure site:

1. Go to www.gillmacmillan.ie/lecturers
2. Logon using your username and password. If you don't have a password, register online and we will email your password to you.

Preface

The third edition of *Communication for Business* has been revised to take into consideration changes in teaching practice and the business environment.

In our colleges there is a growing emphasis on self-directed learning and continual assessment. Increasingly, students are required to formulate their own research objectives, then retrieve, organise and evaluate information and finally present their findings in oral and written reports. It is common for this work to be carried out on a group basis.

These developments are to be welcomed as they encourage initiative and resourcefulness. They also help to develop information management, teamwork and communication skills. As students themselves are aware, such attributes and abilities are now highly valued by business employers.

Two new chapters are included in response to this new approach to learning. *Finding Information* has been written to help students locate and make effective use of the great quantity of information available in libraries and on the Internet. *Groups and Teams* informs students about the nature and structure of groups and should help them become more effective team members when working on group projects.

The business environment also changes constantly. Some of the most dramatic changes have occurred in information technology and hence the chapter on *Electronic Communication* has been extensively revised. Moreover, in recent years the workplace has become increasingly diverse and this is recognised in new sections on gender and multicultural communication.

It is important for students to appreciate that business communication is a practical, real-life activity. Every day, managers and employees face communication problems and complete communication tasks. To show communication in context, I have included a series of short features entitled 'Spotlight on Irish Business' in which business practitioners from some of Ireland's best-known companies talk about their experiences and approaches.

As with previous editions, *Communication for Business* could not have been written without the help and support of many individuals and organisations. In particular, I would like to thank the companies and their representatives who provided examples of best practice and who responded with great courtesy to my requests for information. These are: Aer Rianta, Bank of Ireland, the Industrial Development Authority, Intel, Jurys Doyle Hotel Group, KPMG, Superquinn and Tourism Ireland.

I would also like to acknowledge the support given by colleagues in the Faculty of Business, Dublin Institute of Technology. A special word of thanks is due to Ms Anne Ambrose, Faculty Librarian, whose expert knowledge was freely shared and whose encouragement proved invaluable.

Henry McClave

Acknowledgments

For permission to reproduce copyright material, grateful acknowledgment is made to the following: *The Irish Times* for two extracts; the *Sunday Tribune* for one extract; Methuen for an extract from *Advertising as Communication* by Gillian Dyer; and Routledge for an extract from *Social Skills in Interpersonal Communication* by Hargie *et al*.

The publishers have made every effort to trace copyright holders of materials used in this book. They will be glad to hear from any copyright holders who were not found before publication.

PART 1

Communication and Organisations

1 Introduction to Communication

It has long been recognised that good communication and interpersonal skills are vital for success in business. The ability to communicate clearly and persuasively is often cited as the key characteristic of the effective manager or administrator. High-level communication skills are also essential in specialised functions such as marketing, human resource management, public relations and secretarial work.

However, all employees (not managers or specialists alone) need to interact effectively if a business is to thrive. Communication is the means by which the individual employee conveys his or her wants, ideas and feelings to others. Without this sharing of information it would be impossible to make sound management decisions or co-ordinate the activities of the organisation as a whole.

The aim of this book, therefore, is to identify and describe the key communication skills that employers now demand. A number of features are included to help you achieve both understanding and proficiency in this vital area.

- **Explanation**
  Each chapter contains a full description of underlying communication concepts, ideas and principles. New trends and developments are identified.

- **Models**
  Many models of letters, reports, memos and other forms are provided. These suggest the most appropriate structure and style to use when communicating in writing.

- **Practical advice**
  Useful strategies and tips for improving communication skills are highlighted throughout the text.

- **Real-life examples**
  In a series called 'Spotlight on Irish Business', we give examples of best communication practice in Irish organisations.

- **Exercises and activities**
  Each chapter concludes with extensive suggestions for revision, discussion and practice.

In later chapters we will concentrate on specific communication skills in writing, speaking, working in teams and so on. First, however, it will be useful to gain insight into the nature and complexity of human communication, and so we begin in this chapter with an analysis of the communication process itself. The chapter continues with an account of common communication barriers and concludes with ten basic principles that should guide all communication activities.

THE PROCESS OF COMMUNICATION

Communication can be defined as the process by which ideas, information, opinions, attitudes and feelings are conveyed from one person to another. The *communicator* or *sender* is the person who initiates communication by sending a message. The *receiver* is the person who completes the communication by receiving the message and responding to it.

Most human communication is *two way*, that is, a person is both communicator and receiver at the same time (as in face-to-face communication) or alternates between the two roles (as in an exchange of letters). Moreover, many theorists extend the idea of communication to include the continuous 'inner conversation' each of us conducts in his or her own mind (*intrapersonal communication*).

Early models tended to describe communication as a linear process in which one step or phase followed another. More recent theories, however, see communication as composed of many components that interact *simultaneously*. These include message, medium, context, noise, etc. Changing any one component has an impact on all the others.

The key concepts in communication theory are illustrated in Exhibit 1.1 and described in detail below.

INITIATING COMMUNICATION

The process often begins with a deliberate intention or decision to send a message. For example, a manager may decide to put up a notice about the safe handling of machinery after seeing a young apprentice operating a machine in a careless manner. He then has to think about the wording of the notice, how many copies to make and where to place them on the factory floor. Most of the forms of communication described in this book are like this. They involve a conscious decision to communicate information, followed by careful thought and planning to ensure that the message is received and understood.

However, not all communication is deliberate in this way. Much communication in business takes the form of casual conversation, which is largely spontaneous and unrehearsed. Conversation is a natural human activity which we

Exhibit 1.1 The communication process

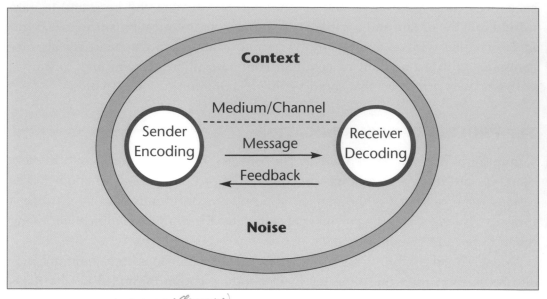

all enjoy. It is a vital source of information as well as a means of pleasure and relaxation, but it also carries risk. During an unguarded moment in conversation we may say something which we afterwards regret. At best, an ill-considered remark may cause temporary embarrassment; at worst, it may lead to a career setback or even dismissal.

Some forms of communication are entirely unintentional or involuntary. Through body language in particular we often leak information we would prefer the observer did not see. A nervous interviewee, for example, may unconsciously reveal his lack of confidence by fidgeting with his hands or sitting on the edge of his seat during an interview. Although unintentional, this behaviour carries a message that may strongly influence the receiver's judgment.

Moreover, the stimulus to communicate may have an internal or external source. Sometimes, thoughts or ideas simply occur to us that we think are worth communicating. Often, however, the desire to communicate is provoked by others' actions. We may be moved to respond by what other people do, conversational remarks they make or written messages they send us.

ENCODING THE MESSAGE

Before any piece of information can be transmitted it has to be encoded, i.e. represented in a set of symbols that make sense to the receiver. The two most important symbol systems we use in human communication are the *verbal* codes of written and spoken language. However, it should also be recognised that a great deal of ordinary communication is *nonverbal*. Even when we are speaking, we convey two-thirds of information through dress, body language and features of the voice. These codes are powerful and important elements in communication and are discussed further in Chapter 11. Other nonverbal codes that may be used include sign language, numbers, computer languages, pictures, photographs and so on.

A selection of communication codes

- Written language
- Spoken language
- Dress
- Body language
- Pictures, photographs and graphic illustrations
- Sign language, Braille, semaphore
- Numbers
- Computer languages.

Several factors may influence the way the sender encodes the message:
- her objectives in communicating
- her knowledge of a particular language
- the receiver's age or linguistic ability
- the medium used
- the context.

Two particular points should be remembered at the encoding stage. First, communication is *dynamic*. Every act of communication affects and develops the relationship between the sender and the receiver in some way. What is said cannot be unsaid, only modified or built on, so we can apologise for a tactless remark or even withdraw it, but never erase it completely. Communication can never be reversed. That is why it is so important to think *before* saying something.

A second, related point is that almost every message has a *content* and a *feeling* aspect. The content of the message is the factual information it contains. The feeling aspect refers to the subjective feeling the message conveys. This is most obvious in oral communication, where the sender's voice may carry clear overtones of sympathy, deference, excitement, etc. However, subjective elements are present even in the most functional pieces of writing. A letter may tell someone factually that her complaint is being dealt with or her query answered, but it will also *please* her if it is prompt, well laid out and has a friendly tone.

Indeed, some kinds of messages are almost wholly concerned with relationships. If someone makes a passing remark such as 'Hi Tom, lovely day, isn't it?' the content is almost irrelevant. The remark is made for another reason entirely: to acknowledge the other person and tell him that his friendship is valued. We make many of these simple but vital social connections every day.

MEDIUM

The medium is the means used to transmit the message. A useful way of categorising media is to group them under five headings: *written, oral, visual, electronic* and *mass* (see Exhibit 1.2 below). A letter, for instance, is a written medium because it depends primarily on the written word to convey the message. An interview is an example of an oral medium because it involves at least two people talking to each other. Television is a mass medium because it reaches millions of people every day.

Some of the factors that influence the choice of medium are:

- purpose of communication
- complexity of the message
- need for a record
- importance of immediate feedback
- distance between sender and receiver
- need for personal touch
- cost.

A written form is usually best if a message is complicated or a record needs to be kept. An efficient business, for example, ensures that all contracts and agreements made with other parties are put down in writing! An oral medium, however, is preferable if an immediate response is required or face-to-face contact is desirable. Often the simplest way to make an enquiry is to pick up the telephone and speak directly to the person concerned. Visual media such as charts and graphs can be used to make the message more easily understood or more visually appealing. Media that combine sound, vision and movement, e.g. television, video and multimedia, have the most powerful impact of all.

In recent years there has been a dramatic growth in the use of electronic, computer-based media such as fax, e-mail and the Internet. At one time it was thought that these would take over entirely and we would have the so-called 'paperless office'. This has not happened, although e-mail is now increasingly used instead of letters and memos. It seems likely that the more traditional paper-based methods will survive along with the newer methods, providing the business user with an ever-widening choice. At the same time, the trend towards electronic communication will no doubt become more pronounced.

Exhibit 1.2 Media checklist

Written media Letter Report Memo Newsletter Press release Company magazine Advertising leaflet	**Features** Provide a written record; can relay complex information; message can be carefully thought out; mistakes can be removed during revision; can be easily duplicated; receiver can reread as required. **But** take time to produce; more formal and impersonal than speech; feedback is slow; once sent the message is difficult to change.
Oral media Conversation (face to face or telephone) Interview Meeting Presentation Oral briefing	**Features** More direct and personal; feedback is immediate; messages can be adjusted in light of feedback; speech can be supported with body language; qualities of voice can be exploited; views can be exchanged quickly. **But** often no record; less time to prepare; impossible to unsay what has been said; interaction more difficult to control.
Visual media Nonverbal Diagrams Charts Photographs Models	**Features** Have immediate impact; support and reinforce verbal presentations; simplify information; stimulate and add interest; can represent reality quite closely; cross linguistic barriers. **But** may give more ambiguous messages; may oversimplify; verbal annotation often required; charts, etc. less easy to produce than text.
Electronic media Video Telephone Fax E-mail Internet	**Features** Provide fast communication over distance; can carry both verbal and visual information; can have powerful impact; information can be easily recorded and stored; can save money by making travel unnecessary. **But** networks and equipment expensive to install; usage costs are high; users may need special training; may be security risk to information.

Mass media	Features
Television Radio Press Film	Important sources of information and entertainment; reach large number of people; have enormous impact; powerful vehicles for advertising and forming opinions. **But** production costs are high; influence on society often questioned and criticised; of limited relevance to small businesses.

CHANNEL

The distinction between *medium* and *channel* is not always clear. For example, either term can be applied to television. It is helpful, however, to think of the medium as the vehicle that carries the message and the channel as the route along which it travels. In oral communication the medium is speech and the channel is the air that carries the sound waves between speaker and listener. Other channels include the postal system, telephone lines, cable television and computer networks. There has been a significant growth in electronic channels in particular, enabling messages to be sent over distance with ever-increasing variety, speed and efficiency.

How information travels

- Television channels
- Radio
- Surface mail
- Computer networks
- Courier services
- Telephone/fax.

DECODING THE MESSAGE

Successful communication cannot be said to have taken place unless the receiver hears, reads or sees the message without distortion and then interprets it correctly. This process of making sense of the message is called *decoding*. The receiving skills of listening, reading and note-taking are important at this stage.

In practice, many messages are misunderstood, sometimes with disastrous results. This may happen because:

- the receiver is careless or inattentive
- the sender has used specialist language that the receiver finds difficult to understand

- the message is ambiguous
- the receiver allows emotion to influence his interpretation of the message.

FEEDBACK

The communication loop is completed when the receiver responds to the message. The receiver may respond positively by acting on the message or storing it for future reference, or it may cause him to change his attitudes or opinions in the way the communicator intended. But the receiver's response may not always be what is expected. For example, he may ignore or discard the message if he is too busy or feels its contents are irrelevant. This happens more often than communicators like to think.

Feedback is an important response as it enables the communicator to judge whether or not the message has been understood and accepted. Feedback can also be either positive or negative. Watch an audience listening to a speaker. Some members of the audience may be encouraging the speaker with nods, smiles and appreciative noises. Others, however, may be showing their lack of interest by yawning or fidgeting. In either case, the feedback they are giving provides the speaker with valuable, if sometimes chastening, information.

CONTEXT

All communication is context bound. This means that *time* and *place* can have a significant impact on its outcome. Give a person an important message late on Friday evening and the chances are he will have forgotten it entirely by Monday morning. Reprimand an employee in front of his peers instead of in the privacy of an office and you will likely make the situation worse. In fact, the whole nature of communication can change as it moves from one context to another. Watch how language, relationships and social interactions change among the members of a group as they move from a meeting room to a more informal setting such as a pub.

NOISE

The concept of 'noise' was first introduced in a famous early model of communication developed by Shannon and Weaver (see Exhibit 1.3). Shannon worked for the Bell Telephone Laboratory and both he and Weaver were primarily interested in improving the transmission of telephone signals. 'Noise' was whatever interfered with or distorted the signal. In later theory, however, 'noise' is taken to mean anything, either physical or psychological, that interferes with the communication process at any point. A noisy background is obviously 'noise', but so are psychological barriers like lack of concentration or mistrust between sender and receiver.

Exhibit 1.3 Shannon and Weaver's model

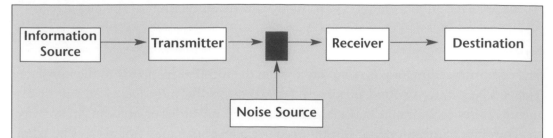

Shannon and Weaver's model has been influential in communication theory. Unlike the diagram in Exhibit 1.1 it is a linear model which shows communication occurring in one direction only.

An *information source* creates a *message*, e.g. a person speaking into a telephone. The message is then formed into a *signal* by a *transmitter* and sent along a channel (telephone line). The signals are reconstructed by the *receiver* and then passed to their *destination* (person listening).

Although imitated and adapted many times, the model has also been criticised. It ignores feedback and fails to introduce many concepts that are now considered important, e.g. code, medium, context, etc.

Good accounts of the many different communication models can be found in Fiske (1990) and McQuail and Windahl (1993).

BARRIERS TO COMMUNICATION

Because human communication is complex, effective communication is difficult and mistakes are often made. We can see this in our ordinary dealings with family, friends, neighbours and colleagues at work. 'Why does she/he never listen?' we complain when someone doesn't respond to our messages in the way we expect. Sometimes we are forced to acknowledge our own inadequacies as communicators. Perhaps we make a tactless remark and then have to withdraw it. 'But that's not what I really meant,' we say.

In business, difficulties with communication can cause considerable disruption. Good business opportunities can be lost or disastrous management decisions made. A serious breakdown in communication can put the very future of a company at risk.

Communication errors can never be completely eliminated. Nevertheless, we are likely to be more successful communicators if we are aware of the factors that cause communication to fail. Here is a brief account of some of the obstacles that stand in the way of effective communication and how these can be avoided or overcome.

PHYSICAL BARRIERS

Some physical problems are internal to the communicator and physiological in origin, while others are located in the communicator's environment. Among the former are conditions such as poor hearing or eyesight, illness, tiredness or stress. Among the latter could be counted distractions such as an excessively warm or cold office, uncomfortable seating, poor telephone connections or the din of traffic heard from outside. If a person's communication difficulties are caused by illness or tiredness, he may need to seek medical advice or learn to manage stress more effectively. External distractions may have a simpler solution – for example, closing a window or altering the thermostat on the air-conditioning system.

LANGUAGE BARRIERS

In order to convey a message to another person we must convert ideas that are often vaguely defined at the outset into language that is clear and precise (the process referred to as *encoding*). Yet we know that it is far from easy to find the exact words that are needed, and that inaccurate or inappropriate use of language is a common cause of communication breakdown. For example:

- Mistakes in *spelling*, *punctuation* and *grammar* invariably harm communication. They make written messages more difficult to understand and damage the sender's credibility. Be careful to eliminate these before you send out any written document.

- Although there is nothing inherently wrong with *jargon* it can disrupt good communication. Jargon denotes the technical vocabulary of a specialised trade or profession and it normally enables fellow professionals to communicate with one another in an efficient way. However, such language should be avoided with nonprofessional receivers, who often find it baffling.

- *Slang* refers to informal expressions, often funny or colourful, that become popular with certain groups for a period of time. The use of slang is acceptable in ordinary conversation (so long as it is inoffensive) but can cause problems in formal business communication where it may detract from the seriousness of the message.

NONVERBAL BARRIERS

It is thought that we convey much more information nonverbally than we do verbally when communicating face to face. Facial expression, posture and eye movement all reveal our feelings and attitudes to the receiver. Moreover, when there is conflict between a verbal and nonverbal signal, it is the nonverbal signal that tends to be believed. For example, an interviewee may assert that she is outgoing and confident, yet unwittingly contradict this claim through nervous or hesitant body language. Thus, business communicators need to be aware of the nonverbal messages they send and to control body language that undermines the message they wish to get across.

POOR LISTENING

Many relationship experts refer to listening as the most important of all communication skills. Good listening gives us a better understanding of the other person's point of view, maintains friendships, helps business collaboration and increases intimacy in personal relationships. Unfortunately, many of us haven't learned to listen well. We are so preoccupied with our own concerns that we don't attend to what the other person is saying. Or we listen superficially – we hear what is being said overtly, but miss important clues about what the other person is really thinking or feeling 'behind the words'. Effective listening is active, empathic and alert to moods and aspirations that may be left unspoken.

'Nelson's sick'

Sometimes simple mistakes can have serious consequences.

In 1996 the South African currency, the rand, fell dramatically on the international money markets because of a rumour that the president, Nelson Mandela, was ill. It is believed the rumour was started when a London stockbroker heard a South African colleague on the telephone saying, 'Nelson's sick.'

He was actually saying 'Yeltsin's sick' (the Russian president) but the damage was done. The rand plummeted twenty per cent against the US dollar and never recovered.

Source: *Time Magazine*

PROBLEMS WITH PERCEPTION

Perception is how we make sense of ourselves and the world around us. We perceive the external world through the senses of sight, hearing, touch, taste and smell. At the same time, we are aware of various internal stimuli. Some of these are physiologically based, such as sensations of pleasure, pain, heat, cold, etc. Others are mental in origin, such as our thoughts, daydreams and fantasies. The brain registers these different stimuli and organises them into shapes and patterns that we can understand. Sometimes these stimuli mislead us, as the well-known optical illusions in Exhibit 1.4 demonstrate.

Perception is both *selective* and *unique to each individual*. Even in our quietest moments we are bombarded with a myriad of stimuli. We cannot possibly attend to all stimuli at once. They would overwhelm us if we tried. Instead we select for attention those that are important to us and filter out those that are not. Moreover, how we interpret a particular set of stimuli depends on a wide range of factors: our knowledge and experience, age, gender, cultural background, even the job we do.

Mistakes can arise if we assume that other people perceive things exactly as we do. Often they don't, and this is a common cause of communication failure. For example, consider how staff may receive a memo announcing a major restructuring of an organisation. Some may welcome the news because they perceive this as an opportunity to gain new experience or enhance their careers. Others, however, may be fearful of change or distrustful of management's intentions. However carefully the message is constructed it is still likely to be perceived differently by different people and to provoke very different (and perhaps quite negative) responses.

Exhibit 1.4 What do you see?

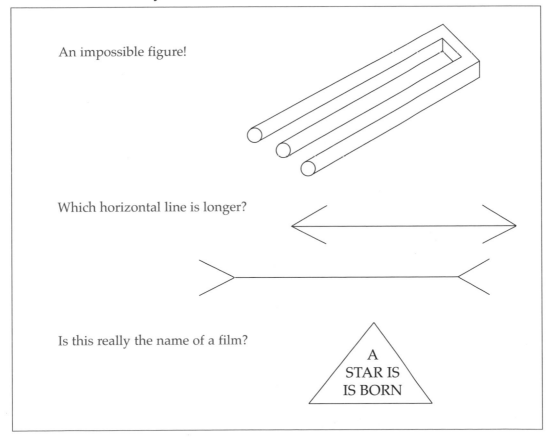

POOR SELF-KNOWLEDGE

Developing a true perception of ourselves and others is one of the most challenging aspects of human understanding and communication. Each person has a self-image built up from his life history. In general, we tend to accept information that reinforces our self-image and shy away from information that conflicts with it. However, we sometimes need to develop a more realistic picture of ourselves if we want to become effective communicators. For example, a person may see himself as rather quiet and shy: 'Don't want to offend anyone, like to mind my own business.' Others may regard him as aloof, distant and unsociable. A strongly extroverted person may not realise that to others he comes across as aggressive and domineering. Thus, learning to become a good communicator is not simply about learning skills, important though these are. It also involves developing a more truthful image of our attitudes and behaviour and how they affect interpersonal relationships.

ATTITUDINAL BARRIERS

Stereotyping, prejudice and *unwarranted attribution* are among the attitudinal barriers that can do the most damage to our ability to relate effectively to others.

- **Stereotyping**
  We stereotype other people when we assume that they will behave in a certain way simply because of their appearance, role or membership of a particular social group. For example, the small, plump person is always 'cheerful and jolly', the person who wears a formal suit is 'conservative', the person with a tattoo or shaven head is 'rebellious, a danger to society'. But are these impressions true? We may be surprised to find that the conservatively dressed individual has radical views, or that the six-foot giant with the studded jacket and the Harley Davidson turns out to be as gentle as a lamb. Judging by appearance only gives an incomplete and often distorted picture of what the person is really like.

- **Prejudice**
  Prejudice is an attitude of hostility based on faulty generalisations such as stereotypes. It may be directed against individuals or groups. The prejudiced person may believe that the other person or group is inferior, subversive, threatening, not fully part of the community and so on. We can see how damaging prejudice can be to communication. If we consider the other person less than ourselves, we are unlikely to value or trust what they say. As

prejudice is often the result of ignorance, more inclusive approaches to education may help reduce its effects.

- **Attribution**

  Even when we avoid stereotyping or prejudice, we may still make the mistake of attributing certain characteristics to a person on flimsy evidence. Even before we meet someone we may have already formed a picture of them from other people's descriptions: 'You'll like Sean, he's very easy to get on with', 'Mary's bright, just finished her MBA', 'Watch what you tell Michael. He has the boss's ear' and so on. Attributions like these should be treated with caution. At best, they give a true but partial account of the person. At worst, they may be seriously misleading. Having an accurate picture of other people is vital for effective communication, but it is something that can only be built up slowly through time, insight and regular contact.

THE PRINCIPLES OF EFFECTIVE COMMUNICATION ▇▇▇▇▇▇

In the remaining chapters of this book you will find much practical advice on how to use specific forms and methods of business communication. First, however, it should be helpful to note a number of broad guidelines that take account of the barriers just discussed and can be applied to almost any situation where careful, planned communication is required.

As communicator

1. **Think carefully about your objectives before communicating**

   Ask yourself what you are trying to achieve. Do you want to inform, persuade, advise or consult the receiver? What kind of response do you need? When you have answered questions like these you can then begin to think about the content of the message and how it is to be delivered.

2. **Put yourself in the receiver's shoes**

   Remember that the receiver's perception or frame of reference may not be the same as your own. You think, 'Any reasonable person would support this proposal', but your boss may be subject to political or budgetary constraints, for example, that you know nothing about.

3. **Choose the right medium or combination of media**

   Difficulties can arise if the wrong medium is used. For instance, when giving a talk, you may leave the audience bewildered if you try to describe a complicated process by means of speech alone. A combination of words and graphics may be necessary.

4. **Organise your ideas and express them carefully**

   Take time to structure your ideas in a logical sequence. In choosing your words, take into consideration the receiver's understanding and linguistic ability. In general, use words that are familiar to the receiver. If you feel it necessary to use a technical term unique to a particular trade or profession, explain it in a way the receiver can understand. Also, try to use language suited to the context in which communication is taking place. Expressions that are acceptable in a formal letter may seem pretentious if used in a note sent to a colleague. Informal language that is appropriate on the shop floor may be inappropriate in a committee meeting.

5. **Consider the context**

   Breakdowns in communication often occur because the receiver is given information at the wrong time or in the wrong place. Even an important message can be promptly forgotten if the receiver is busy or preoccupied in thought. The setting in which communication occurs can also be significant. If you are conducting an interview, for example, you should ensure that the interview environment is private and will facilitate an open exchange of information. In general, always put yourself in the receiver's position and try to anticipate any difficulties or concerns he or she may have.

6. **Check for feedback**

   Make sure your message has been received and understood. For example, when speaking face to face or giving a talk, look out for signs of puzzlement in your listeners. Be prepared to repeat or re-explain if necessary.

Although the main responsibility for effective communication rests with the sender of the message, the receiver also has to contribute. There are two main ways in which the receiver can be responsible for a breakdown in communication: first, by misunderstanding the message through carelessness or lack of concentration; second, by failing to respond in an appropriate manner, e.g. failing to reply promptly to an enquiry or invitation.

As receiver

1. **Give the message your full attention**

   Many messages are misunderstood because the receiver is daydreaming or not concentrating. Focus on the message and try to ignore or remove distractions.

2. **Interpret the message correctly**

   Interpreting the message requires effort. If you are unsure about what is being said, ask for clarification. Check the meaning of unfamiliar words or references. In spoken communication, listen actively and with empathy. Be alert for nonverbal nuances that may subtly alter the meaning of the communication.

3. **Keep an open mind**

You should not allow dislike of the communicator or disagreement with his or her beliefs to influence your judgment. Try to acknowledge your own prejudices and make an objective assessment of the message, no matter what your relationship with the sender. Reflect on the information you are given and try not to jump to conclusions.

4. **Record information you are likely to forget**

'Now what on earth was that telephone number?' This is the kind of despairing remark we all make when we forget to record important details. Listeners in particular should take the time to jot down factual information they are likely to forget, e.g. names, dates, telephone numbers, etc. The information should be recorded in a secure and accessible place – not, for example, scrawled on a scrap of paper that happens to be lying on the desk!

5. **Respond appropriately**

Respond positively to the communicator by providing feedback, following up enquiries or taking whatever other action is required.

ASSIGNMENTS

REVISION

1. With the aid of a diagram, outline the main elements in the communication process.
2. Explain the difference between *intentional* and *unintentional* communication.
3. What does the term *encoding* mean in communication theory?
4. Communication is said to have both a *content* and a *feeling* aspect. What does this mean?
5. Set out the strengths and weaknesses of any *three* of the following media groups: written, oral/aural, visual, electronic, mass.
6. Comment briefly on the role of the receiver in the communication process.
7. Why is *feedback* an important element in effective communication?
8. How can *context* affect the communication process?
9. What is meant by *noise*?
10. Give examples of communication barriers that are (a) physiological in origin (b) located in the communicator's environment.
11. Name *three* aspects of language that can create a communication barrier.

12. Can you define *perception*? How can differences in perception cause problems in communication?
13. Explain what happens when we stereotype other people. Why does this make communication with them more difficult?
14. What is *prejudice* and how does it interfere with good communication between individuals or groups?
15. Set out basic principles of good practice for business communicators.

For discussion

1. Give your views on the following statements.
   - 'You're either a born communicator or you're not. Learning communication skills isn't going to make much difference.'
   - 'I hate people who always think out what they want to say. It's far better to be natural and say the first thing that comes into your head.'
   - 'Most of our communication problems would be solved if people listened instead of talking all the time.'
   - 'I can tell within five seconds what a person is like. All I need to do is look at them.'
   - 'The thing about stereotypes is that most of the time they turn out to be true.'
2. Many job advertisements nowadays specify good communication and interpersonal skills as essential requirements. Do you think the emphasis on communication skills is justified?
3. Discuss the way a change in context can change the way we communicate. For example, why is it easier to talk informally to friends than it is to talk formally in class? Why is a letter to a penpal easier to write than a letter of application for a job? Would it be better if communication with tutors, superiors at work, etc. were less formal?
4. It is sometimes said that spending too much time watching television or playing computer games harms our ability to communicate effectively. Do you think this is true?

Activities and exercises

1. A useful first exercise is to identify your own communication needs. In groups, list the kinds of communication skills that you think will be required in your chosen profession. Then, think about your own individual needs. List those areas where you think you can improve most. Keep the list – it can become your set of personal objectives for the course.

I want to get better at . . .

1. _____
2. _____
3. _____
4. _____
5. _____

2. Look again at the model of communication in Exhibit 1.1. Is this a suitable model for all kinds of communication? Can you devise a better model to represent either of these two situations?

   (a) A public speaker addressing a large audience.

   (b) A newsreader reading the nine o'clock news.

   NOTE This may be a good opportunity to look at some other models in the literature.

3. Try to recall any situation in the recent past where you were involved in or witnessed a breakdown in communication. Share your experience with the group, explaining, if you can, why the breakdown occurred.

4. What precise communication problem is implied in each of the following comments?

   • 'Hold on a minute . . . I think someone's knocking on the door.'

   • 'He said we'd meet sometime this afternoon, but he didn't say where.'

   • 'This room's a bit stuffy, isn't it?'

   • 'We'll be discussing the innovation diffusion hypothesis . . . whatever that is!'

   • 'And don't forget . . . oh, she's gone . . . I hope she heard me.'

   • 'What was that you were saying?'

   • 'Imagine sending me a memo! You'd think he'd have taken the trouble to talk to me in person.'

   • 'Did we get any reply from McCann's yet?'

5. In groups, write a script for and then role-play one of the situations below. In some scenarios, the businessperson should handle the situation well; in some, badly.

   (a) A shop assistant dealing with a difficult customer who is complaining about faulty goods.

   (b) A supervisor reprimanding an employee who believes he or she is being wrongly blamed.

   (c) The manager of a public transport company talking to a very irate customer on a radio programme.

   (d) A shop assistant explaining how a camcorder works to a customer who is slow to understand.

   In a follow-up discussion try to answer these questions: was the person

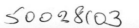

dealing with the problem a good or bad communicator? How do you distinguish between the two?

6. Interview the person sitting beside you. Ask about their place of origin, school, hobbies, likes and dislikes, favourite films, etc. You might then use this information to introduce your colleague to the rest of the group.

    Has your perception of the other person changed now that you know a little more about him or her? Were there any things you learned that surprised you?

7. Write a short essay on *one* of the following topics.

    (a) Communication is much more complex than we think.

    (b) The main barriers to effective interpersonal communication.

    (c) The importance of attitudes and perception in communication.

2 Communication in Organisations

In Chapter 1 we looked at the process of communication and described its components and principles. We now turn our attention to communication in organisations and consider the nature and processes of *internal* communication.

An organisation may be defined as a *'system which is designed and operated to achieve specific organisational objectives'* (Tiernan *et al.*, 1996: 2). Organisations are everywhere; indeed, it would be impossible to imagine modern life without them. Think how many organisations you belong to. You may be a student at college or working in a business. It is probable that you are also affiliated to one or more social or sports organisations – perhaps a college club or a voluntary organisation like the Red Cross. Organisations enable their members to achieve goals they could not achieve by themselves. All organisations need effective communication systems in order to function efficiently.

Internal communication refers to the exchange of information that occurs among people *within the organisation*. For example, a business manager is communicating internally when she briefs her chief executive, consults with other department heads or passes instructions down to her subordinates. Such communication is essential. Executives need timely and accurate information in order to make correct decisions. For their part, junior staff expect to be given clear instructions and need to be able to express their wishes and concerns to management.

INTERNAL COMMUNICATION CHANNELS

Look inside any business organisation, large or small, during the working day and you will find that internal communication is continuous and all pervasive. In her office, the managing director is meeting with the head of information technology to discuss the introduction of a new computer system; in the main entrance, a secretary is pinning up a notice about new fire regulations; on the shop floor, a supervisor explains to an apprentice how a machine works; in the canteen, the catering staff are gossiping about the new canteen manager over their morning cups of coffee and so on throughout the building. It is this buzz of communication that keeps the activities of the business and the relationships among people within it in a constant state of change and development.

Internal communication channels are the lines along which information is transferred. Traditionally, these channels have been described in terms of the formal organisation chart (Exhibit 2.1).

Exhibit 2.1 Information flow

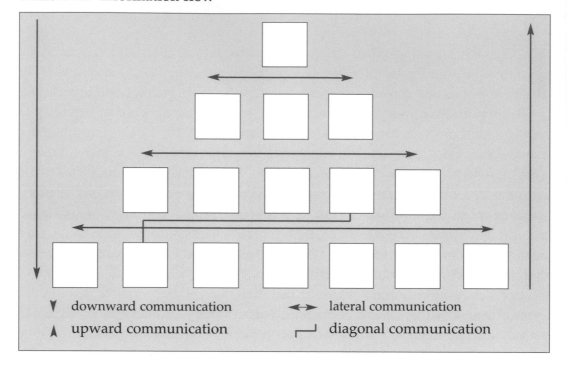

The hierarchical structure of most organisations causes information to flow in *four* directions:

- *downwards* from higher to lower levels of authority
- *upwards* from lower to higher levels
- *horizontally* between peer groups and people at the same level of power and responsibility
- *diagonally* between different levels of different departments.

Downward communication

This describes the transfer of information about management decisions, policies and attitudes to those lower in the hierarchy. Sometimes information travelling along this line will originate with the board or top management and be passed on to middle management only. Sometimes it will cascade all the way down to the most junior staff.

In this process of transferring information downwards, heads of department and supervisors have a crucial role. They themselves are often the source of the message. At other times, they have the difficult task of receiving instructions from above, interpreting them correctly and then passing them along the line in such a way that junior staff can understand what is required.

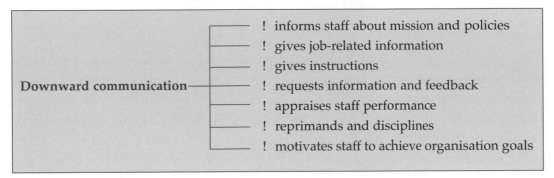

Downward communication
- ! informs staff about mission and policies
- ! gives job-related information
- ! gives instructions
- ! requests information and feedback
- ! appraises staff performance
- ! reprimands and disciplines
- ! motivates staff to achieve organisation goals

UPWARD COMMUNICATION

A good internal communication system should also promote a free flow of information and ideas upwards from subordinates to superiors. There are practical advantages in encouraging employees both to give feedback and to initiate communication of their own. For instance, facilities such as grievance meetings that allow staff complaints to be dealt with in a fair and sympathetic way provide a useful safety valve in industrial relations.

But a good system should do more than allow staff to 'let off steam'. It should also encourage them to contribute to the efficiency of the business by putting forward suggestions based on practical knowledge and experience that superiors may not have. Sometimes, employees can suggest quite simple improvements that prove invaluable to their organisations.

It is particularly important to provide opportunities for middle and junior managers to communicate upwards. They have responsibility for putting company policy into practice in the departments under their control and for ensuring that the daily routine work is carried out. They quickly become disenchanted if used merely as a vehicle for downward flow of orders and information. Their expertise needs to be tapped – otherwise their talents are just being wasted.

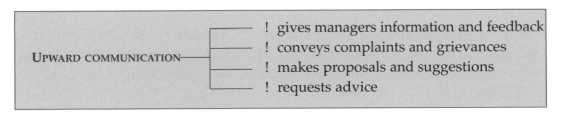

UPWARD COMMUNICATION
- ! gives managers information and feedback
- ! conveys complaints and grievances
- ! makes proposals and suggestions
- ! requests advice

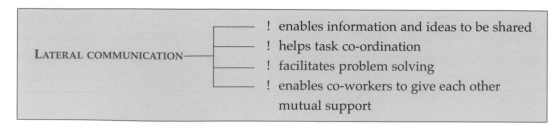

LATERAL COMMUNICATION

This describes the flow of information between people or departments at the same level in the organisation. The increasing use of specialised departments makes effective lateral communication essential. Whether this happens or not often depends on the attitudes of the various department heads. Too much competition between departments can lead to suspicion and hostility, and eventually to whole areas of the business being shut off from each other. Further problems arise if the organisation is large or departments are in different geographical locations.

Teamworking is a modern way of facilitating contact between the various departments in an organisation.

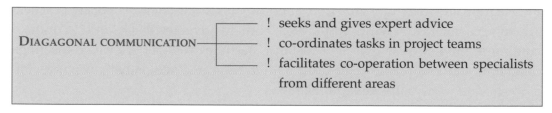

DIAGONAL COMMUNICATION

Situations often arise at work where a person needs help from someone in another department who is senior or junior to herself. For example, suppose a supervisor is having problems with an operative, perhaps over poor timekeeping. Before taking disciplinary action she seeks advice from the head of personnel, someone to whom she does not normally report. This is a case of diagonal communication.

One of the dangers in diagonal communication is that the person immediately above in the chain of command may not be informed about what is going on. This should be avoided as it can lead to misunderstanding and resentment.

FORMAL AND INFORMAL COMMUNICATION

Communication in organisations can be either formal or informal. Formal communication generally follows the formal organisation structure and uses methods that are officially sanctioned by management. Messages sent by report, memo, bulletin or official briefing are all examples of such communication.

The benefits of formal communication are:

- Information is distributed in a predictable way, usually following the chain of command.
- The message is carefully prepared and less likely to be distorted in transmission.
- The message carries authority.
- A record of the message is often retained.

The disadvantages are:
- Preparing and delivering the message may take time.
- The information given may have a management bias.
- Some employees may find formal channels intimidating to use.

THE GRAPEVINE

Few aspects of organisational behaviour are so vilified as the grapevine. Yet like the weeds that keep reappearing in your garden, it is impossible to eliminate.

An organisation chart shows the formal reporting relationship between managers and employees. What the chart cannot show is the informal organisation, that is, the ever-shifting network of informal contacts and relationships that exists largely outside management control (Exhibit 2.2). It is the grapevine that maintains and develops these contacts. Two employees whispering in a corridor, raucous laughter in the canteen, someone dropping into the office for a chat – these are all indicators of the grapevine at work.

Despite the many criticisms that are made of it, the grapevine has several positive features.
- It is the social glue that holds groups together at work.
- It is often the only source of vital information for employees.
- It is fast and used far more frequently than formal channels.
- Contrary to a widely held view, grapevine information has been found to be mainly accurate.
- Managers often use the grapevine both as a source of information and as a means of floating ideas and proposals before they are made official.
- Communicating informally is a natural, human activity which enlivens the workplace and gives pleasure to many people.

However, there is a negative side to the grapevine which should always be taken into account.
- As the diagram on the next page shows, grapevine information travels an unpredictable path that is dependent on social relationships, chance meetings and so on. Some people may be bypassed either by accident or by design.
- Information is transmitted mainly by word of mouth. Small inaccuracies and

distortions may creep into the message as it travels from one person to another.

- The nature of grapevine information may cause problems. Some of it consists of rumour and gossip, which can be damaging either to individuals or to the organisation as a whole.

These problems indicate that the grapevine should always be treated with caution. It tends to expand in closed and secretive organisations where official communication is relatively sparse. It also flourishes at times of major organisational change when employees become uncertain and anxious. The most effective way to counteract any damage it may do is to provide regular, up-to-date information to staff using official channels.

Exhibit 2.2 Informal communication network

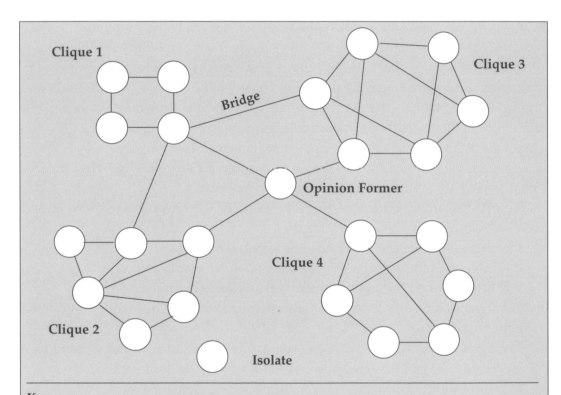

Key:
Clique: Informal group with close ties
Opinion former: Informal leader who links between different groups
Isolate: Person who has minimal contact with others
Bridge: Person who belongs to one clique and has contacts in another

Adapted from Kreps (1990: 223)

BARRIERS TO EFFECTIVE INTERNAL COMMUNICATION ▬▬▬

While some organisations have an outstanding record in providing for the exchange of information between management and staff, many others have done relatively little in this area. The following are some of the main organisational barriers to effective communication.

OPPOSITION FROM SENIOR MANAGEMENT

Senior managers may be afraid that:
- information may be used by employees in negotiating over pay and conditions
- if they brief employees they may be faced with awkward questions about company plans or about their own performance
- giving some information may lead to increasing demands for more
- information may be leaked to competitors.

A more unworthy reason for withholding information may be the claim that employees have no interest in management information or cannot understand it. Yet progressive organisations have found that none of these objections are justified.

PROBLEMS AT MIDDLE MANAGEMENT LEVEL

Middle managers such as department and section heads occupy an important place in the communication chain. Problems that can arise at this level are:
- **Information overload**: The manager has too much information to cope with and is incapable of distributing every message she receives. Messages are mislaid or forgotten about until they are no longer relevant.
- **Gatekeeping**: The manager deliberately withholds information. This may happen because of rivalries or personality conflicts among staff. The manager may think that holding on to information confers a power which she is unwilling to surrender.

PROBLEMS AT STAFF LEVELS

Junior staff and shop floor workers may have little understanding of or interest in the work done by their superiors. They may be apathetic towards communication initiatives or suspicious of management's intentions in giving information. They may also lack confidence in making suggestions or complaints. If they make mistakes they may be fearful of reporting these to their superiors.

ORGANISATION SIZE AND MANAGEMENT STYLE

The larger and more complex the organisation, the more difficult it becomes to establish and maintain effective communication links. Where there are hundreds or perhaps thousands of employees, senior management can seem remote to the ordinary worker. Departments can become so specialised that experts in different areas have difficulty understanding each other. If the organisation is geographically dispersed, people working in branches and subsidiaries can feel cut off from the decision-makers at headquarters.

In addition, as organisations increase in size they tend to add more levels of authority. This leads to what is called *tall organisation structure*. Information may have to travel through several levels before it reaches its intended receivers. This increases the chances that the message may be distorted or blocked off completely as it travels up or down the chain of command.

The particular management style that is characteristic of the organisation can also have a profound effect on communication. If an 'open' management style is practised, information that is not commercially sensitive is disseminated as widely as possible. In more traditionally managed organisations, however, managers keep their distance and information is more likely to be restricted.

A charter for effective internal communication

1. Effective communication is a top management priority. Senior managers are actively involved in promoting good communication throughout the organisation.

2. Communication activities are carried out systematically, not on an ad hoc or fire-fighting basis. A communication planning process exists.

3. There is a stated policy that all employees are entitled to honest, open and accurate information that is relevant to their needs.

4. Bad news will not be filtered out. Employees are entitled to hear about controversial or negative issues such as decline in profit, impending redundancies, etc.

5. Management listens as well as tells. There should be clear routes for effective upward communication.

6. Information is given in a manner that is clear and easy to understand.

7. Resources are made available, including, if necessary, the appointment of a communication officer or manager.

8. The effectiveness of the communication system is regularly monitored by means of a communication audit.

9. Personnel are trained in communication skills where appropriate.

INTERNAL COMMUNICATION MEDIA

There is now a considerable range of devices available for use in internal communication. In deciding which method to use, a manager must take into account such factors as purpose, cost, time, complexity of message and numbers to be reached. Exhibit 2.3 shows how different internal media might be organised and used in a typical medium-sized engineering firm. The main alternatives are then described in greater detail.

Exhibit 2.3 Communication media in Foxworth (Ireland)

Name	Description	Circulation	Frequency
Connect	Internal employee magazine	Free to all staff	Quarterly
Foxworth News	Internal magazine for customers	Available to staff	Quarterly
Service report	Information on current projects	Available to staff	Monthly
E-mail/Internet	Internal and external access	Selected staff only	As required
Noticeboard	One in each department	Visible to all staff	Updated monthly
Tannoy system	Used by security and reception	Covers whole facility	As required

ELECTRONIC COMMUNICATION – E-MAIL AND INTRANET

There has been a huge increase in the use of e-mail for internal communication. The reasons for this aren't hard to find. E-mail is a cheap, flexible form of communication that can be responded to immediately or printed out if required.

However, many organisations are now discovering that it can exercise a kind of tyranny. Recent research in the UK indicates that the average office worker spends three hours a day sending and responding to electronic messages. This can give rise to what researchers call 'information fatigue'. In response, some companies are introducing strict codes to prevent copying irrelevant memos to colleagues. They are also experimenting with 'e-mail-free' days to encourage staff to talk to each other.

Internal communication can also be greatly enhanced with the use of a staff intranet. This is a private Internet that exists only on a company's computers and cannot be accessed by outsiders. It provides a fast and secure means for updating staff about company activities and has proved particularly useful for large multisite organisations. A difficulty is that staff may have neither the time nor inclination to read every piece of news provided. To counteract this, managers can use e-mail or the intranet home page to flag urgent or important messages. (For further discussion of electronic communication, see Chapter 4.)

TRADITIONAL METHODS – MEMOS, CIRCULARS, ETC.

Despite the increasing dominance of electronic communication, most organisations continue to use traditional written forms. These include:

- memoranda (memos)
- circulars
- letters
- pay packet inserts.

Although they take time to produce and distribute, these methods have several advantages. They can be precisely targeted, they provide a record that the message was sent and they have a permanence that is lacking in e-mail and telephone communication.

- Memos and circulars can be used for many purposes: to pass on information, to instruct, to direct or to make enquiries.

- Letters have always been used to communicate with people outside the organisation, but they can also have a valuable role in internal communication. A letter is individually addressed and may sometimes be sent to the employee's home. This gives it a more personal touch than a memo, so it is particularly suited to building the employee's goodwill, just as it would if sent to a customer or client. Suitable subjects for letters include welcoming a new member of staff, appreciating a job well done or sympathising with someone who has suffered a bereavement. They can also be effective in informing staff about major new developments in the organisation and encouraging their support.

- Pay packet inserts are useful for conveying simple but urgent pieces of information that all employees need to know, e.g. a change in benefits or a new health and safety procedure. The message is printed on a small card or slip of paper and attached to the payslip.

NOTICE OR BULLETIN BOARDS

Bulletin boards are an inexpensive and effective communication device. Broadly speaking, they are used for two types of information. The official company noticeboard displays formal announcements about new policies and regulations, new managerial appointments, important company developments, etc. The staff noticeboard is used for information of general interest to staff, much of it of a social nature, e.g. staff parties, sports events, etc. A board may also be provided for the exclusive use of staff associations or trades unions.

Some organisations have experimented with using bulletin boards in a more proactive way to encourage team development. For example, Bose (Ireland) uses a large, centrally placed board to keep its employee teams up to date with progress across a wide range of the plant's activities. High-quality charts and graphs show each employee at a glance whether monthly targets in production, quality control, etc. are being met.

A difficulty with a notice is that it has to work to attract attention, unlike a memo, which is sent directly to the receiver. Some people check the noticeboard regularly; others tend to ignore it. To minimise this problem, boards should be strategically placed and carefully managed. Specifically, they should be:

- pleasant to look at (modern boards have an attractive surface and are nicely framed; some have a glass cover that gives added security)
- located in an accessible place (at the entrance to the staff canteen, in the post room, in staff rest areas, near time clocks, etc.)
- well lit and unobstructed, e.g. not in a dark corridor or directly above seats
- restricted to one subject or, if large, divided into sections
- kept clear from clutter and regularly cleared of out-of-date material.

Notices themselves should be clearly written and concise – for examples see Chapter 10.

MEETINGS AND BRIEFINGS

Meetings are one of the most useful means of communication for an organisation. They provide for a face-to-face exchange of ideas and suggestions, they enable collective decisions to be made, they encourage co-operation and teamwork and they help to make company policies better understood and more willingly accepted.

Many organisations have a briefing system by means of which employees can be given regular information. This is a more direct and personal way of communicating with employees than the formal memo or letter. People attending the meeting can ask questions and seek clarification immediately. Of course, this means the manager may sometimes be put 'on the spot' with a difficult query.

The disadvantage of meetings is that they can be counterproductive if badly run. Very little may be achieved when there is inadequate preparation, uncertainty about the agenda or poor chairmanship.

There are also costs that may not be immediately obvious. The salaries of those attending have to be considered, together with the cost of lost production, secretarial back-up and so on. In the case of a group of senior managers attending, say, a one-day seminar in a hotel, the real and hidden costs are considerable, so it is important that meetings be well organised and time spent at them used wisely. (See also Chapter 16.)

COMPANY PUBLICATIONS

Company publications vary from the slick, colourful house magazine printed on high-quality paper to the one- or two-page newsletter reproduced on a photocopier. Whatever their shape and size, they perform several vital functions in the organisation:
- they give staff information about company developments, new procedures, etc.
- they enhance staff motivation and involvement
- they help to strengthen corporate identity
- they convey a positive image of the organisation to the outside world.

- **House magazine**
  This is usually produced under the guidance of an editor assisted by a small number of staff. Production values are high with lots of photographs, good use of colour and attractive, eye-catching layouts.

  Typical content is a mix of longer articles and lighter topical news, with a strong emphasis on staff affairs. You can expect several pages given over to appointments, long service awards, retirements, engagements, marriages and so on. Sports and social events figure prominently.

  The best examples cover serious news stories from the organisation: new developments, restructuring, industrial relations issues, etc. However, the editor's freedom to deal with controversial matters is constrained. Stories are generally upbeat and usually written from a management perspective.

- **Staff report**
  The annual staff report provides an accessible version of the company's statement of accounts. Financial information is given in a highly graphic and simplified form. In addition, the report usually highlights the main features of the company's performance during the year under review and signposts future developments.

- **Staff induction manual**
  This is an invaluable publication for both existing and new staff. Typically, it

gives information about the company's history, goals, policies and practices and contains a substantial section on employee benefits. It should contain the answers to most questions an employee would want to ask about the organisation.

Spotlight on Irish Business – Aer Rianta

Runway Airports Magazine

Runway Airports Magazine is the award-winning, in-house publication of Aer Rianta cpt. Established in December 1970, this thirty-six page magazine is published bimonthly and is distributed free of charge to all members of Aer Rianta staff at Dublin, Shannon and Cork Airports. The company's subsidiaries, Aer Rianta International (ARI) and the ten Great Southern Hotels, also receive Aer Rianta's flagship magazine.

In 1992, *Runway* won the Irish IPM/AIE Award for Best In-house Publication. Every year since then it has received a variety of publishing prizes for the quality of its content, design and journalistic style. These include Best Internal Magazine awards in the CIB Awards in the UK and Ireland, the Federation of European Industrial Editors Awards (FEIEA) and writing awards both at home and abroad.

Celebrating the magazine's twenty-fifth anniversary in 1995, an independent journalist wrote:

> The most striking aspect of *Runway* magazine is not the many changes that have taken place over the twenty-five years in content, presentation and production – most of them for the better – but the fact that the very first issue in December 1970 provided the 'essential mix' that has remained unchanged and has been the real strength of the magazine up to the present day.
>
> This blend of airport development news, management interviews, 'serious' articles and, most important of all, news and features about and contributed by staff members themselves has been maintained and developed by every editor. It has been said before, but is worth repeating, that the consistent emphasis on staff and 'Staff Matters' is the core strength of *Runway*. This has only been possible through the build-up of a strong team of correspondents at all three airports.

From its initial humble beginnings *Runway* has expanded to provide a range of publications aimed at different internal audiences:

- *GS Quarterly* for the staff and guests of Aer Rianta's hotel group subsidiary, Great Southern Hotels.
- *Employee Report*, a digest of the annual accounts produced for staff.

According to the current editor, 'The magazine's main focus is Aer Rianta's staff. Our aim is to communicate the ever-changing developments in the world of aviation, Aer Rianta's role and the vital part played by our highly talented staff in running our airport business.

It's not all serious, though! Staff are fantastic fun and use their talents in all sorts of ways to help others. It's our job in *Runway* to show them doing what they do best – whether at work, rest or at play!'

SUGGESTION SCHEMES

Many Irish organisations use suggestion schemes to encourage employees to put forward ideas and proposals. A typical scheme works as follows.

1. First, the scheme should be widely publicised and promoted throughout the organisation. Support and commitment from senior management is vital.
2. Staff are invited to complete a suggestion form either as individuals or as teams. The forms should be dispensed in places where they will be noticed, e.g. canteen, bulletin boards, branch offices.
3. Forms are returned to the suggestion scheme co-ordinator, who is usually a member of the personnel department.
4. The ideas are then evaluated. They may first be screened for eligibility or passed to the relevant department head for comment. If they cross these hurdles they are put before an evaluation committee, which will judge their merit.
5. Prompt and positive feedback is essential. It is common practice to give a monetary award for good ideas. Some organisations give a fixed sum, others estimate the value of the idea and make a pro rata award. Winning ideas and their sponsors often feature in the company magazine as well.
6. All ideas should be acknowledged and an explanation should be given when an idea is rejected.

There are some risks in suggestion schemes – for example, the damage to the morale of an employee whose idea has been declined. On the whole, however, schemes can improve efficiency and sometimes generate quite significant cost savings. They are a good method of promoting upward communication and can provide management with useful information.

CORPORATE VIDEO

Many of Ireland's largest companies now make regular use of video for internal communication. Video's ability to present live action, animated graphics, commentary, background music, etc. makes it a particularly powerful communication tool. In addition, it can be shown almost anywhere: to hundreds in an auditorium or one person watching a monitor. The tapes themselves can be reproduced many times and are relatively easy to package and distribute.

Some of the ways in which corporate video is now used include the following.

- **Presenting the annual report**
  A typical example will have a short introduction highlighting the year's achievements, an interview with the chief executive and an explanation of the year's results using animated graphics.

- **Informing staff about company developments**
  Video is sometimes used as a means of enthusing staff about major organisational change.

- **Recording an important corporate event**
  When former US president Bill Clinton visited Ireland he gave an address outside the old parliament building (now owned by Bank of Ireland) in College Green in the centre of Dublin. Bank of Ireland commemorated the event on a fifteen-minute video.

- **Updating sales staff**
  Sales staff can be given information about new products and services.

In conclusion, it is now widely recognised, if not always followed through in practice, that there is a high degree of common interest and interdependence between employer and employee. The working population is now better educated and better informed than in previous generations. It will reject or rebel against an autocratic, secretive style of management. On the other hand, where an effective internal communication system is operated, greater trust and understanding between management and employees develops. Employees are more positively committed to the organisation and the risk of conflict is reduced.

ASSIGNMENTS

REVISION

1. Draw a simple organisation chart showing downward, upward, lateral and diagonal information flow.
2. Downward communication is concerned with giving orders, setting out

procedures, etc. What other types of information are conveyed downward? Why is the word *cascade* used to describe the way the information sometimes travels?

3. Why is upward communication important in an organisation?

4. What are the advantages of formal communication channels?

5. The grapevine has been described as a 'necessary evil'. What is the grapevine? What are its strengths and weaknesses? How can the harm that it may do be minimised?

6. 'Managers themselves can be a serious block to good communication.' Give evidence to support this statement.

7. Describe some other barriers to effective communication in organisations.

8. What are the advantages of using traditional means of communication, such as memos and internal letters?

9. How can a noticeboard be made a more effective communication device?

10. Describe the steps that might be followed in setting up a suggestion scheme.

11. Corporate videos are expensive but are now regularly used by large organisations for internal communication. What kinds of information are videos used to convey?

FOR DISCUSSION

1. Give your views on the following statements.

   * 'My job as a manager is to get people to do things. Communication doesn't come into it.'
   * 'The less you tell your employees the better. They'll only use information against you later on anyway.'
   * 'I like to keep my distance from the people who work for me. If I get too friendly they'll take advantage.'
   * 'Working in a small firm is much better than working in a large one. You get to know everyone on first-name terms and you have a far better idea of what's going on.'
   * 'I just like to get on with the job. I can't see why I should be interested in how the company is doing. All these briefings are a waste of time if you ask me.'
   * 'If the boss tells me one thing and I hear the opposite on the grapevine, I trust the grapevine.'
   * 'Paper-based memos, etc. are old hat. In twenty years' time everyone will be communicating by computer.'
   * 'Suggestion schemes are just a way of getting ideas from employees for nothing.'

ACTIVITIES AND EXERCISES

1. Draw an organisation chart of the school or faculty in which your class is located showing the formal reporting relationships.
2. How is information about class changes, college services, visiting lecturers, etc. conveyed to your class? Working in small groups, identify the different methods that are used. Find out what people think of the system and how it could be improved.
3. Which of the methods discussed in Chapter 2 would you use in the following situations? Justify your choice in each case.
    (a) To announce a forthcoming office party.
    (b) To tell employees about changes in their group pension scheme.
    (c) To publicise the fact that the company has won a national quality award.
    (d) To find out what employees think about a proposed change in work practice.
    (e) To sympathise with an employee who has suffered a bereavement.
    (f) To give information about a major company reorganisation.
4. Put together a collection of company publications and newsletters. Compare their content and layout. What similarities do you notice? What qualities distinguish the best from the worst? (Be patient if companies are slow to respond to requests for material. They get hundreds of these requests every year.)
5. Map out the location of noticeboards in your building. (One floor or section will do if the building is large.) Are the noticeboards well placed? Could they be better displayed?
6. If possible, view a company video or sections of it. (Companies are reluctant to release their internal videos, for obvious reasons. However, it may be possible to get copies of some older videos.) Discuss what management is trying to do in the video. Is the video effective? How does it compare with television? Could it be improved?
7. Write a short article for inclusion in a business magazine about the main barriers to good in-company communication and how they can be removed.
8. Consider the two scenarios set out below, both of which involve making decisions about communication strategies. In each case, write a short analysis of the problem and suggest a solution. Alternatively, use the scenarios as a basis for group discussion.

Scene 1

Jim Sweeney has just returned from a board meeting at company headquarters – with a headache. The board has made a decision to reorganise operations at the plant where he is general manager. This will mean radical changes in work practices and some redeployment of staff. He knows that there will be mixed reactions to this decision. Some staff will be pleased because there will be better opportunities for promotion and more interesting work, but he suspects there will also be strong opposition from one or two shop stewards.

He feels that he must be careful about how the board's decision is communicated to staff. If he makes a mistake he may have a serious industrial relations problem on his hands. As he organises his desk he tries to think out an effective communication strategy for this situation.

What advice would you give?

Scene 2

Mary Sweeney is head of office administration at Intertel (Ireland). Yesterday, just as she was about to go home, she overheard an angry row between Jane Smyth, the new office supervisor, and Margaret Thompson, a clerk.

Mary has already had a complaint from Jane that Margaret is refusing to follow instructions and is generally 'stirring things up'.

Mary suspects that the reason for this behaviour is Margaret's disappointment at not being promoted to the post of supervisor. Although one of the most experienced clerks in the office, Margaret did not meet some of the criteria for selection that the company considered essential. Instead, the job was given to Jane, a much younger but better-qualified applicant.

Mary recognises that Margaret is a good employee whose work has always been exemplary. Yet her behaviour recently is unacceptable and is causing disruption within the department.

All Mary's communication and interpersonal skills will be required to solve this one. What do you think she should do?

3 Marketing Communication

External communication refers to the flow of information that occurs *between the organisation and the external environment*. All organisations are open systems, that is, they must interact with the environment in which they operate. A business has to communicate effectively with many different individuals and groups outside itself. These may include customers, suppliers, government departments, trades unions and the general public.

In this chapter we consider *marketing communication*, a form of communication that is mainly, if not exclusively, used to send persuasive messages outside the organisation. The term *marketing communication* covers a wide range of marketing activities, including advertising, sales promotion, personal selling, PR and sponsorship. However, the chapter will focus on two areas only, *advertising* and *public relations*.

ADVERTISING

Advertisements are paid public announcements. Their importance as a means of communication in our society can hardly be doubted. Everywhere we turn advertising confronts us. At home, publicity leaflets and sales letters regularly arrive in our letter boxes. Outdoor advertising beckons to us from poster panels, illuminated bus shelters, buses themselves and shop windows. Press advertising helps to finance our newspapers and television advertising provides revenue for our national television services.

Among the many uses to which advertising can be put are the following:
- to publicise job vacancies (*recruitment advertising*)
- to promote favourable images of large companies and institutions (*prestige* or *corporate advertising*)
- to inform the public about financial matters, such as new share issues and company trading results (*financial advertising*)
- to promote socially desirable behaviour, such as safe driving or good health habits (*public welfare advertising*)
- to promote and sell products and services (*product advertising*).

ANALYSING A CONSUMER ADVERTISEMENT

The objective of consumer advertising is to create and sustain awareness of and loyalty to the brand. To do this, it tries to give the brand a memorable 'image' or 'personality'. The image is the set of attributes that the consumer associates with the brand, such as reliability, prestige, pleasure or security. A variety of techniques is used in image development (Exhibit 3.1).

Exhibit 3.1 Anatomy of an advertisement

1. **Brand name**: The brand name fixes the product in the consumer's mind. Some brand names have been so successful that they are used as generic titles, e.g. Hoover for vacuum cleaners, Biro for ballpoint pens, Rollerblades for in-line skates and Walkman for personal stereos.

2. **Slogan**: The slogan usually highlights an important feature of the brand's image in an imaginative phrase. There are many memorable examples:

    ▸ Have a break, have a Kit Kat
    ▸ Polo – the mint with the hole
    ▸ Because you're worth it (L'Oréal)
    ▸ The Power of Dreams (Honda)
    ▸ Just do it (Nike)
    ▸ Probably the best lager in the world (Carlsberg)
    ▸ The ultimate driving machine (BMW).

3. **Symbol**: A unique symbol may be used to associate the brand with particular, often intangible, attributes:

    ▸ Esso tiger: power, graceful movement, aggression
    ▸ Dulux dog: warmth, homeliness, loyalty
    ▸ Abbey National umbrella: safety, security.

4. **Headline**: A catchy headline is one of the most effective ways of drawing attention to the ad and contributing to the mood and style of the advertising message. The use of humour or a play on words is a common feature:

    ▸ The art of can (Red Bull)
    ▸ Get fizzical with stains (Persil)
    ▸ Capture every moment (Olympus cameras)
    ▸ You never forget your first time (Mitsubishi cars)
    ▸ Designed for desire (Siemens Mobile).

5. **Copy**: Copy can be used not only to identify the benefits of the product, but to imbue it with certain values.

    The example below shows how potent images of luxury, adventure and snobbery can be intermingled with mundane details about the product's features.

    Whoever it was that said it is better to travel than to arrive must surely have had the Omega Tourer in mind. Perhaps they were thinking about the smooth 2.5 V6 engine that allows you to cruise effortlessly along the autoroutes and autobahns.

    Then again it could have been the advanced multilink suspension that lets you glide around the testing corners of the Kalambaka mountains. Or the air-conditioning that takes the heat out of those scorching days in St Tropez.

6. **Visuals**: The visual element, e.g. photograph, sketch, cartoon, is usually the most prominent feature of the advertisement. This will often work to create a mood or feeling about the product. Marlboro cigarettes, for example, have made extensive use of wilderness scenes, often suffused with strong red or orange colour. These suggest an elemental, 'get away from it all' lifestyle far removed from the dullness of ordinary existence.

How an advertisement works

In order to achieve its objectives an advertisement must get the consumer's attention, hold his or her interest, create desire for the product and promote action. The acronym AIDA (attention, interest, desire, action) is used as shorthand for this process.

- **Attention**
  Getting attention is less easy than may at first appear. An advertisement has to compete with all the other visual and aural stimuli that we experience going about our daily lives. When we read newspapers or magazines our primary interest is in news stories and features. We may not even notice the advertisements. Similarly, when driving our attention is likely to be focused on road conditions rather than on hoardings and billboards. Television commercials are more difficult to ignore, but many viewers regard them as an intrusion and find ways of 'switching off' when the ad breaks occur.

  An advertisement's first task is to provoke us into looking or listening. Many different devices are used for this purpose: catchy tunes, punning headlines, unusual designs, full-page coverage and so on. Some advertisements try to shock the audience into taking notice. The Benetton advertising campaign, for example, has gained worldwide attention by using controversial images that challenge social and cultural taboos.

- **Interest**
  The next task is to hold our interest. To achieve this the advertisement must in some way reflect the consumer's values and attitudes. Thus, for example, advertisements aimed specifically at young men often have a sporting theme or show daring or risky behaviour. Young adults of both sexes are enticed with the promise of excitement or romance. In contrast, advertisements for parents

or older adults may focus on comfort, security or convenience.

At the same time, there must be something appealing or quirky about the advertisement to make it stand out. Press advertisements often draw us in by presenting images of beautiful models, idealised landscapes or stylish interiors. In television advertising a favourite device is to tell a story that upsets expectations or has a humorous 'twist in the tail'.

- **Desire**

  To create desire for the product, the advertisement has to offer a benefit, something that makes our lives easier, makes us healthier or more beautiful or increases our social status. Sometimes an advertisement will emphasise one particular feature, known as the *unique selling proposition*, which is an additional benefit that competitor products don't offer. For example, a recent advertisement for Mercedes-Benz cars highlights a new braking system with the headline:

  > 'Sensotronic Brake Control: only a split second quicker than normal braking. But then accidents can happen in a split second.'

  Claims about benefits may be supported with scientific data to give them greater credibility. Expert or celebrity testimony may be used for the same purpose.

- **Action**

  Because consumers tend to remain loyal to brands they like, it can be difficult to persuade them to try a new product. Moreover, there is usually a time lapse between seeing or hearing the advertisement and having the opportunity to purchase. Some advertisements try to 'prod' the consumer by offering FreeFone numbers, reply-paid coupons, competitions, limited-time price reductions, money-off vouchers and the like. The advertising campaign may also be supported with in-store demonstrations or samples. However, most advertisements influence purchase decisions more indirectly by creating long-term goodwill towards the brand and the company.

THE ADVERTISING AGENCY'S ROLE

A modern advertising agency differs considerably from its nineteenth-century counterpart. Originally, advertising agencies were employed by newspapers and magazines to sell advertising space, for which they received a commission. Gradually, to attract advertisers they began to offer help with copy, layout, typography and illustrations. Eventually they ceased to be space brokers and became what they are now, independent businesses offering a range of services to advertisers.

A full-service agency has three main departments (see Exhibit 3.2).

Exhibit 3.2 Full-service agency

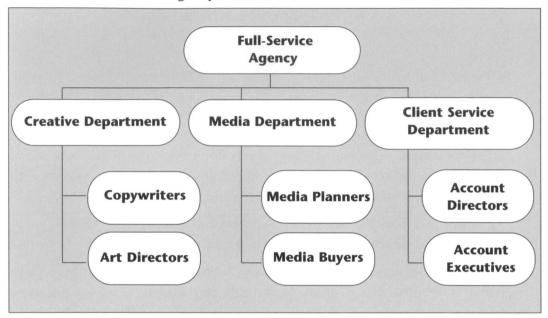

The **creative department** invents the advertisement and is the core of the agency. Copywriters, who are skilled in writing short memorable texts, work with art directors to produce ideas for the campaign. When the concept is agreed with the client the creative department teams up with other specialists to make the advertisements ready for production. In the case of a television campaign, for example, an independent television production company will usually make the commercials, but the creative department will oversee the process of casting, shooting and editing.

The function of the **media department** is to book advertising space in print, radio, television, etc. The media planner recommends a budget for the campaign and prepares a schedule of placements. The media buyer then places the advertisement and monitors its effectiveness. Media staff need to be proficient in analysing extensive media research data. They also need good negotiating skills in order to buy space at the best possible price.

The **client service department** provides the link between the agency and client. It is comprised of the account director and one or more account executives. One of its primary tasks is to prepare an advertising brief that outlines the main features of a proposed campaign. A good advertising brief is vital in winning the client's confidence and getting the business. The department then continues to liaise with the client, ensuring that the work matches the brief while staying on time and within budget.

Full-service agencies in Ireland tend to be small in international terms and have been seriously affected by changes in the industry as a whole. In recent years they have had to contend with increased competition, more sophisticated consumers and changing client demands. One source of competition has come from international agencies that have entered Ireland and taken a substantial part of the market. Another source of competition is the growth of niche agencies that provide specialist services. The rise of media-buying agencies in particular has been spectacular.

Traditional agencies have responded in various ways to these developments. Many Irish-owned companies have forged links with larger overseas groups. Some companies have met the challenge from the media specialists by strengthening their own media departments. Others have transformed their media-buying operations into independent business units which can pursue clients separately from the agency itself. In general, traditional agencies have recognised that they need to become more flexible and customer orientated to survive in an increasingly turbulent environment.

THE ETHICS OF ADVERTISING

Critics of commercial advertising claim that much of it is trivial, irritating, uninformative or misleading. They say that it encourages acquisitiveness and wasteful consumption. It promotes the mistaken belief that many deep human needs, such as the need for security or esteem, can be fulfilled by buying more and more material goods. Different groups (women, men, the aged, etc.) complain about demeaning portrayal in advertisements and there are increasing calls for restrictions on messages aimed at children and young people. There is also much concern about the extent to which the mass media depend for their existence on advertising revenue. Critics argue that this has a subtle but significant effect on newspaper editorial policy and the content of television programmes.

In defence of advertising it is argued that the consumer society has brought many benefits to the public. Mass production has dramatically raised living standards by making a wide range of cheap, labour-saving machines and other products available. Because advertising ensures there is a steady demand for manufactured goods, it gives manufacturers the confidence to buy raw materials, invest in new plant and equipment and provide employment. It also reduces the cost of most goods by helping to bring about economies of scale.

Moreover, supporters of consumer advertising say that the power of advertising to influence consumer choice is greatly overestimated. The public, it is claimed, are now well aware that advertisements emanate from biased sources and may make exaggerated claims. The most advertising can achieve is to persuade the customer to try a new product once. Whether or not the person continues to buy the product depends on the quality of the product itself and on the satisfaction it gives.

Spotlight on Irish Business – Tourism Ireland

'Six p.m. Rush hour, Ireland'

This was the headline over a famous Irish tourism advertisement showing two horses on a three-mile stretch of empty, sandy beach. Although the pace of life has increased a little since the advertisement was used, the idea of Ireland as a relaxed and leisurely place still remains central to the brand message today.

Responsibility for marketing the island of Ireland as a holiday destination now rests with Tourism Ireland, a new organisation established under the framework of the Good Friday Agreement 1998. Tourism Ireland operates on an all-Ireland basis and is jointly funded by the Irish and British governments.

Communicating Ireland's brand message to consumers overseas is a complex task. Indeed, Ireland was a brand long before the concept even existed. Film and folklore created an aura around the name of Ireland that no amount of advertising could match. Tourism Ireland's central mission is to protect the brand as it evolves and manage and develop it to its full potential.

Consumer surveys show that what differentiates Ireland from other destinations is a combination of friendly people, breathtaking scenery and an easy, relaxed pace. Having contact with the Irish way of life leaves the visitor with enriching and memorable experiences. Hence, three core brand values –

The People, The Place and The Pace

– form the basis of Tourism Ireland's new advertising campaign launched in 2002 in ten countries worldwide.

The experience that makes the most indelible mark on visitors to Ireland is encounters with the island's people. Visitors are charmed by the combination of good conversation, friendliness and *craic* that is uniquely Irish. Add in superb scenery from the Glens of Antrim to the mountains of Kerry and the surprise of finding that Ireland offers both the calm of the countryside and the life and vitality of cosmopolitan cities. According to Tourism Ireland, these are things we in Ireland find ordinary but our guests find extraordinary and fascinating.

A few simple facts illustrate the value of overseas visitors to the Irish economy.

> ▸ Almost 800 visitors arrive in Ireland every hour.
> ▸ There are close to two tourists per annum for every man, woman and child on the island.
> ▸ In 2002, overseas visitors spent €3.4 billion, more than half of which went on accommodation, food and drink.
>
> Tourism Ireland says we can add value to the brand by taking a genuine individual interest in visitors and celebrating the things that make Ireland attractive. After all, it seems that the most important motivation for choosing Ireland as a holiday destination is word-of-mouth recommendation.

PUBLIC RELATIONS

In its day-to-day operations a company comes in contact with many different groups, or *publics*. These include customers, employees, investors, suppliers, media and the government. It is always in the company's interest to have the goodwill of these groups. This is where public relations (PR) comes in. The broad aim of public relations activity is to ensure that the company has a good reputation among the people it deals with and is seen as a responsible member of the community at large. Effective communication is at the heart of this activity.

The description of public relations offered by the Institute of Public Relations (see box below) highlights some important features of public relations work. It indicates that effective public relations requires careful planning and sustained effort. It also indicates that two-way communication is involved. Organisations must be prepared not only to give information to the public but also to find out what the public really thinks. The definition emphasises the importance of reputation. People are reluctant to do business with companies that behave in an unethical or unsocial manner. Lastly, the definition makes clear that the company must earn a good reputation before it can acquire it. Favourable images cannot be concocted and it should not be the PR practitioner's job to cover up business malpractice.

Public relations is the discipline that looks after reputation, with the aim of earning understanding and support and influencing opinion and behaviour. It is the planned and sustained effort to establish and maintain goodwill and mutual understanding between an organisation and its publics.

At its best, public relations not only tells an organisation's story to its publics, it also helps to shape the organisation and the way it works. Through research, feedback communication and evaluation, the practitioner needs to find out the concerns and expectations of a company's publics and explain them to its management.

Source: Institute of Public Relations

Like advertising, public relations has become increasingly specialised in recent decades. Today, a large company or organisation is likely to have one or more trained PR practitioners on the staff. Companies can also draw on the skills and expertise offered by PR consultancies. Some of these are independent, while others are off-shoots of advertising agencies. It is now common for PR firms to develop expertise in a particular sector, such as the food industry or computers and high technology.

Thorough planning is needed when putting a public relations programme into action. Objectives have to be carefully thought out and the various publics precisely identified. Research into markets and people's attitudes, opinions and needs must often be conducted. A schedule of activities designed to meet the objectives must be drawn up. An activity could be anything from organising a photocall to setting up an exhibition stand at the RDS, from writing press releases to commissioning a twenty-minute video (see Exhibit 3.3). The whole programme has to be costed before it begins and critically evaluated as it progresses.

Exhibit 3.3 Public relations activities

> ▸ **Programme planning** – analysing problems and opportunities, defining goals, recommending and planning activities and measuring results.
>
> ▸ **Writing and editing** – shareholder reports, annual reports, press releases, film scripts, articles and features, speeches, booklets, newsletters.
>
> ▸ **Media relations** – developing and maintaining a good working contact with the media.
>
> ▸ **Corporate identity** – developing and maintaining an organisation's identity via corporate advertising, presenting the company's name and reputation rather than its products.
>
> ▸ **Speaking** – communicating effectively with individuals and groups, including meetings, presentations and platform participation.
>
> ▸ **Production** – brochures, reports, film and multimedia programmes are important means of communication. Co-ordination of studio or location photography.
>
> ▸ **Special events** – news conferences, exhibitions, facility celebrations, open days, competitions and award days are all used to gain the attention of specific groups.
>
> *Source*: Institute of Public Relations (adapted)

SPECIAL FORMS OF PUBLIC RELATIONS

- **Customer relations**

  It is often said – but not always remembered in practice – that the customer is the most important person in business. A company that cannot sell its products will not remain in existence long, so new customers have to be attracted and the loyalty of established customers retained. A carefully planned customer relations policy can help to achieve both these aims.

  All members of staff dealing directly with customers, e.g. receptionists, telephonists or shop assistants, should be trained to treat members of the public with courtesy and efficiency. They should also be well informed about the company's products and be able to give help and advice when needed. The area where the customer or visitor has to wait should be bright and tidy. All customer complaints should be acknowledged promptly and processed as quickly as possible. Delivery dates should be kept to and an effective after-sales service provided.

- **Community relations**

  There is often a close interdependence between a company, particularly a large manufacturing company, and the community in which it is located. The company depends on the community to provide its workers, buy some of its products, provide its energy requirements and dispose of its waste. It may also need local support if it wants to extend its premises or make increased demands on public services.

  Good community relations can be built up in many ways. Staff can be encouraged to participate fully in local affairs by joining voluntary or professional associations. The company can contribute to community life by supporting charities, sports, cultural events and so on. It can help local schools and colleges by facilitating visits or providing educational material. It can hold 'open days' or 'family days'. Most importantly of all, perhaps, it can avoid irresponsible antisocial behaviour such as dumping dangerous waste or otherwise harming the environment.

- **Media relations**

  The mass media are watched, read or listened to by thousands of people every day. As such, they have considerable influence in forming public opinions and attitudes. They also provide a platform for obtaining wide publicity for a company's plans and activities. For these reasons, media relations is an important part of public relations although not, of course, the whole of it.

  The PR practitioner should know how the mass media operate and should be familiar with their production schedules. He should be prepared to help journalists by giving them truthful information and by being available for comment whenever necessary. Any written material sent by the PR person should conform to accepted journalistic standards.

The main written form is the press release, although letters to the editor or feature articles may also be used. A press release usually contains a story that shows the company in a positive light. As editors reject most press releases it is important to aim the story at the right publication and make sure it says something genuinely newsworthy. (You will find out how to write a press release in Chapter 10.)

ASSIGNMENTS

REVISION

1. Outline *five* different types of advertising.
2. 'The advertising industry in Ireland is going through a period of unprecedented change.' What factors are contributing to that change?
3. How does the AIDA concept help us to understand how advertising works?
4. What is the role of each of the three main departments in a full-service advertising agency?
5. Define *public relations*.
6. Write brief notes on (a) customer relations (b) community relations (c) media relations.

FOR DISCUSSION

1. 'Advertising works.' Do you agree that advertising is an effective method of promoting products? Can you think of alternatives?
2. Do you think that advertising persuades us to buy much more than we actually need?
3. What are the benefits of advertising?
4. Consider examples of advertising that you have seen or heard in the media recently. Which advertisements do you rate highly? What is the basis of your assessment? Is it because the ad:
   • gives a lot of information about the product
   • is very imaginative
   • has a sense of humour
   • is aimed at your age group
   • or has some other appeal?
   Which advertisements do you dislike and why?
5. Advertising has been heavily criticised for promoting behaviour many people regard as undesirable, such as excessive drinking. Do you think drink ads

should be banned altogether?

6. Children are thought to be particularly vulnerable to ads. Should there be stricter controls on advertising directed at children? What controls, if any, would you put in place?

7. Consider some examples of public welfare advertising, e.g. information ads on health, antismoking ads, safe driving ads, etc. Do you think these ads are effective? Do they change people's behaviour?

8. Many public welfare ads make a 'fear' appeal. For example, recent advertisements on Irish television have shown the consequences of drink driving, speeding or not wearing a seatbelt. The appalling accidents that result are shown in graphic detail. Do you think this kind of advertising works? Can you think of other examples?

9. What influence does advertising have on the media? For example, is a music magazine likely to write negative reviews of groups or concerts that advertise in it? Is the media 'controlled' by advertising?

10. One writer on public relations said that there were three ingredients in PR: 'truth, concern for the public interest and dialogue'. Do you think this claim is justified? Or can you think of examples where public relations has perhaps been used to subvert the public interest?

11. Could business companies do without public relations?

12. Is there such a thing as 'free publicity'?

ACTIVITIES AND EXERCISES

1. Replay a selection of TV or radio ads on video or audio tape. How have the ads exploited (or failed to exploit) the medium that is being used?

2. Advertising is used not just to give information about a product but to associate it with certain values. For example, a car might be associated with performance and prestige (BMW), a food product with wholesomeness (Mr Kipling cakes, Kerrygold), a financial product with security, etc.

      Select a number of full-page ads from magazines. What values are being associated with the products? In your view, are these values good or bad for society?

3. There are three advertising industry associations in Ireland:
   • The Institute of Advertising Practitioners in Ireland (IAPI)
   • The Association of Advertisers in Ireland Ltd (AAI)
   • The Advertising Standards Authority for Ireland (ASAI).
   Investigate the role of each of these associations and report to the class.

4. Find out about recent cases where the Advertising Standards Authority gave rulings on complaints against advertisements. Report these cases to the class,

giving your own view on whether the complaints were justified and whether the ASAI made the right decision.

5. Try to find information about any Irish advertising agency. How large is it? How is it structured? Who are its main clients? What advertising campaigns was it involved in recently?

6. Choose a subject for an advertisement (product, event, charity, college society, etc.) and design a poster-sized ad using simple materials such as markers, cut-outs, etc.

7. In small groups, list recent examples of public relations activity that you have become aware of.

8. Intertel (Ireland) Ltd is the Irish subsidiary of a large multinational company. It manufactures computers for the Irish and European markets. It is located on the outskirts of a county town and employs 200 people. Most employees are from the local area, but a substantial number have moved into the community from outside. The company is shortly to announce plans for a major expansion onto a nearby greenfield site.

   Identify a number of public relations objectives for the company and draw up a plan of PR activities.

9. Interview the person responsible for public relations activities in your students' union. Try to find out what he or she does and what plans he or she has to enhance the union's profile. Write an account of this interview in a form suitable for publication in your college magazine.

4 Electronic Communication

In this chapter we consider the impact of **information and communication technology (ICT)** on organisational communication. The principle upon which ICT is founded is that all information, whether voice, text, images or numbers, can be represented electronically. In this form, it can be stored and processed by computers and transmitted along telecommunication networks. Much of today's corporate communication is done using global or local networks of one kind or another. These networks constitute a largely invisible world through which a vast amount of information passes every day.

The topics we will look at are as follows:

- the Internet
- e-commerce
- the web
- e-mail
- landline telephone
- mobile telephone
- video conferencing
- teleworking.

Throughout the chapter technical description is kept to a minimum. Instead, the emphasis is on the benefits (and some disadvantages) of the various technologies as business communication tools. Where appropriate, advice is given on how to use these new applications more effectively.

THE INTERNET

Few developments in ICT have taken greater hold on the public imagination than the Internet. Up to the early 1990s it was mainly used by academics and computer 'buffs'. Now, however, it is a worldwide system used by millions of subscribers. The lack of control over the Internet and its easy accessibility has raised fundamental ethical questions about freedom of information and censorship. This ensures that the Internet is an almost daily topic of discussion in the media.

What is it?

Essentially, the Internet (or Net) is a global network of computers connected by telecommunication links. It has no 'owners'. Instead, it is a service provided by a number of organisations, including government departments, universities and companies, that allows others to connect to their computers and share information.

How did it start?

The Internet's predecessor, ARPAnet, was started by the US Defense Department at the end of the 1960s. Their aim was to develop a computer network that could withstand a nuclear attack. Such a network had to be decentralised so that if any part of it became disabled information would find its way around the damaged part.

However, the system proved unreliable for defence purposes and was soon ignored by the military. It was then taken up by universities and laboratories that recognised its potential for exchanging research information. Progress in the early stages was slow, but large companies gradually became interested and in the early 1990s businesses and individuals of all kinds began to get connected. The Internet is now a vast communication network that is expected to have over 700 million users by 2005.

How do you get connected?

There are two main ways of accessing the Net:
- full network access
- dial-up access.

For full network access, an organisation needs a powerful computer (called a *server*), a *router*, which enables data signals to be transferred from one network to another, and a *dedicated leased line*, which connects you to the Internet. Full access is expensive but it provides a faster means of sending and receiving information than dial-up access.

Most small businesses and individuals use dial-up access. For this you need a personal computer, a telephone link, a modem and an account with an Internet service provider (ISP). This latter is a firm that will connect you to an Internet computer for a fee. The cost of the connection normally includes an initial signing-on fee and a monthly or yearly subscription. You will then have to pay telephone charges (usually at the local call rate) for the time you spend on the network.

E-COMMERCE

The term *e-commerce* can be applied generally to 'any form of business transaction that is conducted electronically using telecommunication networks' (Lewis, 1999). However, it is usually defined more precisely as the trading of goods and services over the Internet. Business interest in the Internet was initially tentative. Now, however, companies are beginning to realise its enormous potential and to consider it seriously as a sales and marketing tool. In Ireland, as elsewhere, e-commerce is developing strongly. According to Forfás (2000) it is likely to be 'one of the most significant drivers of enterprise over the next three to five years.'

THE BENEFITS OF E-COMMERCE

- Gives access to a global infrastructure that even small businesses can exploit.
- Can provide up-to-the-minute information on products and services.
- Is not limited by geographical or time boundaries – products can be sold all over the world and transactions take place around the clock.
- Can reduce overheads by automating operations such as billing and payments.
- Can eliminate the need to maintain costly retail outlets.
- Makes a wider range of products available to the consumer at cheaper cost.
- Enables consumers to purchase from the comfort of their own homes.
- Helps streamline delivery and reduce lead times.
- Helps overcome problems of peripheral location – an e-business can be located anywhere so long as it has reliable access to the Internet, a good delivery system and sufficient stock to meet customer demand.

However, not all businesses are suited to e-commerce. The Internet seems to be particularly well adapted to the sale of merchandise that doesn't need to be seen before purchase, e.g. books, CDs, hotel accommodation, concert tickets, bank products, etc. It is less well suited to selling goods that customers like to examine first. For example, most people will want to try on a fashion item before they feel confident enough to buy it. Despite this, even quite expensive items such as white goods, cars and houses are now sold over the Internet sight unseen.

Cars by mail order

In the spring of 2003, a German mail-order company, Quelle, caused quite a stir in the car retail trade when it offered a batch of Smart cars for sale on the Internet for as little as €1,990 each.

However, the market for Net-based car sales remains small at less than one per cent. Dealers say that most customers still value the personal touch and want to see and test drive a car before purchase. Customers who buy over the Net are also likely to experience problems when it comes to after-sales service and trading in for a new vehicle.

The real value of the Net is that it can tell customers about makes and models before they approach the showroom. According to one sales manager, 'People are coming into dealers armed to the teeth with information.' However, the actual selling of a car is still 'a tactile experience'.

Source: *The Irish Times*, 18 June 2003

THE WEB

The World Wide Web (or web) is the fastest-growing part of the Internet and, for many people, the most exciting part of it. The web is effectively thousands of documents linked by a **hypertext** system. Hypertext allows users to transfer from one web page to another by clicking on key words or pictures. Anyone can set up a document or series of documents on the web. A document can consist of graphics, video and sound as well as text. A program called a **browser** is used to retrieve web pages off the Internet and display them on screen. Two browsers currently dominate the market: *Netscape Navigator* and *Microsoft Internet Explorer*.

When a business wants to exploit the Internet its first step is to establish a **website**. This consists of a number of interlinked web pages that can be used in more or less complex ways.

1. **Electronic brochure**

   The most basic kind of business website provides some limited information about the company or business. For example, the owners of guesthouse accommodation often advertise their product in this way. The website will typically describe the accommodation, include a few photographs, give some information about local attractions and provide a telephone number or e-mail address for making enquiries or reservations.

2. **Online shopping**

   These sites provide all the functions that the customer needs to make a purchase over the Internet. The customer will be able to obtain information about the product she is interested in, select and order it, pay by credit card and have the purchase confirmed. The site is also likely to contain special features, such as gift ideas, promotions, consumer reviews and the like. Some sites mimic a retail outlet by providing the visitor with a shopping cart and taking her on a visual tour of the store.

3.   Corporate marketing

This kind of site requires more effort to design and is much more interesting to view. It has two primary objectives: first, to inform customers about the products or services the company provides and second, to build customer loyalty and brand recognition. In a typical marketing site the company will give information about its history, mission and corporate structure, describe its products, inform about jobs and so on. It may link to other sites or provide a simple search function for finding archived material. Large corporations usually have websites of this standard and complexity.

Exhibit 4.1 below shows the proportion of Irish businesses that had a website in 2002 and their reasons for using this medium.

Exhibit 4.1 Use of websites by Irish businesses (2002)

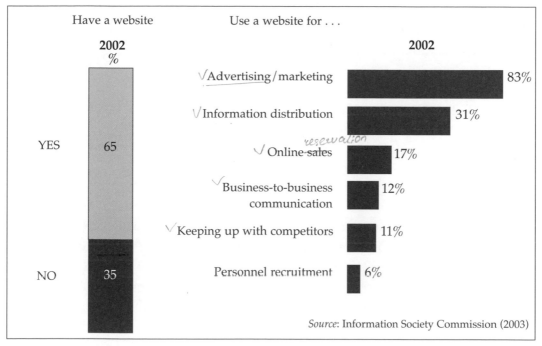

Source: Information Society Commission (2003)

PRINCIPLES OF WEB DESIGN

A business shouldn't make the decision to set up a website lightly. Developing and maintaining a website requires time, effort and money. A variety of software packages can be used to set up the site, but in many cases a better result is achieved with the help of a specialist web development and design service. If a specialist is employed, those who represent the business will still need to decide the content and ensure that the site reflects the corporate image they want to present. Thus, it is useful for all businesses that are planning a web presence to understand the principles of good web design.

1. **Simple, elegant and readable**
    The first rule of good design is that your website should be unfussy and easy to read. Check that the basic elements meet this requirement.
    - **Background:** Light-coloured or white, with an unobtrusive pattern or texture.
    - **Text:** Dark, not too small or large and set out in a standard font.
    - **Images:** Clear (not out of focus, for example) and complementary to the text.
    - **Graphic elements (logos, icons):** Simple, colourful and easy to understand.

    Ideally, pages should fit the size of a computer screen so that the visitor can avoid scrolling up and down. This entails good organisation of content and concise writing.

2. **Consistent**
    If you are reading a report you expect consistency in layout and style throughout the document. The same rule applies to a website. Continue the same fonts, background colours and stylistic devices from page to page. This gives the website a coherent and professional appearance.

3. **Easy to navigate**
    It should be easy for visitors to find their way around your site. The **home page** (first page) should provide a table of contents enabling visitors to move effortlessly to any section they want. Each section should contain a link back to the home page. Hypertext links should be carefully chosen and highlighted so that they are easy to find. Navigational buttons or tabs should be immediately recognisable and have text attached. The 'two to three click' rule applies: a visitor should never be more than two or three clicks away from the information they seek.

4. **Easy to download**
    Visitors lose patience with sites that take a long time to download. Fancy graphics and animation may look clever, but they take up large files and may detract from your core message. The ideal site can be downloaded quickly, has a clean look and uses simple graphics.

5. **Informative and entertaining**
   This is more of a content than a design issue. Nevertheless, it is important for your site to give some 'added value' in the way of attractive images or useful information. For example, a site might provide interview tips for prospective job applicants on its 'Careers' page. An online shopping site might provide consumer reviews or offer free software gifts that can be downloaded immediately.

Having a Net presence is taken as a sign that a business is progressive and up to date. Thousands of small businesses as well as large corporations now include a web address in their promotional material, so it is worthwhile ensuring that your website is well designed, easily navigable and attractive to view. This way it is a valuable and cost-effective marketing tool.

E-MAIL

E-mail (short for electronic mail) is an Internet application that facilitates fast transmission of messages and documents. It may be used for either internal or external communication. It is the most extensively used facility on the Internet. Many companies provide a direct link to their e-mail address on their website so that customers can make inquiries, contact after-sales services, etc.

E-mail has been described as a hybrid medium, having some of the characteristics of both a letter and a telephone call. It is written and sent to an address like a letter, but it also has some of the immediacy of a telephone call. When you press 'Send' the message is transferred at once and the receiver can respond quickly. The language of e-mail messages reflects this – there is less formality and the message is often peppered with abbreviations.

The advantages of email are:
* it provides a printable copy of the message
* the message is transferred quickly and cheaply over any distance
* the receiver can read the message and reply at her convenience
* other documents and computer files, such as graphics, spreadsheets, etc., can be attached to the message
* information is in electronic form and so can be easily edited or reused.

But there are some disadvantages, too:
* Because e-mail can be sent quickly, the sender may take less care with the message (similar to making a spur-of-the-moment remark and then regretting it later).
* Security is poor unless encryption software is used. This is one of the reasons why businesses such as banks are wary of the Internet.

- E-mail printouts are usually less tidy than letters.
- There is no guarantee that an e-mail will be read immediately.
- E-mail accounts attract unsolicited and usually unwanted direct mail shots by advertisers (referred to as *spam*).
- (For tips on writing e-mails see Chapter 10.)

LANDLINE TELEPHONE

The origin of electronic communication can be traced back to the nineteenth century when the telegraph (1833) and telephone (1876) were invented. The telephone in particular has proved an enormously successful technology. Indeed, the ordinary telephone network is still the most extensive telecommunications system worldwide. Today, it is used to carry not only voice communication, for which it was originally designed, but also data, images and text.

BASIC TELEPHONE SERVICES

The basic telephone service itself is being continually upgraded and modified to provide a more comprehensive service for the business user. Some of the facilities now available include the following.

- **FreeFone**
  This enables either local or international customers to call your business and have the call charged to you. FreeFone can be an invaluable way of encouraging customers to respond to your marketing efforts, to develop existing customer relations or to attract new business.

- **Chargecard**
  A chargecard enables calls to be made from any phone at home or abroad and have the call charged to the company telephone in Ireland. It can be of particular benefit when calling Ireland from overseas. It helps avoid the difficulty of using foreign currency or having to communicate with a foreign operator. It also saves the heavy charges that can be incurred by telephoning through a hotel. Using a chargecard is cheaper than using the roaming facility on a mobile phone.

- **Call management services**
  These are a range of add-on features such as call answering and call forwarding that can be used with a touch-tone phone to increase its flexibility and efficiency.

- **Telemarketing**
  A company can provide a telephone information service that the customer accesses by ringing a 15xx number. The messages may be recorded or live.

Each time a customer uses the service the company receives a percentage of the revenue generated, while the remainder goes to the service provider.

HIGH-SPEED TELEPHONE SERVICES

A limitation of the basic telephone system is that local telephone lines still transmit in **analogue** (continuous electrical waves) whereas computers transmit in **digital** (on-off electrical impulses). Therefore, when you wish to send computer data over ordinary telephone lines you have to use a **modem,** which converts between the two types of signals. Moreover, telephone networks use twisted-pair copper cable from the customer to the telephone exchange. Because this cable is designed primarily for voice communication it carries standard modem signals at relatively low speeds.

To overcome these problems telephone companies offer a range of high-speed **broadband** services. Such services are 'broad' because they can be used for many different applications: transferring large data files, voice communication, fax, videoconferencing or even watching television on one's PC.

Until recently high-speed services were based on **ISDN** technology (ISDN is short for integrated services digital network). However, a new technology called **ADSL** (asymmetric digital subscriber line) seems likely to replace ISDN in the longer term. Like its technological competitor, ADSL provides multichannel high-speed network access using existing telephone connections. However, download speeds are many times faster.

MOBILE TELEPHONE

VOICE AND TEXT MESSAGING

It is no exaggeration to describe the growth in mobile telephone usage in Ireland as astonishing. In 1995 approximately 2.5 per cent of the Irish population subscribed to a mobile phone. By 2002, mobile penetration had grown to seventy-nine per cent of the population. Usage is highest among young people, with over ninety per cent of fifteen- to twenty-four-year-olds now connected to mobile networks. In hindsight it is easy to understand the appeal of a phone that is wireless, is carried on the person and can be operated from any location.

More surprising is the appeal of the text messaging application, particularly among teenagers and young adults. Yet research indicates that young people value this feature because it is fast, cheaper than voice and useful for quiet private conversation. It is estimated that over 1.5 billion text messages are sent annually by Irish mobile subscribers. Overall, mobile telephone traffic now exceeds landline traffic, accounting for nearly sixty per cent of telephone calls.

For business users, the basic benefit of the mobile phone is that it enables instantaneous voice contact from virtually anywhere. It has transformed voice communication for people in service industries who spend most of their time working at remote sites. It effectively provides them with a virtual office from which they can answer queries, make arrangements, solicit new business, etc. while continuing with the job in hand. It is also an invaluable communication tool for managers with responsibility for co-ordinating remote teams. For example, a fleet manager can use the mobile network to maintain contact with long-distance drivers, issuing new instructions or receiving information about problems that drivers are encountering.

INTERNET ACCESS

There are two main ways in which mobiles can be used to download from the Internet. First, mobiles can be connected to laptops or **PDAs** (personal digital assistants) with or without cable. Second, the mobile screen itself can be used to display web pages using **WAP** (wireless application protocol) technology.

The most basic way to access the Net is to connect a laptop or PDA to a specially configured mobile phone using a data cable. This enables the user to check e-mails, download files and browse for information at much the same speed as if using a landline phone and home PC. However, ease of access is likely to be further improved by **Bluetooth,** a new technology that enables laptops, mobiles and other portable devices to be connected by short-range radio. The mobile and laptop don't have to be in line of sight – the connection can be maintained even if the mobile is kept in the user's pocket or briefcase.

WAP phones provide easier but more limited Internet access. This technology enables selected content to be downloaded from the Net (or company intranet) and displayed on the mobile screen itself. Companies can set up their own WAP websites but have to bear in mind that mobile phones have limited computer memory, a short battery life and a very small space in which to display characters and graphics. WAP sites are ideally suited to information that is written and concise. Despite these limitations, the range of goods and services promoted via WAP is expected to grow. Consumers will increasingly use mobile phones to book tickets, purchase goods, check their bank account and so on. This area of e-commerce is sometimes referred to as **m-commerce** (mobile commerce).

MULTIFUNCTIONAL MOBILES

As in other areas of telecommunications, mobile phone producers and operators constantly seek to enhance the capabilities of the mobile network and add to the range of services it can provide. New **third-generation** (or **3G**) mobiles promise to integrate e-mail, Net access, voice, text and camera into a single hand-held device.

At present, these so-called smartphones tend to be cumbersome and expensive, but are expected to become more technically refined and affordable as a mass market for them develops. In future, we can expect higher screen resolution, sleeker design and much better integration of the various features.

Flirting by text

Research by Demos, an independent UK think-tank, has uncovered countless examples of people using mobile text messages to flirt and send intimate messages. According to one survey, thirty-five per cent of people in the UK between the ages of fifteen and forty-four admitted to flirting by text, while twenty-two per cent said they had secured a date with someone as a result of text messaging. On Valentine's Day 2002, almost 60 million messages were sent by mobile phone in contrast to 13 million Valentine cards.

Young people like flirting by mobile because it allows the expression of feelings in more discreet and intimate ways. They can overcome shyness and impart uncomfortable information without meeting the other person face to face. As one young woman remarked, 'You can deny sending a flirty message. Say your friend sent it.' There is the further benefit that mobile communication is relatively free from scrutiny by parents and other adults.

Source: Harkin (2003)

VIDEO CONFERENCING

As was noted in Chapter 2, meetings between executives who work in widely dispersed locations are both time consuming and expensive. For example, consider the cost to the organisation of providing accommodation, travel and other expenses for a group of top executives who need to meet regularly but who are normally based in different countries. More difficult to estimate but no less significant is the cost of lost productivity while the executives are travelling to and from the meeting. Video conferencing saves on these costs by enabling executives to participate in 'virtual' meetings while remaining at their own place of work. It can also be a useful facility for those who are engaged in telecommuting, helping to connect employees in the office with those at home.

The essential physical elements of a video conferencing system are:
- **cameras** to capture and send video from your location
- **video displays** to show images of other users
- **microphones** to capture and send audio from your location
- **speakers** to play sound received from other users
- **network connections** of sufficient capacity to support good-quality audio and video transmission.

Video conferencing units vary from relatively simple units that suit one-to-one communication to more complex units that can be used for board meetings and conferences. The more powerful systems allow you to show videos and slides or use whiteboards to display charts. In addition, you can download close-ups of documents, drawings or objects onto your computer.

Video conferencing etiquette

The aim in conducting a video conference should be to make the experience as comfortable and productive as possible for the participants. A virtual meeting is still a meeting held in real time and governed by much the same rules of good conduct as any other meeting. It should therefore start punctually and be chaired in a fair and efficient manner. However, the use of quite sophisticated technological support adds a new dimension to this type of meeting, so there are some behaviours that are specific to video conferencing alone. Trauner *et al.* (2000) advise the following.

1. The first step to take is to make sure that audio and visual conditions are as effective as possible. This might involve a brief rehearsal at the beginning to make sure camera angles are correct, sound can be heard and so on. Most systems enable you to see your own image on the video display. Check that you can be fully seen, that there are no background distractions and that you are looking straight at the camera.

2. Once the initial adjustments have been made, behave as if in normal conversation. Avoid readjusting equipment as this is likely to distract the meeting. If you try to adjust the camera, for example, all other participants may see is a giant hand bearing down on the screen. Trying to move the microphone may cause sound to break up.

3. Like television, video tends to exaggerate body movements. If you look away from the camera or search around on you desk for documents, it will seem as if you have lost control or are no longer paying attention.

4. Avoid side conversations. Microphones are liable to pick these up and magnify them for the whole meeting. It is often a good idea to switch off your microphone when you aren't speaking.

5. Pay attention to dress and appearance. Clothes that have exaggerated patterns or strong colours may not work on video. Remember that we are used to highly professional standards on commercial television and video, so apply these to video conferencing as well.

6.   Making sure that all relevant documents are available is a little more complicated at a virtual meeting. Either these should be sent in advance to all participants or the facility to print them out during the meeting should be available at each site. As far as possible, amenities at each location should be of equal standard.

TELEWORKING

Flexible location work is the term used to describe new forms of work practice in which employees work on the move or from home. For example, a salesperson who travels frequently and uses her hotel room as a temporary office is engaged in this kind of work. Such a work pattern is often referred to as *teleworking* or *telecommuting* because electronic communication is the primary mode of communicating with headquarters. Already an estimated six per cent of workers in the European Union are classified as teleworkers, and this proportion is expected to grow to approximately eleven per cent by 2005.

Teleworking can be advantageous from the perspective of both the worker and employer. For example, employees who work from home avoid the cost and stress of travelling to and from work. They may enjoy greater autonomy and have more freedom to organise their working day according to their own needs. They may be better able to balance the demands of work with other aspects of their lives, such as family commitments or recreation. Employers also benefit in terms of higher productivity, reduced overhead costs and reduced employee turnover.

However, there may also be disadvantages. An employee who is working from a remote location may feel a sense of isolation or may worry about being overlooked for promotion because she is not at the centre of things. From an employer perspective, managing at a distance brings about its own problems, such as how to ensure that work is monitored and everyone has the information he or she needs, what to do if an employee cannot be contacted, how to maintain the morale of a person who is working on their own and so on.

Teleworking creates a more dispersed organisation and requires highly efficient and sophisticated forms of communication if it is to be successful. It also requires a somewhat different communication style from management.

- The primary requirement is for excellent electronic communication links between the worker and head office. It is essential that the teleworker has highly reliable access to office systems via e-mail, intranet or telephone.

- Information has to be more carefully structured and its distribution more efficiently managed. When workers are remote, managing by 'walking around' is impossible and informal channels are unavailable. The worker is off the premises, so the manager cannot drop by and make a comment or ask a question in passing. Because of this, particular care needs to be taken to ensure that information reaches those who need it and no one is forgotten simply because they are physically absent. Likewise, the message needs to be focused and prioritised. E-mailing copies to everyone is a waste of time when the message is relevant only to a few people.

- To overcome the problem of isolation managers need to keep in close contact with remote workers. Constant two-way communication should be encouraged. It is also suggested that managers make more use of the telephone instead of depending entirely on e-mails. Voice communication adds warmth to the interaction and allows for social and personal exchanges as well as purely work-related information.

- Virtual meetings using telephone or video conferencing can replace regular face-to-face meetings. Often this represents a real saving to the organisation by eliminating the cost of travel and accommodation for attendees. Nevertheless, it is recommended that normal face-to-face meetings take place from time to time. These are particularly useful when critical or strategic decisions need to be made. They also give teleworkers an opportunity to mix with their colleagues, share ideas and socialise, so they should be fun as well.

ELECTRONIC COMMUNICATION – SUMMARY OF BENEFITS

SPEED

Perhaps the most important advantage of the new technology is that it enables information to be handled and transmitted with much greater speed and efficiency than before. For example, e-mails can be sent and responded to in a fraction of the time taken by the traditional postal system (now referred to disparagingly as *snail mail*).

CONVENIENCE

New facilities and features help to remove some of the difficulties and inconveniences associated with traditional methods of communication. A few examples illustrate this. E-mail enables the receiver to accept and read mail at convenient times. Video conferencing saves executives the trouble and expense of travelling long distances to meetings. Voice mail ensures that no telephone call need go unanswered or unrecorded. The astonishing growth in mobile phone usage illustrates how quickly a convenient and flexible medium will be adopted by consumers and businesses alike.

ACCESS TO DATA

Because of the speed and efficiency with which it processes data, the new technology is making an ever-increasing range of information available to managers. For instance, analysis of markets, prices, sales figures, etc. that would have been too laborious to prepare can now be accessed in minutes. Used properly, this information should enable managers to make quicker and better-informed decisions.

ENHANCED PRESENTATION

Not only can more information be made available more quickly, it can also be presented more effectively. For example, we have seen how a video conferencing facility not only enables virtual face-to-face communication but also the display of high-quality visuals.

ECONOMY

Although using electronic communication is far from cheap, it may nevertheless be a more economical option than using paper-based alternatives. Systems like the Internet can put the manufacturer in direct contact with the consumer, thereby cutting out the cost of distributors, agents and wholesalers. Video conferencing saves on the expense of travel and hotel accommodation.

FLEXIBLE WORK ARRANGEMENTS

Electronic communication enables workers and employers to choose more flexible work arrangements. Teleworking gives workers greater freedom to work from home if they wish and organise their working day according to their own needs.

To conclude, electronic communication has a profound effect on the way businesses operate. Obviously, the new technology has considerable impact on the forms and methods of business communication, but it also brings about fundamental organisational change as well. Managers and workers have to learn new skills, some jobs may disappear while others are created and work practices have to change and become more flexible. Nevertheless, the new communication technologies are so important nowadays in gaining competitive advantage that few, if any, businesses can ignore them and hope to survive.

ASSIGNMENTS

REVISION

1. Write brief explanatory notes on (a) the Internet (b) e-commerce.
2. Name any five benefits the Internet brings to business.
3. Explain the difference between websites that are used for the following purposes: (a) electronic brochure (b) online shopping (c) corporate marketing.
4. Outline five principles of good website design.
5. What are the strengths and weaknesses of e-mail?
6. Name four services provided on landline telephones.
7. Give reasons for the astonishing growth in mobile phone usage in recent years.
8. How can you use a mobile phone to access the Internet?
9. What are the benefits of video conferencing?
10. Describe some ways in which behaviour during a video conference differs from behaviour during a face-to-face meeting.
11. Define *flexible location work* or *teleworking*. What are the benefits of teleworking for (a) the employee (b) the employer?
12. Working at a distance creates special problems for communication between manager and employee. Describe some of the problems that arise and suggest ways of solving them.
13. Summarise the benefits of electronic communication.

ACTIVITIES

1. Access the websites of well-known telecommunication providers in Ireland, e.g. Eircom, Esat BT, Vodaphone Ireland or O$_2$ Ireland. Find out what new products are on offer and how the products and services described above have developed.
2. Contact your local Internet service provider and find out what services are offered.
3. A number of ways of using the Internet in business are described above. Can you think of any other business uses? In small groups, brainstorm for new ideas.
4. Access the websites of three or four well-known Irish companies. Rank the sites according to:
    • content – is it interesting and informative?
    • navigation – is it easy to use?
    • design – is it easy to read, attractive to look at?
    What improvements can be made to the site you think least effective?
5. Select a product that you might want to buy from a website. Find companies

in Ireland or the UK offering this product for sale. Compare prices, shipping costs, etc. Estimate how much you are likely to save by buying online rather than from a conventional retailer.

6. Access the website of the Information Society Commission at www.isc.ie. The ISC, an independent advisory body, monitors Ireland's evolution as an information society and highlights the opportunities and challenges the new technology offers. Click 'ISC Reports' to find their most recent discussion documents and statistical summaries.

FOR DISCUSSION

1. How do you think global telecommunication links will affect the way businesses are organised? Do you think the nature of work will change radically? What are the social consequences likely to be?

2. There is now a serious public debate about whether or not the lack of control of the Internet is a good thing. Do you believe anyone should have the right to use the Internet as he or she pleases, or should there be some form of regulation?

3. Consider the benefits and drawbacks of electronic communication when compared with paper-based communication. Does paper communication have unique advantages that will ensure its survival, or is it likely to disappear altogether?

4. An increasing number of workers are choosing to work from home. Discuss the advantages and disadvantages of working away from the office, with particular reference to communication. Do you think teleworking would appeal to young people?

PART 2

Research and Writing Skills

5 Finding Information

WHY DEVELOP RESEARCH SKILLS?

It is often said that we live in the 'information age'. New communication technologies such as the Internet give us access to information on a scale that former generations could not have imagined. The great benefit of this is that information once hidden away in libraries or guarded by professional elites can now be reached at the touch of a key on a personal computer. But the task of dealing with all this information can sometimes seem daunting. What do we do when an enquiry about even the simplest topic on an Internet search engine brings up hundreds of possible information sources? How do we make sense of it all? Clearly, to succeed in the 'information age' we need be become efficient in finding, organising and *limiting* information among the vast amount that is available.

Increasingly, business students are required to develop information-handling skills by engaging in self-directed learning and presenting their findings in written or oral presentations. In later years of the course there may be substantial projects or dissertations to complete. If you are given such assignments you may be uncertain at first about sources of information and how to locate them. As work progresses you may face the problem of interpreting what is found and evaluating its usefulness.

The aim of this chapter is to help you approach research in an informed and organised way. Specifically, this chapter:

- suggests a step-by-step research strategy
- identifies some of the key resources that can be accessed in a college library (or library website)
- gives useful guidelines for organising and using the information you find.

Given that businesses must also deal effectively with the modern explosion in information, the research skills you develop in college should prove a valuable accomplishment in your professional life.

A STRATEGY FOR RESEARCH

There are two essential things to do when researching for an essay or dissertation. First, you should start as soon as possible. There are several reasons for this. It may prove more difficult than you think to identify the research questions you want to answer, finding information may take longer than expected or some of the material you want to read may not be immediately available and you may have to wait several weeks for your library to locate and deliver it. Then, you will need to leave sufficient time at the end for writing up, revising and printing your submission.

Second, you should carry out your research as systematically as you can. Taking a planned approach makes the whole process more efficient and hopefully more enjoyable. It should be noted, however, that the different stages of research are not so discrete that one must be completed before the next begins. For example, you may find that the first definition of your topic needs to be revised several times in light of the evidence you uncover. Something you notice at writing-up stage may send you back to look for more information. Research is a cyclical and sometimes messy business. With this proviso in mind, a plan for research consisting of six stages is suggested below (see Exhibit 5.1).

Exhibit 5.1 The research process

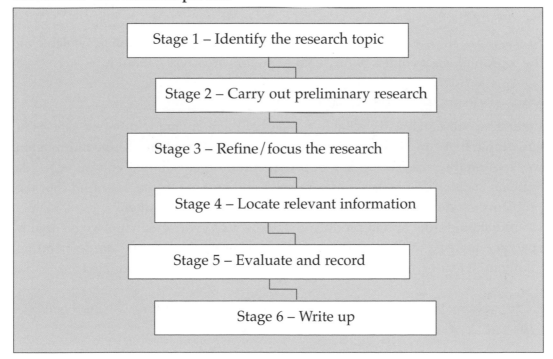

Stage 1 – Identify the research topic

Stage 2 – Carry out preliminary research

Stage 3 – Refine/focus the research

Stage 4 – Locate relevant information

Stage 5 – Evaluate and record

Stage 6 – Write up

STAGE 1 – IDENTIFY THE RESEARCH TOPIC

The first step is to find a topic that interests you. Sometimes you will be given a topic by your tutor and perhaps some guidelines as to the approach he or she would like you to take. At other times, however, you will be expected to choose a topic yourself and identify your own research questions. You may have trouble settling on a topic initially. If this is the case, you can look for inspiration in the course subjects that you like, or scan newspapers, business magazines or journals for ideas. It is important to choose a topic that you can feel enthusiastic about, otherwise you will find the research very hard work indeed.

STAGE 2 – CARRY OUT PRELIMINARY RESEARCH

At the beginning, it is common to state the research topic in broad terms. For example, you may want to specialise in human resource management – you are interested in the problem of motivating team workers in industry. You now have at your disposal three key concepts to help you with preliminary research (motivation, teamwork, industry). Using these keywords, you can search for information in:

- reference books, such as specialised encyclopaedias and dictionaries
- library catalogues
- journal indexes (for relevant articles)
- websites.

At this stage the aim should be to find out how much information is available on the topic and what contemporary commentators are saying about it.

STAGE 3 – REFINE/FOCUS THE RESEARCH

Preliminary research will probably reveal that there are many different aspects of your topic that can be addressed. For example, the problem of motivating team workers might raise issues of group dynamics, organisational culture, rewards systems, gender differences, different roles and so on. Or you may find that the problems in one industry or country differ from those in another.

   You should now aim to produce a statement of your research objective that is specific, focused and manageable. For example, the initial topic heading 'motivating team workers in industry' may eventually be reformulated as:

> 'To evaluate the impact of reward and recognition systems on the motivation of team workers in the Irish financial services industry.'

You can see how this has significantly narrowed the research problem. It is now concerned with just one clearly defined aspect of motivation and is restricted to a particular region and industry sector.

STAGE 4 – LOCATE RELEVANT INFORMATION

Armed with a precise research objective, you can now be more rigorous and purposeful in your search for information. In the example above, you will need to review the literature on reward and recognition systems in employment. You will probably want to find out how individual reward systems differ from group systems. You will also need to research the extent to which teamwork is used in the financial services sector, what its perceived benefits are and so on.

Books, journals, reports and conference proceedings are the best resources to use when carrying out research at this stage. In the case above, relevant material is likely to be found under the general headings 'human resource management', 'personnel management' or 'organisational behaviour', e.g. *Personnel Review, Human Resource Management Journal*. Use the full range of resources available and ask library staff for help if you need it.

STAGE 5 – EVALUATE AND RECORD

It is important that you assess the value and relevance of the information you read. It is also important that you record the details of all your sources as well as taking note of the content. Useful tips on criteria for evaluation and techniques for recording are given later in the chapter.

STAGE 6 – WRITE UP

When writing up, try to follow a recognised academic format. (If in doubt, ask your tutor what he or she expects.) Always acknowledge when you have used other people's material in quotations or paraphrases, set yourself high standards in layout and style, avoid simple but obvious mistakes in spelling, etc. and make sure to leave enough time at the end for final review and last-minute corrections.

HELPFUL HINT – USE THE LIBRARY!

At every stage of research the most valuable source of information you have is your college library. As you become familiar with the library, you will find that it provides an astonishing range of material in both print and electronic form, including:

- books and general reference
- periodicals and electronic journals
- indexes and databases
- information on film, video, microfilm, audio tape and CD-ROM.

If material cannot be found on-site, the library can arrange interlibrary loans or provide letters of introduction to other libraries. In addition, many ancillary services are provided, such as access to inexpensive photocopying or the loan of laptop computers. Library staff are invariably accommodating and helpful. They will gladly give expert advice on where and how to find the resources you need. Lastly, the library will provide at least some seating space and can be a quiet, pleasant place to study.

Many libraries arrange an introductory tour or a short series of tutorials for new students. If such a service is offered, make sure to avail of it. The few hours this takes will be among the most productive you spend in college!

Let us now look in more detail at the kind of resources libraries make available.

RESOURCES IN PRINT

Although an increasing amount of information can be found on the Internet, college libraries still hold a large stock of print material that supports the curriculum. In addition to books and periodicals, there will be collections of newspapers, theses, official publications, conference proceedings and photocopies. Some items may be stored on open shelves while others are held in archives or storage.

Each item is assigned a call number that identifies its subject and location. In Irish libraries, call numbers are usually based on the Dewey Decimal Classification System (see Exhibit 5.2 below).

Exhibit 5.2 Dewey Decimal Classification System

> 000 Generalities
> 100 Philosophy/Psychology
> 200 Religion
> 300 Social Sciences
> 400 Language
> 500 Natural Sciences/Mathematics
> 600 Technology
> 700 The Arts
> 800 Literature/Rhetoric
> 900 Geography

The easiest way to find a book or print journal is to use the OPAC facility (Online Public Access Catalogue) on your library website. By searching under 'Author', 'Title', etc. you can quickly find out if the library has the item you want and whether or not it is currently on loan. Note that while OPAC will tell you if the library owns a particular publication it will say little or nothing about its content. To discover more you will need to consult journal indexes or databases (see below) or visit the library itself.

GENERAL REFERENCE

As research usually proceeds from the general to the particular, the reference section of your library can be a good place to start. Here you may be able to obtain a broad overview of your topic, check definitions or find useful names and addresses.

* **Encyclopaedias** give excellent background information and are usually written in an accessible style. Some encyclopaedias, such as the *Encyclopaedia Britannica,* are general whereas others, such as the *International Encyclopaedia of Communication,* are specialised.
* **Dictionaries** can provide definitions of specialist terms you may need to understand for your research.
* **Directories** give information and contact details for companies and other organisations.

Once you have obtained a basic understanding of your subject and identified the main terms to use in searching you can then begin to explore more widely in books and journals.

BOOKS

Books are an excellent resource if you want a detailed and comprehensive understanding of a topic. Each of your tutors will probably recommend one or more key books to ensure you have a solid foundation in the subject and you should certainly read these carefully. Obviously, there is great demand for recommended books, so libraries often restrict access to them, e.g. holding them at the library desk or releasing them on short loan.

Important though books are, they also have some limitations. They take time to read, tend to be inflexible and often contain out-of-date information. It is a good idea, therefore, to use them selectively. You rarely need to read a book from cover to cover – instead, only read those chapters or sections that are truly useful. A quick glance through a book can tell you a great deal about its value and relevance.

So what should you look for when you take a book off the shelf?

* **Title:** Gives a broad indication of what the book is about.
* **Author:** Is the book written by a respected expert, someone your tutor has mentioned?
* **Date:** Some books, particularly those in the technology field, go out of date very quickly.

- **Table of contents:** Are there individual chapters that interest you?
- **Index:** Tells you where particular topics are dealt with in the book.
- **References/bibliography:** May guide you to other books or journal articles.
- **Style:** Is the style popular or academic, accessible or more difficult, modern or somewhat old-fashioned?

Having carried out this initial appraisal you can then decide whether to read the book in full, in part or not at all.

PRINT JOURNALS

Academic journals are published regularly (often quarterly) in every discipline and may be available in either/both print and electronic form. You will need to consult journals for up-to-date information and to read reports on the most recent primary research in your subject. Your library will subscribe to a range of print journals that you will find listed on the library website. Periodicals such as newspapers and journals are held separately from books, and in most libraries only current issues are displayed. Earlier issues may be kept in boxes or shelved in bound volumes, while some material, particularly newspapers, is stored on microfiche or microfilm. As a general rule libraries do not release periodicals on loan, so you will probably have to photocopy or take notes on the articles you want.

It can be useful to visit your library and look through the latest issue of a relevant journal. This will alert you to 'hot' topics that currently engage the academic community. However, browsing on library shelves is not a particularly efficient way of finding and evaluating journal articles. Instead you should:

- look specifically for articles recommended on your reading list or by your tutor
- track articles from one publication to another by scanning references and bibliographies
- use a **journal index.**

A journal index provides a key to the contents of many journals at once and will indicate which articles may be relevant to your research topic. In each case it will tell you the article title, the name of the author, the journal in which the article was published and the date of publication. In addition, it may provide a short summary (or abstract) of the article. Most journal indexes are now accessible online and many also provide the articles themselves in full text (see the **databases** section below).

When you have identified the journal you want, you can then use the OPAC facility to see if your library has it in stock. If your library does not carry the journal it may nevertheless be able to locate a copy using the interlibrary loan system.

USING THE INTERNET

The Internet gives access to an enormous amount of information provided by governments, colleges and universities, companies, associations, interest groups and private individuals. This information is being added to all the time and much of it is free and up to date. However, the Net has some limitations that you need to be aware of before using it for research.

- First, the Net contains such a mass of material that finding a particular piece of information can seem like looking for a needle in a haystack. It is easy to waste time browsing and getting sidetracked into irrelevant websites.
- Second, the quality of material on the Net is very uneven. Anyone can post information and there is no independent verification of its truth or value. Documents can be altered or removed at will. Those who write them don't need to have any academic or professional qualifications. While there is much information to be found that is reliable and trustworthy, equally there is much that is badly written, naïve or prejudiced, so beware!
- Last, the Net is only *one* source of information and is unlikely to meet all your research requirements. Many books and journals are unavailable on the Net because they have not been digitised or because their publishers want to make money selling them in print format.

The lesson to draw from this is that you can save considerable time and effort by navigating websites efficiently and making accurate judgments about the quality and relevance of the information you find there. Let us now look at three Internet facilities that can help: search engines, directories and gateways.

SEARCH ENGINES

The quickest way to find information on the web is to use a search engine such as Google, Altavista, Lycos or Yahoo. Search engines trawl the web using robot software called harvesters, crawlers, etc. To find information, type keywords in the 'Search' box and then click on 'Go' or press the return key on your keyboard. The search engine will almost immediately present you with a long list of web pages containing the words you have chosen.

Keywords can be linked with connectors, usually AND and OR. For example:

- entering 'telework AND childcare' will return web pages containing **both** words
- entering 'telework OR childcare' will return pages containing **either** word but not both together.

As many of the pages displayed will be of doubtful relevance you should try to make the search as focused as possible. One way to achieve this is to use the 'advanced search' option. This allows you to select pages from a particular time period, in a particular language, etc. Another good idea is to use progressively more precise terms. For example, 'capital taxation' will return a much smaller number of hits than the general word 'taxation'. It can also be useful to enter the words 'definition', 'article' or 'report' along with your other search terms as this often helps to remove nonacademic or trivial information.

DIRECTORIES

Most search services provide directories that classify web resources under generalised subject headings. A directory differs from a search engine in that websites are selected by a human being rather than a machine. This means that some element of judgment has been used and the quality of information is likely to be more reliable. Directories are arranged hierarchically so that the user is able to move steadily towards more specific information. Thus, for example, websites relating to Irish credit unions can be located in the Google directory by clicking on successive headings as follows: Business>Financial Services>Banking Services> Credit Unions>Ireland.

Commonly used directories like those provided by Google and Lycos contain a mix of popular and serious subjects, e.g. 'Shopping' along with 'Science'. They use their own method of classification. In contrast, BUBL Link, a directory run by the University of Strathclyde, lists only academic subjects and uses the Dewey Decimal Classification System familiar to library users everywhere. As a general rule, web resources indexed in academic directories are much more carefully evaluated – and hence likely to be more useful – than those found in commercial directories.

GATEWAYS

A gateway is a classified directory for one specific subject or discipline. For example, SOSIG, the Social Science Information Gateway, provides selected Internet resources in the social sciences, business and law. The websites listed in gateways are rigorously evaluated by librarians or academics, and therefore you can be sure of obtaining high-quality, structured information. In addition, gateways usually provide other facilities, such as search engines and online tutorials teaching Internet skills. If you want to browse for general but reliable information at the beginning of a research project, a subject gateway is an excellent place to start.

Useful gateways and directories

BUBL: Internet information service provided by Strathclyde University at *http://bubl.ac.uk*.

EEVL: The gateway to engineering, maths and computing at *http://www.eevl.ac.uk*.

FINFACTS: The gateway to Irish business information at *http://www.finfacts.ie*.

HEANET: Irish academic gateway at *http://heanet.ie*.

NISS: Provides a gateway for the UK education community at *http://niss.ac.uk* and *http://www.educserv.org.uk/niss/*.

RDN: The Research Development Network provides a subject directory as well as an interactive Internet skills training module at *http://rdn.ac.uk*.

SOSIG: The Social Sciences Information Gateway (including business) at *http://sosig.ac.uk*.

ELECTRONIC JOURNALS AND BIBLIOGRAPHIC DATABASES

ELECTRONIC JOURNALS

An electronic journal (or e-journal) is a publication supplied electronically via web pages. Most e-journals available from your library are likely to be electronic versions of print journals. They are published at regular intervals, are properly refereed and contain the most up-to-date information available on a subject. Their accessibility means that they can be an excellent resource for research students.

Access to e-journal articles is provided at three levels.

- **Full text:** The complete article can be read.
- **Abstracts:** A summary of the article is given. Sometimes the summarised article is available only in print. However, an abstract can help you decide whether or not the full article is worth reading.
- **Table of contents (TOC):** This lists the titles of articles only. As titles give an initial indication of the content's relevance, a table of contents is a useful guide when you are simply browsing for information.

The most common formats for downloading full text articles are **html** (web page) and **pdf** (portable document file). Documents displayed in html are easy to read but may not print out so well, e.g. they may be wider than a standard A4 page. In contrast, pdf reproduces documents on screen in much the same format as they would appear in print. Note that you will need to have Adobe Acrobat Reader or RealPage software on your computer in order to access full text documents. The software may be supplied by your library or downloaded from the proprietors' websites.

Useful e-journal subscription services

Ingenta, founded in the United States, indexes 27,000 international journals and gives access to more than 5,000 full text journals.

SwetsWise is an off-shoot of Swets Blackwell, one of the largest journal subscription management services in the world. It provides the table of contents for more than 17,000 journals and full text for over 7,000 publications.

Zetoc is the British Library's Electronic Table of Contents service.

It is likely that your library has an account with these services. Note that the library must subscribe to publications in hard copy before you can avail of them in electronic format. To access e-journals, check your library website or ask your librarian for help.

BIBLIOGRAPHIC DATABASES

A bibliographic database contains descriptive information about publications such as books, periodical articles, newspaper and magazine articles and so on. This information is presented in a highly structured form consisting of a series of **records** (much the same as a library catalogue). Each record gives information about an individual item, e.g. an article on brand management in a marketing journal.

Bibliographic records normally contain the following elements:
- the **citation,** i.e. information about the author, title, date of publication, source, etc.
- **subject headings** or **descriptors** that give an indication of the content
- an **abstract** that summarises the content in greater detail.

The first step is to find out which databases can be accessed from your library. Then, having chosen one that meets your needs (see list below), you simply enter keywords in the 'Find' or 'Search' box. This will bring up a list of relevant articles, documents or news items. You can then click on any titles that seem interesting or relevant. You can usually refine or limit your search to particular time periods, publications or publication types, e.g. scholarly journals only. When you have found reference to an article that you want to read in full you can ask your library to locate it for you. Increasingly, however, bibliographic databases link to **full text databases** that enable you to read articles online.

Useful databases

ABI/INFORM

One of the first electronic databases, ABI/INFORM provides abstracts and full text for over 1,000 titles in business. It is an excellent source of information on market conditions and business trends worldwide.

Business Source Premier

This database is designed specifically for business schools and libraries. It contains more than 3,000 full text journals and periodicals in a range of business areas.

Emerald

Emerald databases, e.g. **Emerald Fulltext** and **Emerald Management Reviews,** are smaller in scale but review articles in a range of useful business journals and periodicals, including *Harvard Business Review* and *The Economist*.

FACTfinder

This database indexes business-related articles and news items in the Irish print media. It also provides useful information about Irish companies.

EVALUATING INFORMATION

Let us assume that you have located a number of sources of information related to your topic. Indeed, given the amount of information available, you may have discovered that there are hundreds of articles, news items, etc. that could be relevant. The problem now is to find the right information and eliminate material that might damage the credibility of your research. In other words, you need to *evaluate*.

The nature of the topic will have a bearing on the quality of information required. If your task is to write an essay, it may suffice to read articles in good-quality newspapers or business magazines, e.g. *The Irish Times* or *The Economist*. However, if you are writing a research paper or dissertation, it is certain that you will need to refer to current academic journal articles, government reports and the like. In all academic work your sources must reach a relatively high standard, and the use of popular articles, quizzes, advice columns, etc. as source material is nearly always unacceptable.

There are a number of tests that can help you make an effective assessment of the information before you.

1. **Author's credentials**

    Is the article written by an acknowledged authority? Is the publisher well respected? Have you located the article using a reputable academic or business database?

2. **Year of publication**

    Is the article up to date, i.e. published within the last few years? Even if you are relying on classic texts, you may still need to find out how these are interpreted in current journals.

3. **Validity**

    Is the information reliable? Are the methods used to gather data of an acceptable standard? For instance, if the writer has carried out survey research, has he or she used a sufficiently large and representative sample? Are correct conclusions drawn?

4. **Objectivity**

    Does the information come from a biased source? For example, is the article written by someone who has a particular ideological viewpoint or who represents a particular interest? Remember that bias need not invalidate the work – after all, it is difficult if not impossible to write from a truly neutral standpoint. However, be alert for bias that causes important facts to be misused or overlooked.

5. **Style**

    Is the quality of writing good? Is the article written in a serious or academic style? Note that a journalistic or popular style is often the first indication you have that the article is not suitable for research.

ORGANISING AND USING RESEARCH

Soon after you begin research you need to organise the information you collect into a form that can be easily recalled and managed. The importance of good organisation cannot be emphasised too strongly. Here are suggestions for what you should do.

1. **File printouts and photocopies carefully**

    Try not to let photocopies and web page printouts accumulate in an indiscriminate mass. File them under appropriate subject headings and discard those that are of no value to your research. Use highlighters to mark passages that you particularly want to remember. This will save having to read the whole article again.

2. **Take notes**

    Use brief, structured notes to summarise the main points of books and articles. Store these under subject headings in a file or folder. Be highly selective. It is rarely necessary to summarise the *whole* book! (See also tips on note-taking from lectures in Chapter 13.)

3. **Record sources**

    It is vital that you keep a record of sources as you go along. Write down the complete citation to include:
    *   article or book title
    *   author
    *   volume and issue number (if a journal article)
    *   publisher
    *   date of publication
    *   page number
    *   date of access (if a web page).

4. **Mark word-for-word quotations**

    Be careful to copy word-for-word passages exactly as they appear in the text. Mark them with quotation marks and record the page numbers where you found them.

5. **Build your bibliography**

    It is a good idea to start compiling your bibliography from the very beginning. Use a standard referencing system (see below for an example) and enter the details of books, articles, etc. immediately after you have identified them as useful. It is much easier to delete a superfluous entry than search for a reference you came across weeks ago and failed to record at the time.

Avoiding plagiarism

Research involves reading other people's work and incorporating some of it into your own essays and projects. It is important to credit words and ideas that are not your own and that are not part of the store of common knowledge. To copy without acknowledgement is plagiarism, which is regarded as a serious offence in academic writing. It is important to note that copyright applies to the Internet as well, so the easy availability of web information doesn't mean that it can be used freely.

You should cite the source in any of the following cases:

- when referring to an idea or theory that another person has originated
- when quoting word for word
- when paraphrasing what another person has said
- when using statistics, graphs or charts that someone else has generated.

However, you don't have to reference information that is commonly known and appears in many different sources. For example, the basic elements of communication described in Chapter 1 can be regarded as part of a common understanding of the communication process, so no acknowledgments are needed.

WHEN TO QUOTE

Quoting or paraphrasing another writer provides evidence that you have read around your topic and have become familiar with current ideas and opinions in the area. You are also helping readers who may wish to follow up references for themselves.

Word-for-word quotations should always be used sparingly and only when there is clear justification. You might typically use a quotation when you want to enlist the support of important experts for your argument, or when the words the other person has used are particularly vivid or provocative. Short quotations should be integrated into the text and enclosed in single quotation marks. Longer quotations, e.g. forty words or more, should have no quotation marks but should be separated from the text, indented from the left and right and typed in single spacing.

Paraphrasing can be used more extensively. Essentially, you paraphrase when you convey the sense of what someone else has said without quoting them. It is important to use your own words as much as possible while remaining true to the meaning of the original. Changing one or two words or phrases does not suffice.

CITING AND REFERENCE

Citing is the means by which you give formal recognition to sources in your text. A **reference** is a detailed description of the source. It may appear at the bottom of the page as a footnote, at the end of the chapter or at the end of the complete work.

Finally, a **bibliography** is an alphabetical compendium of all the sources used. The Harvard author-date citation system is straightforward and one of the most widely used. Each time you refer to a source you simply insert the author's surname followed by the year of publication. A direct quotation should also include the page reference. For example:

> 'An electronic market can be viewed as a direct parallel of the familiar shop, store or emporium. It is, in essence, a virtual trading area, where deals are struck through a computer screen, over a network.' (Norris and West, 2001:18)

When the author's name occurs naturally in the text it is not bracketed. For example:

> According to Barrett (2002), senior communication staff should have a central role in strategic decision-making and should be represented on the senior management team.

Bear in mind, however, that there are several different conventions for citing and reference so it is advisable to ask your tutor which one is preferred in your department. Likewise, if you are writing a paper intended for an academic journal you will need to find out and use the publisher's house style. For a complete guide to the Harvard citation system or any other style you should consult style manuals in your library. (References for the two citations above are given in the bibliography at the end of the book.)

As a final word, it is worth remembering that research, while undoubtedly demanding, can also be an adventure. The American journalist Franklin P. Adams once remarked that most of the knowledge he had accumulated came from 'looking up something and finding something else on the way.' The information age has made a wealth of information available, so learn to use research tools well and enjoy the journey, even if it takes you along some unexpected paths.

ASSIGNMENTS

REVISION

1. This chapter has suggested a research plan in six stages. What are these stages?
2. Name three types of general reference books that can help research.
3. It is advisable to appraise a book before deciding to read it. What features of a book can help you assess its relevance to your work?
4. What is a journal index?
5. While the Internet enables researchers to access vast amounts of information it also has some limitations. What are these?

6. Give a brief description of the following Internet facilities: (a) search engine (b) directory (c) gateway.

7. A bibliographic database contains descriptive information about books, journals, magazine articles, etc. in a series of records. What information does each record normally contain?

8. What tests can you use to evaluate the usefulness or reliability of information found during research?

9. This chapter makes some suggestions for organising information. What are these?

10. What is plagiarism? When should you cite another author? What is common knowledge?

11. Quotations should be used sparingly. Describe two circumstances in which quotation can be justified.

12. State clearly what each of the following means: (a) citation (b) reference (c) bibliography.

ACTIVITIES

1. Access your college library home page to find out the range of services provided and how to use them. Explore the basic library catalogue, e-journal indexes, databases, etc. Look for extra features such as online tutorials or a library newsletter.

2. Explore the library itself and find out how books are arranged, where journals are displayed, etc.

3. Using a search engine such as Google, you can find many useful online library skills tutorials. Just key in the search terms 'library skills tutorial' or 'library search tutorial'.

4. The RDN Virtual Training Suite provides excellent online tutorials on how to use the Internet for research across a wide range of subjects. It also lists other useful Internet sites. RDN is short for Resource Discovery Network and its website can be found at www.vts.rdn.ac.uk. Start the tutorial by clicking on 'Business Studies'.

5. From the library catalogue select one book dealing with business communication. Find the book in the library and look at the author's credentials, date of publication, table of contents, index, bibliography and style. How useful is this book likely to be for your studies? Give reasons for your assessment.

6. You want to find recent statistics on the extent to which teleworking occurs in Ireland. Using a **search engine,** search for the terms 'teleworking statistics Ireland'. Open the first website listed and evaluate its usefulness on a scale

from one (not useful at all) to five (very useful). Give reasons for your assessment, then repeat the exercise using a **directory** and a **gateway**, e.g. SOSIG.

7. Find out if a particular referencing system is preferred by your department or tutor. Obtain a copy of the style manual and learn to use its conventions consistently.

Effective Writing (1): The Writing Process

There are many different written forms in business – e-mails, letters, reports, notices and press releases, to name but a few. Each form has its own distinctive characteristics. A press release looks different from a memo and a sales letter will not be written in the same style as a formal report. Nevertheless, there are certain basic rules and principles that can be applied to all functional writing. No matter what it looks like an effective document:

- will have clear objectives and will keep the reader in mind
- will be logically organised and written in a clear, persuasive style
- will be presented in a manner that attracts the reader and enhances the message.

Basic principles and guidelines for effective functional writing are set out in this and the following chapter. This chapter covers each main stage of the writing process, from early preparation to final presentation. The next chapter deals with aspects of style.

THE WRITING BACKGROUND

PURPOSE

The first essential step in writing is to clarify objectives. There are a few broad objectives that are common to all documents – giving information, asking for information, etc. However, writers in business usually need to be more precise than this.

For example, suppose you wish to write a letter of reply to a customer who has made a complaint. The letter might have the following specific objectives:

- to accept responsibility and apologise to the customer for the inconvenience caused
- to offer an explanation for what has gone wrong
- to say what you will do to remedy the situation.

You will find the actual letter in Exhibit 6.3 on p. 96. Notice how the identification of the objectives gives shape and structure to the message.

Most of the time it is sufficient to think about objectives and clarify them mentally. Sometimes, however, it is a good idea to write them down in what is called a *statement of purpose*. This can be particularly helpful when the document to be written is complex and there is a danger of it becoming unfocused if the objectives are in any way unclear.

Here are some examples.

1. The aim of this report is to examine the reasons for the high level of absenteeism among young apprentices at ABC Ltd and to suggest how the problem can be solved.

2. The purpose of this letter is to inform XYZ Ltd about the current state of its group pension scheme, to make it aware that its scheme is now underfunded and to recommend that premiums be raised.

3. In this report I am required to compare the OPA/A and OPA/A1 operating systems and to recommend to management which should be adopted.

4. The purpose of this memorandum is to list, describe and cost the audio-visual equipment that will be required for our new training centre.

READERS

Finding out as much as you can about the reader and trying to look at the message from his perspective is a vital element in effective written communication. If you fail to do this, you may not get the results you want. Useful questions to ask are:

- Am I writing for fellow professionals or the general public?
- What is my audience's status? Are they my juniors, peers or superiors?
- How much do they already know about the subject?
- Will they understand the technical terms I take for granted in my work?
- How busy are they? Will they have much time to read what I write?
- Are their priorities different from mine? What do they believe to be important? What information will need special emphasis?
- Do they like documents in a particular format, e.g. short/long, detailed/main points only?

The closer you can match your written messages to your readers' needs and concerns, the more effective those messages will be.

CONTEXT

People like to put information in context. If they cannot see the relevance of a document, where it originated from or why it was needed, they are unlikely to give it much attention, so you should always be aware of the context yourself and make it clear to the reader when necessary.

For example, is your report or memo referring to a completely new development? If so, you will have to give full background information and explain why the development is necessary at this time. Alternatively, it may refer to something that has happened in the past. Then you will need to remind the reader of this so that she knows immediately what the document is about.

People may also be worried about the *consequences* of the document, for example, how a proposal may affect them personally or their part of the organisation. It may be necessary to reassure them about the way the information will be used or about confidentiality.

Finally, you should remember that a document is a written record. If someone takes the document from the files after, say, six months or a year, will they understand what it is all about? You may need to make the context clear not just for present readers but for future readers as well.

GETTING STARTED: THE WRITING PLAN

Writing, like many other human activities, is a rather untidy affair. A complex document may be restructured many times before it is finished. New ideas may be added, paragraphs moved around, dozens of words deleted or changed. There can be many false starts and changes of direction. However, this is not to say that writing is unplanned. On the contrary, all good writers plan, even if they do so only in their heads. Some types of plans are useful at an early stage in writing, some are useful later. You do not have to use any particular plan; choose those that work for you and that suit the job at hand.

LISTING

One way to begin planning is to make a list of points as they come to mind. The points need not be in any particular order and may include a mix of quite specific details and more general ideas. Listing in this *random* way can help to free up your thinking. It tells you what you know about the subject and what further research needs to be done.

MIND MAP

Some writers find it useful to put down their first thoughts in *diagrammatic* form. In a *mind map* the writer begins with the main topic and then works outwards to subtopics. The advantage of this method is that it indicates how ideas are connected to a central theme.

The mind map in Exhibit 6.1 below shows an initial plan for a circular letter to staff about the proposed introduction of flexible working.

Exhibit 6.1   Mind map

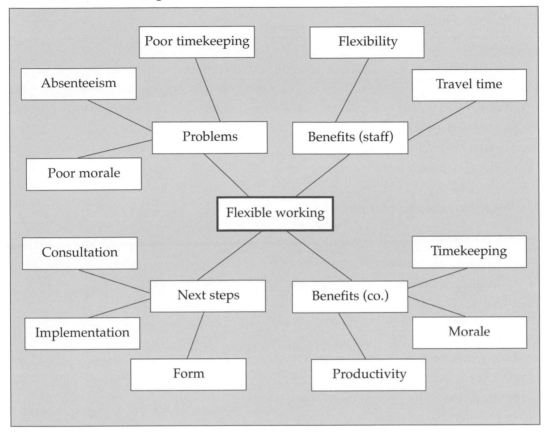

OUTLINE PLAN

This is a plan that shows main topics and subtopics in a neat, logical sequence. It can provide a framework for gathering information or a structure for writing. It ensures that the document follows a clear sequence and that there is no overlapping (see Exhibit 6.2).

DETAILED PLAN

This is similar to an outline plan, but with information points listed for each section. It is time consuming to do, but can be helpful when writing long reports in which there is a wealth of data to be included. It can be used to check that no essential point has been omitted before you write the first draft.

A plan does not have to be written down – some writers prefer to plunge in and organise ideas mentally as they go along. Word-processing packages make it tempting to do this because they allow headings to be changed and blocks of text to be moved around without too much difficulty. Even here, however, some planning must take place. If it does not, then a great deal of time can be wasted and the end result may be a badly organised document.

Exhibit 6.2 Outline plan

SUBJECT

Proposal to introduce flexible working system

OPENING
- ▸ give background
  - – suggestion from board of directors
- ▸ state purpose of letter
  - – to describe the system
  - – to invite comments from staff

INFORMATION

- ▸ description of system
- ▸ benefits for staff
- ▸ benefits for company

ACTION

- ▸ ask staff to fill in and return form
- ▸ give final date for receipt
- ▸ give date for implementation if agreed

RESEARCH

The value of many business documents, particularly reports, depends crucially on the thoroughness of the research that is done. A report that is incomplete or that contains inaccuracies is fatally flawed no matter how good it may be in other respects.

Sometimes the information you need may be found within the organisation itself, perhaps by consulting company files, by sending round a questionnaire or by interviewing members of staff. At other times you will have to search outside the organisation. There are many sources of information – indeed, as the previous chapter has shown, the problem is not so much to find sources as to decide which ones to use. The most obvious places to start are libraries, newspapers and journals, computer databases, reference books and directories.

It is important to do research well but not to waste too much time on it. Having clear objectives and an outline plan to begin with can prevent you from chasing down blind alleys.

STRUCTURE

Structure is what emerges at the end of the planning process – it is the final overall shape of a document. This shape should make sense to the reader and provide him with information in a logical sequence. The four-part structure described below will suit many different written forms, in particular letters, memos and notices. The structure of reports is somewhat different and this will be described in Chapter 9.

OPENING

All documents must have one or two opening paragraphs even though the heading *Introduction* need not be used. Openings are used in two main ways:
- to set the document in context by giving essential background information
- to make the purpose of the document clear or the reason why it is being sent.

Introductions should be kept as short and direct as possible. For example, if the document is one of a series and the context is already well known, the opening need only be a couple of sentences long.

INFORMATION

This section should set out in a clear sequence the information you wish to convey or questions you want to ask. In a long document it may be divided into a number of subsections, each with its own heading. It should contain all the reader needs to know, without repetition.

ACTION

In this section you say what you intend to do next and/or what you expect the reader to do.

CLOSE

You may wish to end with a polite 'one-liner' if required, although this is more common in letters than in other forms.

This structure is illustrated in the letter below (Exhibit 6.3), which is written in reply to a customer complaint.

Exhibit 6.3 Four-part structure

Dear Ms Whelan,

We were sorry to learn from your letter of 4 October that you were **Opening**
dissatisfied with the quality of the Irish Prize frozen chips which you
purchased recently (**context**), and we must apologise for this occurrence
(**purpose**).

Unfortunately, the quality of potatoes has not been as good as we would **Information**
wish this season and this has led to some black spots appearing on the
chips. We assure you that these represent no danger to health. In any
case, we are now in the process of installing new machinery which
should remove this problem entirely.

We are grateful that you took the trouble to contact us about this matter, **Action**
and enclose coupons to the value of €10 which you may exchange at
your local supermarket for any of our products. We hope this will
compensate you for the inconvenience caused.

Close

We look forward to your continued custom.

Yours sincerely, etc.

WRITING

The actual task of writing a document is an absorbing activity which requires
much concentration, so try to find a space for yourself where you can work in solid
blocks of time without interruption. This may not be so easy if you work in an
open-plan office or have to share the kitchen table with the rest of your family.
However, it is difficult to write efficiently if you have to stop and start constantly
or if there are distracting conversations going on in the background.

Getting on with the job is made much easier if you have planned well and have
an effective structure in mind. Having said that, we are all familiar with those
times when ideas seem to dry up or we struggle to complete a paragraph. Our
brain is really telling us that we need a rest, so when progress slows right down,
it is better to take a break. Go for a walk, do something different – you will come
back to the document refreshed and with new inspiration.

A plain, direct style is now recommended for all business and technical writing. (The main features of this style are discussed in detail in the next chapter.) One of the many advantages of a plain style is that it allows you to write quickly. You do not have to search for impressive words or construct complicated sentences. However, you do have to group your sentences into well-constructed paragraphs. Each paragraph should deal with one topic only and there should be a clear progression from one paragraph to the next. Think of paragraphs as links in a chain, each link complete in itself but joined to the link before and after it.

REVISION

Revision is an essential part of the writing process. The first draft you write will almost certainly contain mistakes, omissions, awkward sentences, etc. Careful revision will give you an opportunity to eliminate these and get your message across clearly and persuasively. Even a short, routine letter should be reread at least once to ensure that it is correct. A long, complex document, on the other hand, may need many revisions before it is of good enough quality to be sent out.

Distancing yourself from the document can be helpful at the revision stage. One way to do this is to let it 'cool off' for awhile: for example, leave it on your desk overnight and reread it the next morning. You will be surprised how a gap of even a few hours will enable you to approach the document with more self-critical eyes. Another idea is to ask your colleagues to read what you have written. They will bring an independent point of view to bear on the document and may be able to see problems and mistakes you have overlooked. Listen to their advice, as they may suggest useful changes.

PRESENTATION

Presentation is the final stage in the writing process. An attractive, balanced, uncluttered layout is important because this is the first thing a reader notices about a document. If the document looks interesting and easy to read, the reader will be motivated to read on; if not, it may simply be filed away and forgotten about.

One of the many benefits of computers is that they put a whole new range of presentation tools at the writer's disposal. Fonts (typefaces) can be varied, lines centred, graphics integrated with text and so on. These facilities represent both an opportunity and a danger. When used carefully and in moderation they can transform a document's appearance. When overused, however, they lose their value and make a document fussy and untidy.

Let us now look in more detail at some of the basic elements of good document design.

USE OF SPACE

A cluttered-looking document in which there is little white space is visually unappealing. Frame each page with good-sized margins, at least 2 cm left and right, 3 cm top and bottom. Avoid long, unbroken stretches of text and leave plenty of space for headings. Subsections in the text can be inset or indented to make them stand out.

You can choose between justified or left-aligned formatting (Exhibit 6.4). Justified text has a straight right margin whereas left-aligned text has a ragged right margin. Justification is achieved by adding extra white space between the words and thus stretching out the line. However, this destroys the natural space between words and can sometimes make the text difficult to read.

You will notice that this textbook has a straight right margin (justified).

Exhibit 6.4 Formatting

Justified	Left-Aligned
Revision is an essential part of the writing process. The first draft you write will almost certainly contain mistakes, omissions, awkward sentences, etc. Careful revision will give you an opportunity to eliminate these and get your message across clearly and persuasively. Even a short, routine letter should be reread at least once to ensure that it is correct. A long, complex document, on the other hand, may need many revisions before it is of good enough quality to be sent out.	Revision is an essential part of the writing process. The first draft you write will almost certainly contain mistakes, omissions, awkward sentences, etc. Careful revision will give you an opportunity to eliminate these and get your message across clearly and persuasively. Even a short, routine letter should be reread at least once to ensure that it is correct. A long, complex document, on the other hand, may need many revisions before it is of good enough quality to be sent out.
Distancing yourself from the document can be helpful at the revision stage. One way to do this is to let it 'cool off' for awhile: for example, leave it on your desk overnight and reread it the next morning. You will be surprised how a gap of even a few hours will enable you to approach the document with more self-critical eyes. Another idea is to ask your colleagues to read what you have written. They will bring an independent point of view to bear on the document and may be able to see problems and mistakes you have overlooked. Listen to their advice, as they may suggest useful changes.	Distancing yourself from the document can be helpful at the revision stage. One way to do this is to let it 'cool off' for awhile: for example, leave it on your desk overnight and reread it the next morning. You will be surprised how a gap of even a few hours will enable you to approach the document with more self-critical eyes. Another idea is to ask your colleagues to read what you have written. They will bring an independent point of view to bear on the document and may be able to see problems and mistakes you have overlooked. Listen to their advice, as they may suggest useful changes.

FONTS

Word-processing packages offer a bewildering variety of fonts which can be set at different sizes and produced in upper or lower case, bold or italics. Always choose plain, legible fonts as opposed to decorative ones. Avoid using many different fonts in the same text. A simple but effective variation is to use a *serif* font for text and a *sans serif* for headings. In *serif* fonts each letter has a small projection at the end of the stroke whereas in *sans serif* fonts the projections are absent (e.g. **T** compared with **T**).

Font styles such as **bold**, *italics* and <u>underscoring</u> can be used for emphasis. They can mark out headings or draw attention to words and phrases in the text. The law of diminishing returns operates here. The more often they appear in the document the less effective they become, so use them sparingly.

NUMBERING

Number all pages clearly and consistently. Sometimes it can be useful to indicate the total number of pages, as follows: 'Page 1 of 3, Page 2 of 3', etc. This will help the receiver if the pages are likely to become separated in a busy office.

Numbering in the text should be simple and consistent. You should not switch needlessly from one numbering system to another, e.g. from 1...2...3 to (a)...(b)...(c). The decimal system (1.1...1.2...1.3) can be used in more complex documents. Use asterisks or dots instead if the items marked are of equal importance and you do not need to refer to them again in the document.

HEADINGS

Headings help to signpost different topics, break up large blocks of text and catch the reader's eye. Headings should be short and give a precise description of what is to follow. If possible avoid headings such as 'Miscellaneous' or 'General remarks'.

Headings of equal value should be set out in the same style:

1. **Operating Procedures**	**Not**	1. <u>Operating Procedures</u>
2. **Rules of Settlement**		2. **Rules of settlement**.

TABLES AND GRAPHICS

The inclusion of tables or charts often helps to package information more efficiently and makes it easier to understand. This is particularly true when dealing with numerical or statistical information. In addition, tables and charts make the document more interesting to look at because they break up large bodies of text. Like other aspects of document design, however, they should be used only when they have a genuine contribution to make and not just for show.

In conclusion, a well-written business document should make a good first impression by being pleasing to look at, but it should also be clearly written, carefully planned and show evidence of thorough research. If it does all of these things it will serve its purpose well.

Spotlight on Irish Business – Bank of Ireland

Technical writers at work

Bank of Ireland Group has its head office in Dublin and provides a broad range of financial products and services for Irish customers through its extensive branch network.

The Branch Communications section in Bank of Ireland occupies a key position in the Group as a whole. This section employs trained technical writers who have responsibility for preparing and sending out procedural information to staff. The process begins when a department or project team in the bank needs to introduce new operating procedures for one of its initiatives, e.g. new computer system instructions, new lending procedures, etc. A draft of the procedures is sent to Branch Communications, which is tasked to write the final document and then disseminate it via the company intranet.

An overriding objective is to ensure that the message is clear, concise and well structured. The writers check for mistakes in English and make sure that jargon is avoided wherever possible. They keep documents concise by removing irrelevant or replicated information. If supplementary information is considered appropriate it is attached as an appendix. The most up-to-date desktop technology is used to ensure all documents are formatted to a consistently professional standard.

Awareness of the reader is always an important consideration. Branch Communications has to interact with a diverse audience: there are many different groups, levels of experience and job types within the Group. When communicating, the section tries to encompass all these levels of knowledge. For example, summarised information rather than detailed may be sent to experienced members of staff or hyperlinks can be embedded in the document to provide more in-depth information for those who need it.

At every stage in the writing process, Branch Communications must liase closely with the information 'owners' to make sure that the new procedures are accurate and complete. Expert reviewers may check that content is correct and documents must be signed off by all interested parties before publishing. Diplomatic skills can also come in handy. Different interest groups may have different ideas about the content of the document or how it should be presented. The technical writer often has to bridge these differences and find common ground between competing points of view.

Finally, the timing of publication has to be agreed with the 'owning' department or project team. For example, a message may need to be sent out urgently, e.g. to alert staff to fraud, or it may be timed to coincide with an event such as a product launch. The section tries to publish all material as soon as possible, but a document requiring many revisions may take up to ten days to finalise.

Clearly, technical writing at this level requires a high level of skill, tact and professionalism. A current member of staff has this to say about his role:

> The core task of Branch Communications is knowledge dissemination. Because we face the challenge of communicating new ideas to a wide audience we must have a flair for writing, layout and design allied to a keen awareness of desktop technologies. Seeking ways to exploit technology and continuously improving the quality and effectiveness of documentation forms part of this challenge.

All this and diplomacy as well!

ASSIGNMENTS

REVISION

1. What is a *statement of purpose* and how can it help when writing a document?
2. Outline six key points about the reader that the writer needs to keep in mind.
3. Briefly describe the four planning techniques mentioned in this chapter.
4. A four-part structure is recommended for business documents. Name the four parts and state the function of each.
5. Why is the careful revision of a document so important? Why is it a good idea to leave a gap between writing and revision?
6. Explain the following elements of document display: (a) justification (b) serif and sans serif fonts (c) bold and italic style (d) decimal numbering system.

ACTIVITIES AND DISCUSSION POINTS

1. In business writing it is important to keep the reader in mind. A common complaint is that the examination texts recommended for subjects such as English or Irish at school are not well suited to those who have to read them. Do you agree?
2. What kind of plan do you use when you write? Do you think it is possible to write well without planning?
3. Choose any topic on which it is possible to get a wide variety of views, e.g. how your school/college/students' union could be improved. Carry out a

group *brainstorm* and record the ideas on a board or flipchart. Then try to reorganise the ideas into groups, each with a common theme. Find a suitable heading for each section.

4. Some students claim that listening to music or having background noise actually helps them to write. What do you think?

5. How important is good presentation in writing? Is it the most important aspect of all?

ACTIVITIES AND EXERCISES

1. Each branch of Bestbuys supermarket chain holds regular feedback meetings with a representative group of customers. The members of the group are asked to focus on the quality of service they receive and to express their views frankly. They are also encouraged to make recommendations for improvements. All comments are noted and the facilitator then writes a report which is sent to the head office. The following comments are recorded from one such meeting. They are in random order.

    In this planning exercise your task is to:

    (a) reorganise these comments into **four** or **five** groups, each with a common theme

    (b) write a suitable heading for each group.

    NOTE   You may wish to write a report based on this exercise when you have read Chapter 9 on report writing.

    1. The car park is far too small – by midmorning on Saturday it is impossible to get a space.
    2.   I find the staff very helpful and efficient.
    3. Automatic doors at the entrance would be a good idea.
    4. The staff change around too often – I've no sooner got to know someone than they are moved to another branch.
    5. One of the things I like is that there are unusual products you can't get anywhere else. Yesterday I bought something called an uglifruit. It was delicious.
    6. It would be good if the staff wore name badges – then I would know who I was talking to.
    7. I like all the samples of food that are on offer. Sometimes I come into the store for my breakfast.
    8. My car was broken into once – surely there should be a security guard outside the premises.
    9. Who is the manager? He or she never seems to be available when you want to make a complaint.

10. There should be more parking spaces for disabled people.
11. I think some products are a lot dearer than in Wonderbuys. Why is this?
12. The aisles are very narrow. It is difficult for two trolleys to pass.
13. What's an uglifruit?
14. Couldn't the basic things you want like bread, sugar, tea, etc. all be placed together so you don't have to walk around the whole store to find them?
15. The passageway leading from the entrance to the car park is very steep – I find it difficult to push a full trolley up the slope.
16. There are some good special offers.
17. The queues are far too long on Saturday. Would it not be a good idea to open up a few more checkout points?
18. It's about the size of an orange and has a kind of crinkly skin.
19. Some of the checkout assistants seem to work too slowly.
20. Most of the trolleys seem to be damaged. They're impossible to push along. Isn't it time Bestbuys bought some new trolleys?
21. I hate the way the layout of the store is changed every so often.
22. One week the bread is one place, another week it is somewhere else and I just get lost.
23. Customers with money-off coupons and club cards really annoy me. They take so much time at checkouts. Couldn't this system be improved?
24. What I like best about Bestbuys is that someone packs your bags for you on the way out.
25. I think the checkout assistants are excellent. They are only slow while being trained in.

2. The following circular letter is badly structured. Reshape the letter making use of the four-point plan: opening, information, action, close.
   NOTE Some small changes in sentence structure may be needed to make the letter read fluently.

Dear colleagues,

The AGM of the Staff Association will take place on Wednesday 15 September. I am writing to you to inform you about this meeting and to urge you to attend. One of the most important functions of the AGM is to appoint an Executive Committee which will be responsible for the day-to-day running of the Association for the coming year.

The principal items of business will be: chairperson's address, secretary's report, treasurer's report, election of executive officers, motion to increase annual subscription. The meeting will take place in the Martin Hall from 6:00 pm to 8:00 pm.

A number of vacancies now exist on the Executive Committee. If you are interested in becoming an officer please put your name forward, properly nominated and seconded, to the Secretary by Friday 10 September at the latest. The normal term of office is for two years and no special experience is needed. The committee meets once a month. As it is becoming increasingly difficult to find people who are willing to contribute to this work we would very much like to hear from volunteers.

We look forward to seeing you on the 15th.

7 Effective Writing (2): Style

In all kinds of communication, as we have seen, a fundamental aim is to convey information clearly and persuasively to the receiver. In writing, this is made a little more difficult by the fact that the reader is usually elsewhere when the message is being composed.

Because of this it is essential that all written messages in business are appropriate in tone and easy to understand. You should not aim solely to impress the reader. It is far more important that your message be as clear, concise and persuasive as possible.

This chapter sets out *four main objectives* and *ten simple rules* that will help you achieve a more direct, economical style. You should try to follow these guidelines when writing letters, memos or any other business or technical documents.

You should also have a good grasp of the basics of English usage, that is, grammar, punctuation and spelling. Employers and examiners regularly express concern about deficiencies in these areas so it is worthwhile making the effort to get them right. If you need to improve your basic English you will find rules for punctuation and grammar provided in the appendices, along with short exercises and model answers.

THE IMPORTANCE OF STYLE

When we speak to another person and express ourselves badly the situation can be remedied on the spot. The receiver can ask a question or ask for the message to be repeated. We may notice nonverbal signs of puzzlement or uncertainty about what we have said and we can respond immediately. In writing, however, this vital feedback is missing and we may find out only indirectly that the message has failed. By then the damage may be done. Too late we hear that the memo sent to staff is causing offence because it is considered high handed. Too late we realise that the report on which we spent so much time is being ignored because it is long winded and obscure.

It is important to realise that a piece of writing may be poor even though it contains no faults in English usage. Consider the following message sent out by a well-known multinational company.

> A spot check of randomly selected directories indicated that a number of the directories contained blank pages.
>   In view of the foregoing it is suggested that each user review the issue directory and ascertain whether the directory is complete.
>   In the event the directory is incomplete, the user should return the directory to issue source for disposition.

There are no mistakes in grammar here, but the writing is pretentious and repetitive. Would it not be better to write instead:

> If you find that your directory contains blank pages please return it to us and we will send a replacement.

One plain sentence instead of three verbose ones!

WRITE DIRECTLY AND PERSUASIVELY

Businesspeople and professionals simply do not have time to peruse long-winded documents, so your first aim should be to write uncomplicated sentences and use a direct, no-nonsense style.

There is no such thing as a 'correct' sentence length. Long, heavily qualified sentences make the writing difficult and time consuming to read. However, a series of short sentences with the same structure and stress pattern can be monotonous, making the writing sound like a repetitive drumbeat. The ideal style is one in which there is some variation in sentence length, but where sentences are generally short. An average sentence length of fifteen to twenty words is a good rule of thumb to follow.

Let us now look at some ways of giving impact and vigour to sentence structure.

RULE 1: USE THE ACTIVE VOICE

All well-written documents use a mixture of active and passive constructions, but with a preference for the active voice.

In the active voice the *doer* or *agent* of the action is the subject of the sentence.

> *The board* (subject) will appoint a new office manager on Tuesday.

> *We* (subject) have obtained Central Bank approval.

In the passive voice the person or thing to whom the action is done is the subject of the sentence. The doer or agent is either named later in the sentence or not named at all. For example:

A new office manager (subject) will be appointed *by the board* (agent) on Tuesday.

Central Bank approval (subject) has been obtained. (agent not named)

There are two reasons for preferring the active voice. First, active constructions are more dynamic and usually contain fewer words. Second, they always name the agent or doer of the action, so the reader is not left wondering who was responsible.

In the following example you can see how changing from passive to active voice makes the writing more direct.

Passive:

It was announced yesterday by Mr Jim Hegarty, president of Seafield Technology, that a further investment of €150 million would be made in its Waterford plant and the workforce would be doubled over the next two years. This decision had been taken after a number of alternative investment sites had been considered, but Waterford was chosen because it was the company's most profitable location. (64 words)

Active:

Mr Jim Hegarty, president of Seafield Technology, announced yesterday that the company intended to invest a further €150 million in its Waterford plant and double the workforce over the next two years. The company had looked at a number of alternative investment sites, but chose Waterford because it was its most profitable location. (53 words)

RULE 2: USE PERSONAL PRONOUNS (WHEN APPROPRIATE)

Quite often when writing a formal report it is advisable to maintain a distance between yourself and the reader or to be cautious in putting forward proposals or recommendations. In such cases, it may be best to use impersonal constructions like the following:

The committee is of the opinion that . . .
It is recommended that all staff should . . .

All managers are advised . . .
The results of the investigation show . . .

However, an impersonal style can be off-putting if used in letters or internal memos and circulars. Personal forms using *I, you, we, us,* etc. are livelier and establish a friendlier relationship with the reader.

We believe that . . .
You should . . .
You are advised . . .
Our (or my) results show . . .

The example below shows how to improve a bureaucratic message by speaking more directly to the reader.

Impersonal:

It has been brought to the attention of management that some members of staff are continuing to smoke in the canteen. Staff are advised that the canteen is a nonsmoking area. In the interests of nonsmoking patrons, all staff are requested to observe the no-smoking regulation.

Personal:

We have received some complaints that a small number of staff are continuing to smoke in the canteen. We wish to remind staff that the canteen is a nonsmoking area. Please observe the no-smoking regulation, as this is in everyone's interest.

WRITE PLAINLY

Developing an effective style depends not only on using suitable constructions but on finding the right words. Business writers sometimes use jargon or long, inflated words because they think this makes them appear more impressive or dignified. Nothing could be further from the truth. Far from being impressed, readers may simply fail to understand the message or they may suspect that the writer is setting out to baffle them. Thankfully, there has been a movement in recent years towards using plain English in all kinds of functional writing, which is a trend that you should try to follow.

RULE 3: AVOID JARGON

The Concise Oxford Dictionary defines jargon as 'words or expressions used by a particular group or profession' but also as 'barbarous or debased language' and 'gibberish'. This points out that jargon can be acceptable when used in the right context, but that it becomes confusing or meaningless when used incorrectly.

Quite often, it is necessary to use some jargon, particularly when writing technical reports. Each profession has its own specialist terms and it makes sense to use these when you are writing for fellow professionals. For example, phrases such as *hard disk cache, local bus* (not the 46A!), *auto-increment field* and *bitmap editor* are part of the stock in trade of the computer world and will make sense to a computer expert. However, these phrases will probably be completely unintelligible to a layperson. This is why you should try to reduce jargon as much as possible in technical writing aimed at nonspecialists. It can also help the reader if you provide a glossary of unfamiliar technical terms or explain them the first time you use them in the text.

Going nuts!

The following extract from the Ground Nuts Order shows how even the simplest words can be made unintelligible in the hands of bureaucrats.

In the Nuts (unground) (other than ground nuts) Order, the expression Nuts shall have reference to such nuts, other than ground nuts, as would but for this amending Order not qualify as nuts (unground) (other than ground nuts) by reason of their being nuts (unground).

Courtesy of *Have I Got News for You* (Hat Trick Productions)

RULE 4: AVOID LONG, POMPOUS WORDS

English has borrowed extensively from other languages. As a result, it is rich in **synonyms**, that is, words that have nearly the same meaning. In place of the word *home*, for example, you could use *abode, domicile, residence* or *habitation*. However, *home* is the simple, ordinary word, and the one that is normally used in conversation. The others have their place, but sound too formal or pompous in most contexts, including business writing. As a general rule, therefore, using big words makes writing pretentious, and it is better to use simple, plain words instead.

We must *try to use* our resources to the *full*.

instead of

We must *endeavour to utilise* all of our resources to the *maximum advantage*.

Regretfully, I *need* to *resign* because my family is *moving* to Cork.

instead of

Regretfully, my decision to *terminate my employment* has been *necessitated* by the *change of residence* of my family to Cork.

Sometimes, the use of pompous words can make a simple message so inflated that it loses all credibility, as in the following examples.

partial restructuring of information transmission procedures (the noticeboard has been moved to a new location)

company rest and recreation area (canteen)

panorganisational gathering (seminar)

multifaceted problem that does not admit of a unidimensional solution (simple problem that management cannot solve)

RULE 5: USE VERBS INSTEAD OF ABSTRACT NOUNS

Another way of invigorating a piece of writing is by removing abstract noun phrases and putting equivalent verbs in their place. An abstract noun may be recognised by endings such as *-ment, -tion, -ance, -ence*, etc.

assessment (assess)	*preparation* (prepare)
entitlement (entitle)	*possession* (possess)
assurance (assure)	*expectancy* (expect)
avoidance (avoid)	*suitability* (suit)
necessity (need)	*preference* (prefer)

All these nouns express abstract ideas and overusing them can make a document seem slow and lifeless. In contrast, the verbs from which they come denote action. Using the verb instead enlivens and energises the writing, as in these examples.

Most of our customers *prefer* standard cheques.

instead of

Most of our customers *express a preference for* standard cheques.

Many home buyers *need* a bridging loan.

instead of

The use of a bridging loan *is a necessity* for many home buyers.

WRITE CONCISELY

All the rules that have been discussed so far help towards achieving a clear, direct, plain style. As you looked at the examples, you may have noticed a further benefit from applying these rules: they lead to fewer and shorter words.

Conciseness is increasingly valued as a quality of good business writing. It not only aids clarity but saves on stationery, storage space and typists' time. As you will see in Chapter 8 it is a particularly noticeable feature of business letters, where the modern tendency is to be as brief and to the point as possible.

The following rules will help you to reduce words still further without in any way reducing the impact of your message.

RULE 6: AVOID WORDY PHRASES

There are many long-winded phrases in English which perform the function of prepositions or adverbs. It is often possible to replace these with one or two simple words. For example:

Instead of:	**write**
with reference to	*about*
in the event of	*if*
in the course of	*during*
in respect of	*for*
at the present time	*now*
in the near future	*soon*
during the time that	*while*
with the minimum of delay	*quickly*

Instead of:

Tenders should be submitted *with the minimum of delay* and by 15 July at the latest.

write:

Tenders should be submitted *promptly* and by 15 July at the latest.

There are also quite a number of introductory phrases that can be shortened or omitted without loss of meaning.

In view of the fact that . . .
As far as we are concerned . . .
We must point out that . . .
We are obliged to remind you that . . .

Instead of:

>   *As far as we are concerned* delivery is to be in two weeks.

write:

>   *We expect* delivery in two weeks.

RULE 7: AVOID REDUNDANCIES

In both speech and writing we often use words that repeat an idea. Sometimes these words are justified because they add an important emphasis or qualification. Usually, however, they add nothing to meaning, in which case they are said to be redundant.

One type of redundancy is where two synonyms are used in the same phrase.

> You should try to *look* and *appear* confident during an interview.

> I would like you to find out *exactly* and *precisely* what is required.

In another type the same word (usually a pronoun or conjunction) is repeated unnecessarily.

> In the introduction you should explain *from* where you got your information *from*.

> It was thought *that* if we had free education *that* we would have a better society.

A third type occurs when adjectives and adverbs are used without justification.

> Unemployment has many *undesirable* disadvantages.

> I am happy to tell you that you have been *successfully* chosen for the part.

> We must discover the *real* facts.

Redundancy in writing is usually inadvertent and can be easily corrected once you are aware of it.

AVOID 'LOOSE' WRITING

Throughout this chapter, we have advocated a particular approach to writing that values directness and simplicity. Be careful, however. Plain writing does **not** mean loose, informal writing, so it is not permissible to get words mixed up or to use colloquialisms or slang. And care should always be taken to choose words that convey an appropriate tone in the message. Remember that business is a professional occupation and your use of language must reflect this.

RULE 8: Use words in their correct sense

One form of loose writing is to confuse words that are the same or similar in sound but different in meaning, e.g. *accept – except, continual – continuous, council – counsel, elicit – illicit, stationary – stationery.*

> Copies should be forwarded to the *personnel* (NOT *personal*) officer before 15 May.

> I hope that this will not *affect* (NOT *effect*) our profits for next year.

Often it is the simplest words that cause most problems. Take care with: *have – of, lead – led, of – off, raise – rise, its — it's, loose – lose, quiet – quite, their – there – they're.*
    Equally troublesome are words which are close in sound and meaning but different in tone.

> The chairperson should be the *dominant* (NOT *domineering*) person at a meeting.

> We have received an *official* (NOT *officious*) request for further information.

Take care also with words that have a more restricted application in writing than in speech. These include *less* (often confused with *fewer* in colloquial speech), *between* (confused with *among*), *amount* (confused with *number*) and *aggravate* (confused with *annoy*).

> *Fewer* people turned up than we expected.
> **But** We expect to make *less* money this year.

> Divide this portion *between* the two of you.
> **But** She wandered *among* the crowd.

> We will need a large *number* of chairs.
> **But** A large *amount* of cash was collected.

> I was *annoyed* by the high-pitched noise.
> **But** She *aggravated* (made worse) the injury during the race.

RULE 9: AVOID COLLOQUIAL EXPRESSIONS

Another form of loose, and lazy, writing is the use of colloquial idioms and expressions. These are words and phrases that belong to informal conversation but are not accepted in formal business and technical writing. Here are some examples.

> We have still to decide whether *to go for* (CORRECT *choose*) leasing or buying.

> The chairperson has the power to *throw unruly members out of meetings* (CORRECT *remove unruly members from meetings*).

> It will be *a bit longer* before we know *whether agreement is on or not.* (CORRECT It will be *some time* before we know *whether or not agreement can be reached.*)

RULE 10: USE A FRIENDLY, UNDERSTATED TONE

It is the tone of a piece of writing (cheerful, patronising, serious, etc.) that conveys the writer's attitude to both subject matter and reader. Most business writing has a calm, friendly tone that in other contexts might be considered artificial. There is a tendency to avoid exaggerated expression and excessive claims. Choosing words to convey this tone is often a matter of following well-established conventions. Thus, you would write:

> *I should be grateful if you would deal with this matter immediately.* (NOT *I want this matter sorted out immediately.*)

> I am *pleased* (NOT *overjoyed*) to accept the post of assistant clerk . . .

> We expect to make *substantial* (NOT *huge*) profits in our dairy products division next year.

> Figures for this quarter show a *significant* (NOT *massive*) decline in industrial stoppages.

Sometimes it may not be easy to maintain this understated tone. For instance, in letters of complaint it can be difficult to strike the right balance between strong feeling on the one hand and the need for restraint on the other. Nevertheless, the safest course is to remain polite and to let the facts speak for themselves. You have nothing to lose in business writing by treating the reader with courtesy and respect.

ASSIGNMENTS

REVISION

1. What are the four main characteristics of an effective business writing style?
2. Describe three steps that can be taken to make sentences more direct and vigorous.
3. What is jargon? Is it ever acceptable in business writing? Why should jargon be avoided when writing to nonspecialists?
4. What are synonyms and why is English so rich in these? Why is it usually better to use the simple word when you have a choice?
5. Why is conciseness valued in business writing?
6. Briefly explain and give examples of the following aspects of style: (a) redundancies (b) colloquialisms.
7. What is meant by the tone of a piece of writing?
8. What tone would be appropriate in the following: (a) a formal report (b) a letter of condolence (c) a written complaint?

ACTIVITIES AND DISCUSSION POINTS

1. Collect excerpts from both popular and serious newspapers and magazines (ideally dealing with the same topic). Discuss the differences in style. Is it possible to say that one style is better than another?
2. Popular magazines are usually written in a colourful and breezy style. Collect some examples and identify the techniques used to hold the reader's attention. Do you think some of these techniques would help to make business writing more effective?
3. Find some examples of writing that contains a lot of jargon – computer and games magazines are good sources. Do you think that jargon works here or does it make the writing more difficult to understand?

EXERCISES

1. Make the following message more reader friendly – and more concise – by replacing impersonal expressions and passive constructions (in italics) with more direct, personal forms.

> *It has recently come to the notice of office management* that there has been a significant increase in the cost of staff photocopying. *It is believed* that this is due to *the overuse of* the office photocopiers, which are designed for short runs only. In addition, the heavy use of the machines is causing them to break down on a frequent basis. In order to reduce costs and

provide a more efficient service *it has been decided* to introduce a new 'swipecard' system as from 1 September.

Each member of staff will be issued shortly with *his/her* individual 'swipecard' which will record the number of photocopies *he/she* makes over a monthly period. Each card will be programmed for a monthly total of not more than 500 copies. Accordingly, to ensure that this limit is not exceeded, *staff are strongly advised* to use the office photocopiers for short runs only (no more than ten copies).

If longer runs are required, the originals should be sent to support services together with the appropriate requisition form. *It should also be brought to staff's attention* that support services require three clear days to complete any work submitted to them.

Staff who may wish to make their views known about the new system or who would like further information about its operation should contact . . .

2. Shorten and invigorate the following sentences by substituting verbs for abstract noun phrases (in italics).

    Production has increased significantly since *management brought about the introduction of* the new bonus scheme.

    We will not be able to *make an assessment of* the programme until all the results are known.

    There is an expectancy among staff that redundancies will follow any takeover.

    The union will *engage in consultation with* its members before *reaching a decision* on industrial action.

    It seems inevitable now that there *will be a postponement of the project by the company*.

    I *give you my assurance* that this will not happen again.

3. What simpler words can be used instead of the following?

assistance	commencement
conflagration	despatch (verb)
endeavour	encounter
indigenous	initiate
manufacture (verb)	merchandise
predominantly	procrastinate
purchase (verb)	residence
termination	utilisation

4. Can you find shorter equivalents for the following phrases?

A large majority of . . .

A percentage of . . .

In the initial stages . . .

In the neighbourhood of . . .

In the not-too-distant future . . .

Due to the fact that . . .

I am inclined to the view that . . .

There can be no doubt about . . .

Should the situation arise that we are unable . . .

We are prepared to admit . . .

5. Identify redundant expressions in the following sentences.

There is no cause for undue alarm.

This was certainly and definitely the wrong decision.

We were not told what the meeting was about or what it centred on.

He could not say what possible opportunities there were for promotion.

A whiteboard is more preferable to a chalkboard.

'To whom should I give this to?' she asked.

Today there are better improved methods of conveying information visually.

This system has been adopted by almost every country in the world, with a few exceptions.

6. In each of the sentences below, one word is used incorrectly. Identify the misused word and suggest the correct alternative.

The evidence must be either accepted or objected.

The quality of service seems to have decreased recently.

The driver collided with a stationery vehicle.

A large amount of people turned up for the meeting.

You should not loose your temper so easily.

I got quiet a good return on my investment.

You should write to the personal manager for an application form.

To do this would be wrong in principal.

It is very regretful that the accident happened.

7. Comment critically on the italicised words and phrases in the following sentences and suggest more acceptable alternatives.

The managing director spoke for half an hour *off the top of his head*.

You have just sent me *a lot of bad coal*. Can you *do something about it*?

It's a bit much having to wait three weeks for delivery.

The marketing manager *dropped a real clanger* at the meeting.

We can give you a *ballpark figure* of €2,000.

If I hear further news I will *give you a buzz* on Friday.

He dropped his wallet, *lost his head* and ran into a busy road to find it.

8. The following letter is adapted from students' work. What criticism would you make of its tone? How can it be improved?

Dear Sir,

It is with the utmost pleasure that I accept the post of junior clerk in your company. I did not know what to expect when I received your letter. When I learned that I had been successful and would be working with such a pleasant crowd of people I was over the moon.

As regards the date of commencement I will, I am pleased to inform you, be available to take up the post on that day.

Looking forward to meeting you all.

Yours sincerely,

PART 3

Business Writing

8 Business Correspondence

Business correspondence is the principal means by which a business organisation communicates in writing with customers, suppliers, agents and so on. Its primary value lies in providing a permanent record of the many and varied transactions between the company and its associates. Typically, a letter is used for enquiries, quotations, requests for payment, complaints and replies to complaints. There are also many special once-off cases that arise in business, e.g. answering a request for sponsorship, where a letter will be the most effective response.

The letter is also said to act as an ambassador for the company or individual who sends it. If it is carefully composed and well presented it will enhance the sender's reputation; if it contains mistakes or looks somewhat untidy it will have the opposite effect. An executive will look closely at the first letters sent by a new customer or supplier. Is the letterhead well designed? Is there a fax number or e-mail address? What kind of printer has been used? Is the stationery of good quality? From such observations the executive can obtain useful clues as to the reliability and standing of the firms she is dealing with. Accordingly, the letter writer needs to take great care with the letter's content and appearance if he wants to make a good impression.

The same care with letter writing needs to be taken by young people seeking employment. An employer is likely to scrutinise letters of application for mistakes in spelling, poor expression and shabby presentation. A badly written letter may destroy any chances of success from the outset. For reasons such as this, students need to be well informed about the conventions of business correspondence and conscious of the need for excellence in their own letter writing.

It is possible that in time letters will be replaced completely by e-mail or other forms of electronic communication. As we have seen, e-mail is now used extensively for both internal and external messaging. Nevertheless, not everyone has access to the Internet and we are still a long way from the paperless office, so for the foreseeable future the letter is likely to remain an essential method of business communication.

ELEMENTS OF A BUSINESS LETTER

Exhibit 8.1   Sample letter

Letterhead ———▶	**Trim Ceramics Ltd** Unit 16, Navan Road Industrial Estate Trim, Co. Meath, Ireland Tel: 046-33225 Fax: 046-33268 E-mail: info@trimceramics.com Web: www.trimceramics.com
References ———▶	Your ref: DK/RS Our ref: MW/JR
Date ———▶	10 October 20—
Inside name and address ———▶	Ms Donna Ward J.H. Anderson Ltd Head Office 60–64 Leeson Square Dublin 2
Salutation ———▶	Dear Ms Ward,
Subject ———▶	Re: 'The Burren' Dinner Service

Message
———▶
	Thank you for your enquiry of 7 October concerning our new range of tableware which we displayed at the recent Ideal Homes Exhibition in the RDS.
	    'The Burren' is an elegant earthenware dinner service handcrafted to the highest standards and reflecting the colours and contours of one of Ireland's most beautiful areas. It complements our growing range of quality tableware and is proving extremely popular with our existing customers.
	    I enclose our catalogue and price list as requested. As you can see we offer a generous discount for large orders and can supply most items from stock.
	    Please do not hesitate to contact me if you would like further information.

Complimentary close ———▶ Signature ———▶	Yours sincerely, *Mary Murphy* Ms Mary Murphy Sales Manager
Enclosures ———▶	Encls. (2)

LETTERHEAD

Almost all business letters are typed on headed notepaper. The letterhead gives the name of the company, its address, the address of the head office or registered office (if different) and its registration number. In addition, it may give the company's telephone and fax number, along with e-mail and web addresses. Spaces are usually provided for references and the date.

As well as giving useful information, the letterhead has an advertising and public relations value. A well-designed and attractive letterhead helps to convey a positive image of the company to its customers.

SENDER'S ADDRESS

This must be given in correspondence that does not have a printed letterhead. It is placed on the top right-hand corner of the page and may be blocked or indented.

REFERENCES

The purpose of references is to enable the letter to be quickly routed through to the person or department dealing with the correspondence.

A reference may be made up in various ways. For instance, it may indicate the file where the correspondence is kept, e.g. Our ref: T45, or it may consist of an order or quotation number, e.g. Our ref: Order No. 3165. Most commonly, it consists of the initials of the person who has drafted the letter followed by the initials of the typist, e.g. Our ref: JMC/KM.

When writing a letter of reply you should always quote the reference given to you by your correspondent.

THE DATE

The date should be separated by a space from the sender's address and should be typed or written in full, e.g. 10th September 20— or 10 September 20—. Do not abbreviate the month, e.g. 10th Sept. 20—, or use numbers only, e.g. 10/9/20—.

ATTENTION HEADING

A 'FOR THE ATTENTION OF . . . ' heading is used when you are writing to a company but want your letter to be directed to an individual member of staff. Traditionally, this heading is placed between the inside address and the salutation. However, many letter writers now place it above the inside address and type it in capitals, as shown in Exhibit 8.3.

THE RECEIVER'S (OR 'INSIDE') NAME AND ADDRESS

In business correspondence the name and address of the intended recipient should always be given. The normal place for this is on the upper left-hand corner of the page underneath the date. It is usually typed flush with the left-hand margin, i.e. 'blocked', to give the letter a neat, compact appearance.

You may address your letter directly to a firm (Northern Insurance Ltd) or to an individual in the firm by title (The Marketing Manager) or to an individual by name (Ms C. Thomson).

The titles normally used when addressing a person by name are *Mr* or *Ms*. The use of *Mrs* or *Miss* for women or *Esq.* for men, e.g. J.D. Marron, Esq., is becoming increasingly rare.

In the address itself words such as *Road*, *Street*, *Avenue*, etc. should not be abbreviated. *County*, however, is usually abbreviated to *Co.* and if you are writing to an address in Britain you may abbreviate the names of counties there, e.g. *Bucks.* instead of *Buckinghamshire*.

In all letters within or to Northern Ireland and Britain you should quote the appropriate postcodes as this helps speed up delivery. The postcode should be the last item on the address and may be set out as follows:

Mr M. McCartan
113 Ellesmere Road
Belfast
BT4 1SD

THE SALUTATION

The most common forms of greeting are the following:

Dear Sirs (when you are writing to a company)

Dear Sir (when writing to a man)

Dear Madam (when writing to a woman)

Dear Mr . . . Dear Ms . . . (when writing to a named person)

Dear Susan, Dear John, etc. (when writing to a person you know well).

SUBJECT/SECTION HEADING

If a subject heading is used it is placed between the salutation and the first paragraph. Its purpose is to enable the recipient to identify the subject of the letter at a glance. Section headings can be helpful to the reader in a long letter dealing with a number of distinct topics (see Exhibit 8.7).

THE MESSAGE

For a professional appearance the main body of the letter should be typed in single spacing with paragraphs separated by double spacing.

THE COMPLIMENTARY CLOSE

Only two closes are now commonly found in business letters: *Yours faithfully* (more formal) and *Yours sincerely* (less formal). If you have begun *Dear Sir(s)* or *Dear Madam*, you should end *Yours faithfully*. If you are addressing the recipient by name you should end *Yours sincerely*.

THE SIGNATURE

The letter is signed underneath the complimentary close. Because many signatures are difficult to read (for no good reason, it might be added) it is standard practice to type the signer's name and position in the organisation underneath the signature. For example:

> Yours faithfully,
> (*Signature*)
> Alice Smith
> Local Office Administrator

When the signer wishes to indicate that he is signing on behalf of another person he may use the word *For* or the initials *pp* (*per pro.*) as in the example below.

> Yours faithfully,
> (*Signature*)
> For T. Meehan
> Managing Director

ENCLOSURES

When a brochure or other document is enclosed this is usually indicated by typing *Enclosure(s)* or *Encl.(s)* on the left at the end of the letter.

COPIES

The most common way of indicating that copies are being circulated to a number of recipients is to write *cc* (originally a reference to carbon copies being made) followed by the names in alphabetical order.

LETTER FORMATS

There are a number of well-recognised formats in common use, two of which are illustrated in the text. There are no fixed rules about layout, but there are generally agreed conventions which change from time to time. Within these conventions each firm will have its own individual approach to displaying its letters. All the visual elements of the letter – the letterhead, typescript, layout – should combine to produce a result that is both readable and pleasing to the eye.

Exhibit 8.2 Fully blocked layout

Daly & Cronin Ltd
Engineering Consultants
34 Ennis Road, Limerick
Tel: 061-34567
Fax: 061-34589
E-mail: brian@dalycronin.com
Web: www.dalycronin.com

Your ref:
Our ref: BD/RL

5 March 20—

Mr V. McAvoy
General Manager
Icefoods Ltd
Longmile Road
Dublin 12

Dear Mr McAvoy

At our last meeting you mentioned that you were building a new cold store but had not yet decided which type of condensing unit to install.

I thought you might be interested to know that a company in Northern Ireland, Hebert Ltd, is now supplying and installing Aercal units. As you are aware, these units are manufactured in Germany and have a very good reputation for reliability.

The full address of the company is Hebert (NI) Ltd, North Road, Armagh. I believe the sales manager there is Mr Jim Donnelly.

I hope this information will be useful to you, and I look forward to meeting you again in the near future.

Yours sincerely

Brian Daly

Brian Daly

Fully blocked layout

In the fully blocked layout all lines begin at the left-hand margin. This style is becoming popular in business because it saves considerably on the typist's time. It is often combined with open punctuation, where punctuation marks are omitted in the date, the line endings of the address, the salutation and the complimentary close, but not, of course, in the body of the letter itself. This style is illustrated in Exhibit 8.2 above.

Semi-blocked layout

This is an attractive style well suited to handwritten letters, where it is still widely used. It is not often found in typewritten letters. Its main features are:
* date near right margin
* inside name and address on left and blocked
* subject heading centred
* first line of paragraphs indented
* complimentary close placed right of centre.

Exhibits 8.3 and 8.4 illustrate the semi-blocked style, one on headed notepaper and one on unheaded notepaper. Note that in the handwritten letter the **sender's address** is placed at the top right of the page and that the more traditional **closed punctuation** is used. The sender's address may be blocked or indented, although some think that blocking gives a more balanced effect.

TYPES OF BUSINESS LETTERS

Enquiries

Brief enquiries can be made by telephone, but if you require more detailed information you will need to put your enquiry in writing. You should state clearly and concisely what you want – and no more. Make sure to give the relevant reference if enquiring about goods you have seen advertised or promoted, e.g. title and date of magazine, name and date of exhibition. If you need the information urgently say that a prompt reply will be appreciated.

Exhibit 8.3 Letter of enquiry (1): semi-blocked layout

Icefoods Ltd

Longmile Road, Dublin 12
Tel: 01-4564567 Fax: 01-4564321
E-mail: info@icefoods.com
Web: www.icefoods.com

Your ref:
Our ref: VM/ST   12 March 20—

FOR THE ATTENTION OF MR JIM DONNELLY, SALES MANAGER

Hebert (NI) Ltd
North Road
Armagh
BT61 3SJ

Dear Sirs,

We understand that you are agents in Ireland for the supply and installation of Aercal condensing units.

We are soon to begin construction of a cold store with internal dimensions 8 m 7.5 m 4 m and feel that the Aercal unit may be suited to our requirements. We would like to know plant specifications, details of installation, price, terms of payment and delivery.

As our plans for the cold store are already well advanced we would welcome an early reply.

Yours faithfully,

Vincent McAvoy
Vincent McAvoy
General Manager

Exhibit 8.4　Letter of enquiry (2): semi-blocked layout

14 Rathdrum Avenue,
Rathdrum,
Co. Wicklow

12 July 20—

The Principal,
International Business Institute,
35 Rossmore Road,
Ballsbridge,
Dublin 4.

Dear Madam,

I am interested in the evening course leading to a Bachelor of Business Studies (BBS) which you advertised in *The Irish Times* today.

Could you please give me further information about the course: entry requirements, subjects offered, course fee, etc.

I should point out that I do not have a Leaving Certificate although I have worked for many years at management level in a business environment. Would I still be able to gain entry to the course?

I look forward to hearing from you soon.

Yours faithfully,

Margaret Lowry

REPLIES

Often it is not necessary to write a letter of reply. For example, routine requests for catalogues, price lists, etc. can be answered by enclosing the relevant document and a 'with compliments' card. However, a reply should be written if the enquirer wants specific information or is likely to place a valuable order.

In the opening paragraph thank the writer for his enquiry, mentioning the date of his letter. Give the relevant information in a clear, logical sequence. Use the opportunity to promote the goods or services you are selling. If you cannot help, e.g. you do not have the goods in stock, make this clear from the outset but suggest alternatives. Conclude the letter by offering further help or information if required. (See Exhibits 8.5 and 8.6.)

Exhibit 8.5   Letter of reply (1)

Hebert (NI) Ltd
North Road
Armagh
BT61 3SJ
Northern Ireland
Tel: 01861-34567
Fax: 01861-34589
E-mail: sales@hebert.co.uk
Web: www.hebert.co.uk

16 March 20—

Mr V. McAvoy
General Manager
Icefoods Ltd
Longmile Road
Dublin 12

Dear Mr McAvoy,

Thank you for your letter of 12 March concerning the Aercal condensing units.

From the details you have given us, we feel sure that the Aercal unit is ideally suited to your needs. These units are manufactured by Bremen GmbH in Germany and have an outstanding reputation for economy and reliability. They are also relatively easy to install and maintain.

Our engineer, Mr Tom Smith, will be pleased to visit your plant at any time to discuss the matter further. He should be back from an assignment in Scotland next week and will contact you immediately on his return.

In the meantime we enclose a brochure giving the Aercal's specifications. Please do not hesitate to contact us if you require any further information.

Yours sincerely,

Jim Donnelly

Jim Donnelly
Sales Manager

Exhibit 8.6 Letter of reply (2)

International Business Institute
35 Rossmore Road
Ballsbridge
Dublin 4

Tel: 01 660 2211
Fax: 01 660 2256
E-mail: admissions@ibu.edu
Web: www.ibu.edu

17 July 20—

Ms Margaret Lowry
14 Rathdrum Avenue
Rathdrum
Co. Wicklow

Dear Ms Lowry,

Further to your enquiry of 12 July 20—, please find enclosed our prospectus for evening courses for next academic year. Please note that all course fees quoted are inclusive of examination fees.

Normally, a Leaving Certificate is a minimum requirement for all our evening degree programmes. However, a number of places are reserved for mature students who do not meet this criterion but who have relevant work experience.

Applications for the evening BBS course must be submitted no later than 5:00 pm, Wednesday 20 August and interviews will be held in the first week of September.

If you would like further information please contact Ms Áine Hogan, course director, ext. 3245, who will be very glad to hear from you.

Yours sincerely,

Kathleen Graham

Kathleen Graham
Principal

QUOTATIONS AND ESTIMATES

Usually quotations and estimates are set out on specially designed forms and forwarded together with a covering letter. A quotation gives information about the nature of the goods in question, prices, conditions of sale, terms of payment and delivery dates. An estimate describes the labour and materials required to complete a job, together with price, terms of payment and so on.

If there are any special qualifications or conditions attached to the terms of the contract these should be made clear to avoid any subsequent disagreement with the customer. For instance, it should be stated if the price quoted is not fixed but may vary according to, say, fluctuations in the exchange rate.

The letter in Exhibit 8.7 illustrates how to set out an estimate in a detailed and carefully ordered manner. Note that the estimate is contained in the body of the letter itself, and section headings are used to make the information easier to follow.

Exhibit 8.7 Estimate

Dear Mr McAvoy,

Further to our telephone conversation of 30 March we have pleasure in submitting an estimate for installation of two Aercal units as follows.

Installation
We will deliver, offload and position the units, connect the refrigerant pipework, provide an electric control panel and pressure test when installation is complete.

In order to give a good safety margin we recommend that two units be used, each capable of performing approximately sixty per cent of total duty. We suggest that these units be mounted on steelwork above the ceiling of the store.

Price
The price for delivery, installation and commissioning of the plant is £15,450 inclusive. This price is based on the current cost in sterling of materials, labour and transport and is subject to amendment before the contract commences.

Terms of payment
Terms of payment are thirty per cent on order and the remainder on completion.

Delivery
Delivery of plant is approximately ten weeks from date of order.

We hope that these particulars meet with your requirements. If you have any further queries please do not hesitate to contact us. We look forward to hearing from you.

Yours sincerely,

ORDERS

Orders are usually made out on printed order forms and sent with a covering letter. In Exhibit 8.8, however, the order is included in the letter itself. If two or more items are required they should be tabulated, all necessary details, such as catalogue numbers, should be given and the agreed prices, terms of payment and delivery should be confirmed.

Exhibit 8.8 Order

Dear Ms Murphy,

Thank you for forwarding your current catalogue and price list.

We are pleased to place an order for the following items at the prices and terms stated.

CAT. NO.	DESCRIPTION	QUANTITY	PRICE (per item)
BD01	Dinner plate	30	€19.95
BD02	Dessert plate	30	€16.95
BD03	Tea plate	30	€14.50
BD04	Soup/cereal bowl	30	€17.50
BD09	Pasta bowl	20	€17.95
BD10	Salad bowl	20	€16.95
BD17	Teapot	10	€69.95
BD18	Coffee pot	10	€82.95

We would appreciate an acknowledgment and look forward to delivery within the next week.

Yours sincerely,

LETTERS OF COMPLAINT AND ADJUSTMENT

Although you may feel annoyed when you write a letter of complaint, you should not be tempted into abuse or sarcasm. You are likely to get the best results if you adopt a reasonable tone. Always assume, in the first instance, that the person or organisation against whom you are making the complaint is willing to put the matter right. In Exhibit 8.9 the writer makes clear at the outset what she is complaining about, gives additional helpful information, makes clear that the problem is causing inconvenience and is precise about the action she wants taken. The tone of the letter is firm but polite and restrained throughout.

Exhibit 8.9 Letter of complaint

> Dear Sir,
>
> I purchased a Netcell PX computer (Model No. NPA-7L) from you on 17 April 20—. Since buying the computer I have had to replace the monitor and motherboard under warranty and it now appears that the hard disk will also have to be replaced.
>
> While I appreciate that the computer is now out of warranty, I feel that you should fit a new disk free of charge as the performance of this machine has been unsatisfactory from the beginning.
>
> I should point out that the frequent breakdown of the computer is causing considerable disruption to my business.
>
> I look forward to an early reply.
>
> Yours faithfully,

The reply to a complaint is called a letter of adjustment. When a complaint is justified you have no alternative but to acknowledge the difficulty, offer an explanation if you can and state how you intend to remedy the matter. Depending on the circumstances, you may propose a discount, a refund, the replacement of defective goods or whatever compensation you feel to be appropriate.

Note that the writer in Exhibit 8.10 does not waste time in excessive apologies. Instead he tells his correspondent what she most wants to hear: that prompt action is being taken to deal with the complaint.

Exhibit 8.10 Letter of adjustment (1)

> Dear Ms Nolan,
>
> Thank you for your recent letter regarding a faulty computer which you purchased from us in April 20—.
>
> I appreciate the difficulty this is causing you and have taken the matter up with our customer service department. I am now pleased to advise you that we will be able to replace the hard disk without charge.
>
> I should be grateful if you would contact our service department to arrange for the computer to be collected from your premises. We will make every effort to have the PC returned to you as soon as possible.
>
> In the meantime, should you have any additional queries please feel free to contact me at any time.
>
> Yours sincerely,

When a complaint is unjustified the writer has the delicate task of rejecting it without making the correspondent look foolish. The letter below from an estate agent shows how this task can be approached. Begin by acknowledging the letter you have received, then tactfully explain why you have no case to answer and end with a positive remark that shows you are still sympathetic to your correspondent's feelings.

Exhibit 8.11 Letter of adjustment (2)

Dear Mr and Ms Lambe,

We note from your letter of 10 February that you feel we are not making sufficient efforts to complete the sale of your property.

We would respectfully point out that negotiations have been in progress for only two months. Given that the average period for completion of a sale is three months you may be assured that the transaction is proceeding normally.

Of course, we shall do everything in our power to expedite matters but we doubt if it will be possible to exchange contracts in the coming week. However, we shall see what can be done.

Yours sincerely,

COLLECTION LETTERS

Collection letters should be written with care in order to avoid giving offence. There may be a simple explanation for the customer's failure to pay, e.g. he may have overlooked the account or sent a cheque that has not been received. The first and second collection letters should be no more than brief, polite reminders that payment is overdue. Copies of relevant invoices and statements should be enclosed.

Exhibit 8.12 First collection letter

Dear Mr O'Sullivan,

I notice from our records that your account no. JS/896 amounting to €1,763.50 has not yet been settled.

I should be grateful if you would send a cheque for this amount as soon as possible.

Yours sincerely,

Exhibit 8.13 Second collection letter

> Dear Mr O'Sullivan,
>
> We have still not received payment for your account no. JS/896 amounting to €1,763.50 despite a reminder sent on 3 March.
>
> As you are usually prompt with payment, I am sure there is some special reason for this oversight.
>
> I should be grateful if you would settle this account within seven days or at least offer an explanation for the delay.
>
> Yours sincerely,

Only in the third or fourth letter should you propose to take further action if payment is not made by a fixed date. You may consider legal action, although this may not always be appropriate.

Two different approaches to a final collection letter are illustrated in Exhibits 8.14 and 8.15. In the first, the writer has decided to use a friendly and helpful tone because he is dealing with a customer of long standing. Nevertheless, he puts the recipient under considerable pressure to respond. In the second, the writer takes a tougher approach which includes the threat of legal action.

Exhibit 8.14 Final collection letter (1)

> Dear Mr O'Sullivan,
>
> I write to advise you that your account no. JS/896 amounting to €1,763.50 has not yet been settled despite a number of reminders.
>
> I am surprised at this as you have always cleared your accounts on due dates in the past.
>
> Perhaps in the near future you could come in and have a chat with me about the matter. You are a most valued customer and I hope we may be able to clear up whatever problem exists.
>
> Could you telephone me in the next day or two to arrange a time when we can meet?
>
> Yours sincerely,

Exhibit 8.15 Final collection letter (2)

Dear Mr O'Sullivan,

We note from our records that your account no. JS/896 for the amount of €1,763.50 has not yet been settled despite reminders sent on 3 March and 24 March.

As our previous dealings with you have been most satisfactory we are surprised that, on this occasion, you have not at least offered an explanation for nonpayment.

We feel we have been very reasonable and must now point out that if payment is not made within a further seven days the matter will be placed in the hands of our solicitors.

Yours sincerely,

GOODWILL LETTERS

Letters dealing with actual business transactions are the bread and butter of business correspondence, but they are not the only letters that need to be written. At various times a businessperson may be called on to offer congratulations, express condolences, write references, make representations on behalf of the local community and so on. Such letters should arise out of a sincere desire to help or express appreciation. The return is in the valuable goodwill created for the business.

A lively, informal tone is often appropriate in such letters. The letter in Exhibit 8.16, for example, has a lightness of touch that is largely absent from the more functional letters that precede it.

Exhibit 8.16 Goodwill letter

Dear Susan,

I am delighted to hear that you have won a Special Category Award in the Irish Quality Mark competition.

I know very well that there is great competition for this award from all parts of the country so your success reflects tremendous credit on yourself and your staff.

Congratulations to all concerned. You have done the county proud.

Best wishes,

Of course, the mood in letters expressing sympathy or condolences should be sombre, but even here the writer should strive for the personal touch that shows the letter is not being written to a formula.

Other types of business letters are illustrated in Chapter 10 (sales letter) and Chapter 17 (letter of application).

GUIDELINES FOR EFFECTIVE LETTER WRITING

Effective business correspondence should conform to the guidelines on planning, style and presentation set out in Chapters 6 and 7. Here is a recap of some of the key points to bear in mind when writing a letter.

PURPOSE

The first step is to define your purpose in writing. For example, suppose that you are in your final year in college and you decide to write a letter of introduction to a potential employer. What exactly do you hope to achieve by it? Do you simply want the employer to put your letter on file in the hope that you will be notified should a vacancy arise? Or do you want to be sent useful literature? Or are you hoping for an interview, perhaps? Until you are sure about the kind of response you require from the reader you cannot begin to plan the letter itself.

CONTENT

The next step is to decide what to say. List the points you want to make and arrange them in a logical sequence. Generally the content of a business letter will fall into the four divisions described in Chapter 6.

- The first paragraph introduces the subject of the letter (**opening**).
  We note from your letter of 14 June that you are concerned about . . .
  I wish to apply for the post of . . .
- The middle part, which may consist of one or more paragraphs, develops the subject (**information**).
- The concluding part indicates what needs to be done (**action**).
  Please confirm your acceptance by signing the enclosed . . .
  We will be sending you replacement units within the next few days . . .
- The final paragraph expresses goodwill or offers further help (**close**).
  We look forward to hearing from you . . .
  We hope you will find this information useful . . .
  Please contact us if you experience any further problems . . .

Style

The third step is to compose the letter. Remember that you may have to revise the initial draft a number of times before you are completely satisfied with the result. Business correspondence is a highly functional form of writing, so you will need to be careful with the following aspects of style.

- Try to write clearly and simply. There has been a welcome movement in recent years towards a simple, direct use of language in business letters and most of the old-fashioned 'commercialese' has disappeared. Thus, today one would write *Thank you for your letter of 4 July* instead of *I am in receipt of your letter of the 4 inst.*, i.e. this month, or *We acknowledge receipt of your esteemed favour.* However, some remnants of commercial jargon persist and should be avoided:

  We enclose herewith (say *We enclose*)

  at your earliest convenience (say *as soon as possible*)

  your good selves (say *you*)

  Thanking you in anticipation and

  Assuring you of our best attention (both worthless tags that should have been abandoned long ago)

- Be as brief as possible. Far too many business letters are twice as long as they need to be. They become much crisper in style and easier to type when padding is removed and rambling sentences shortened. For instance, take the following excerpt from an actual letter sent by an Irish company.

  As you know there are other products in our range, some of which we do not wish to market under the 'own', i.e. generic, brand label as these particular products we require identified under our own brand name for marketing purposes. (39 words)

  Remove the dead wood and this becomes:

  There are many other products in our range, some of which must be sold under our own brand name. (19 words!)

The shortest correspondence on record was that between Victor Marie Hugo (1802–85) and his publisher, Hurst and Blackett, in 1862. The author was on holiday and anxious to know how his new novel, *Les Misérables*, was selling. He wrote '?' The reply was '!'

Source: The Guinness Book of Records

- Be polite at all times without being obsequious. Conventional phrases such as *Please let us know if we can be of any further help* or *We will be happy to make other arrangements if these are unsuitable* may be somewhat clichéd but at least they indicate an interest in the reader's needs and a willingness to put yourself out on her behalf.

PRESENTATION

The final step is to type or write by hand a good copy of the letter before sending it out. Use good-quality stationery and aim for an attractive layout. If the letter is handwritten it should be neat and legible. If typewritten there should be as few typing errors as possible. Finally, proofread carefully for mistakes in spelling, punctuation and grammar.

ASSIGNMENTS

REVISION

1. Describe the function of the following elements of a business letter: (a) letterhead (b) references (c) attention heading (d) inside name and address (e) subject heading.
2. When do you use these salutations: (a) *Dear Sirs* (b) *Dear Madam* (c) *Dear Sir* (d) *Dear Ms*?
3. What is the purpose of these abbreviations: (a) *pp* (b) *Encl.* (c) *cc*?
4. Describe the main differences between the following letter layouts: (a) *fully blocked* (b) *semi-blocked*.
5. What are the main areas that should be covered in a quotation? Why is it important to specify any conditions or qualifications?
6. How should you write a letter of adjustment (a) if the complaint is justified (b) if the complaint is unjustified?
7. Why are collection letters written in series? What are the main differences between a first request and a final request?
8. Describe the steps that need to be taken when planning and writing a business letter.

FOR DISCUSSION

1. In your opinion, what are the most important characteristics of a good business letter?
2. Why are business letters described as *ambassadors* for the business? How important is this aspect?
3. The postal system is sometimes disparagingly referred to as 'snail mail' nowadays. Is this a fair comment? Do you think electronic communication will eventually replace the business letter?
4. In Exhibit 8.10 the writer agrees to repair the complainant's computer free of charge even though it is out of warranty. Is he right to do this?
5. Compare the final collection letters in Exhibits 8.14 and 8.15. In your opinion, which letter is likely to get the result the writer wants?

6. It could be said that goodwill letters are a waste of a businessperson's valuable time. Do you see any merit in this view?

ACTIVITIES

1. Each firm has its own house style for letters. Collect a number of business letters and compare them in terms of letterhead, layout, style, etc. Decide which are most effective and give reasons.

2. Do you feel strongly about any social, political or environmental issue? If so, find out the name of the person, journal or organisation you should write to, e.g. local politician, national or local newspaper or radio, pressure group, business. Support your point of view with careful research and write a well-argued letter. Do not be disappointed if you get little or no response – national newspapers, for example, get many letters every day and cannot publish them all. However, you may be surprised by how positively your letter is received – letters can be a very persuasive form of communication! Discuss the results in class.

WRITTEN EXERCISES

1. The following advertisement has appeared in the 'Articles for Sale' section of the *Evening Reporter*:

   Ladies Quality Fashions, stock clearance, 100 lots for sale, normally retailing €2,000, now clearing for €750, contact Threads Cash & Carry, Bow Street, Dublin 2.

   You own a small retail outlet specialising in fashion for the young adult age group. Write to the wholesaler seeking further information about the above offer. Use the *fully blocked style*.

2. Write a letter of quotation for a bulk tanker based on the following information: single compartment – capacity 3,000 m^3 – €30,000 ex. VAT, ex. delivery – price subject to change – payment fifty per cent on order, remainder on completion – delivery fourteen weeks – specifications, drawings enclosed.

3. You have bought a stereo hi-fi system from a well-known retailer during the January sales. When you unpack the hi-fi you discover that the remote control is missing. Write to the retailer asking for the control to be supplied. Use the *semi-blocked style*.

4. As head of customer services, reply to the above letter in *fully blocked layout*. Point out that the model concerned is currently out of stock and will have to be ordered from abroad.

5. You have bought several rolls of carpet on special offer from a warehouse. When the carpet is being laid, the fitters point out that one roll is noticeably different in shade from the others. The manager of the warehouse inspects the carpet and agrees that there may be a slight variation in shade. However, he refuses to accept that any further action is warranted on his part. You are still dissatisfied and decide to put your complaint in writing. Write the appropriate letter.

6. You are the manager of the carpet warehouse. On receipt of the letter of complaint, write a letter of adjustment in which you EITHER make a conciliatory offer in order to keep the customer's goodwill OR refuse to take further action because you genuinely believe the customer is being unreasonable.

7. A good customer has an outstanding debt of €7,000 which he has failed to pay after a number of reminders. He has now sent in a further order for goods valued at €1,500. You have heard privately that he is in financial difficulty and are anxious to interview him before agreeing to supply the goods. Write an appropriate letter.

8. A small, two-teacher primary school near your factory is threatened with closure. As manager of the factory, write a goodwill letter to your local newspaper in which you argue the case for keeping the school open.

9. You are the principal of a secondary school. Write a letter to the personnel manager of a large company in the locality, inviting her to give a talk to a group of students about job opportunities in the industry concerned.

10. As the personnel manager, reply to the principal accepting the invitation. Give details of date, time, etc. when you will be available.

9 The Business Report

WHAT IS A REPORT?

A report is a formal presentation of information given by one person or group to another. It often contains the results of a specific investigation together with conclusions or recommendations derived from the findings. It may also be a record of work in progress or an account of something attended, such as a conference or an exhibition.

Reports may be written or oral. Indeed, sometimes the reporter is required both to submit a written report and subsequently to give a brief oral summary of it to a committee. The reporter can then be questioned about matters that are still unclear or challenged on points that need further justification. Oral reports by officers such as the secretary or treasurer are a regular feature of formal meetings.

Written reports may be broadly classified into two groups: *routine* and *special*.

ROUTINE REPORTS

Examples of routine reports include sales reports, production reports, etc. These are made out at regular intervals and have a predetermined structure that enables them to be completed quickly. They often consist of a short written introduction or commentary followed by pages of numerical information. Sometimes, the report writer simply fills in a form on which headings and spaces for writing are already set out.

SPECIAL OR ONE-OFF REPORTS

This is a report for which there is no exact precedent. Usually it is prepared following instructions from a superior or a client who needs special information but has neither the time nor the expertise to carry out the work herself. Special reports have a unique status in organisations and need to be approached with particular care because they are often the basis for important decisions about people's lives or about spending large sums of money. Since they are such influential documents they must be meticulously researched and written in a mature and balanced style.

A break from routine

A problem with routine reports is that they get taken for granted. As time goes by, they may contain increasingly irrelevant or incomplete information. Their layout may begin to look stale and old-fashioned. In some cases, they continue to be produced even when no longer needed. To combat this, organisations should conduct regular audits of routine reports to ensure they are still serving a useful purpose. Questions to ask include:

- What was the original reason for the report? Does that reason still exist?
- Who is using the information?
- Could new or more relevant information be provided?
- Could the format of the report be improved?

REPORT FORMATS

As you become familiar with a range of special reports you will notice that they take many different forms. Reports serve a wide variety of objectives (see Exhibit 9.1) and vary greatly in length. A short summary report may take up just one page whereas a government report may consist of several volumes. Because of this there is no single way in which all reports should be set out. Broadly speaking, however, the following four formats can be distinguished.

LONG FORMAL REPORT

Long reports are usually commissioned by the government, semi-state bodies or large corporations. Typically, they result from:

- government reviews of existing policy and legislation in a particular area
- inquiries into matters of major public concern
- in-depth studies of company operations, often conducted by management consultants.

They involve extensive investigation and may run to many pages. The contents are always highly structured.

SHORT FORMAL REPORT

Short reports that can be investigated and written in a matter of days are commonplace in business. A formal layout may be used when one or more of the following conditions applies:

- the nature of the investigation suggests a formal approach
- the findings are detailed or complex
- the report is intended for the chief executive or senior management.

An example of a short formal report is given in Exhibit 9.3.

SHORT INFORMAL REPORT

This format is used when the information does not have to be highly structured or when the writer is reporting to someone at or near the same rank as himself. An example is given in Exhibit 9.4.

LETTER OR MEMORANDUM REPORT

Mixed formats are quite common in reports. For example, property surveyors' reports are often sent out to clients in letter form. Short internal reports, particularly those written on the report writer's own initiative, are often set out as memoranda.

Exhibit 9.1 Report objectives

1. **To inform or explain**

    Information and *progress reports* fall into this category. The purpose of an information report is to record facts and ideas that may be useful to the organisation now or at a later date, e.g. report on a visit to a conference, report on a course attended, economic report on a country or region with which the company intends to trade. Progress reports may be written at various stages in the life of a project and are intended to tell management how the project is faring.

2. **To investigate and present findings**

    Investigative reports are usually written when a problem arises in the organisation and action has to be taken to solve it, e.g. high absenteeism, fall in output, failure to meet quality standards, etc. The writer investigates the causes and effects of the problem and then puts forward proposals for a solution.

3. **To provide a record**

    Some reports, such as *accident reports* or *disciplinary reports*, are primarily 'for the record'. They are written at the time of a particular event, discussion or decision and remain in the files as an account of what took place. They can be referred to again if further action is required or if the facts of the case are later brought into question.

4. **To evaluate**

    Valuation reports and *feasibility studies* belong to this category. In a valuation report, the writer examines a property, a piece of equipment, etc. and estimates its quality, usefulness or worth. Alternatively, she may compare one thing with another, e.g. competing software packages, and set out the advantages and disadvantages. Such reports usually end with a recommendation.

Feasibility studies may have to do with a planned expansion or the introduction of new systems or procedures in the organisation. The writer investigates the costs and practical implications involved and then recommends a course of action.

5. **To persuade**

In a *persuasive report* the main objective is to put forward a proposal and argue the case for it, e.g. an increase in a department's budget for the coming year. The writer must make sure the proposal is feasible and must set out the arguments in a persuasive sequence. She should provide supporting evidence and, if necessary, counter likely objections.

STRUCTURE OF A REPORT

The recognised parts of a report are:
* title page
* table of contents
* executive summary
* introduction
* findings or information (body of report)
* conclusions
* recommendations
* appendices.

TITLE PAGE

The title page enables the report to be easily identified, distributed and filed. It usually contains:
* the report title, which briefly states the subject
* the date on which the report was presented
* the report writer's name
* the name of the individual, department or organisation who the report is submitted to
* a reference number for filing.

In addition, it may indicate that the report is confidential or give a circulation list. Because it is the first page the reader will see, it should have an attractive and balanced layout.

TABLE OF CONTENTS

The table of contents (often shortened to 'Contents') lists the chapters or main sections as they appear in the report and gives the page number for each. The writer should make sure that the headings in the contents page are the same as those in the text. Page numbers should be set in a neat column.

EXECUTIVE SUMMARY

In most long reports a summary or abstract is provided at the beginning. It is intended to give the busy executive who does not have time to read the report itself a general idea of what it contains. Then, later on when she has more time at her disposal she can read the entire report or whatever part of it interests her.

Usually the summary makes a brief statement about the report's objectives and goes on to outline the main findings, conclusions and recommendations. Sometimes, however, it lists the main conclusions and recommendations only. Its length is relative to the length of the report (perhaps half a page in a fairly short report and two or three pages in a long report).

INTRODUCTION

The purpose of the introduction is to provide important information about the nature of the report and how the writer went about the task. It may act in any or all of the following ways:

- to state the terms of reference and make whatever comment on them is felt to be necessary (the terms of reference are the initial instructions given by the client)
- to give relevant background information
- to explain the writer's approach to the subject if this differs in any way from what the reader might expect
- to explain the procedure used in collecting data
- to acknowledge help given by others
- to indicate sources of information.

Note that in a short formal report (see Exhibit 9.3) there are separate headings for 'Terms of reference' and 'Procedure'.

FINDINGS OR INFORMATION

Here the report writer gives the results of the investigation. The findings should be set out in a clear, logical sequence in order of importance or according to any principle of organisation that suits the material and helps the reader.

Normally, a system of headings, subheadings and numbers is used. The advantages of such a system are that it makes the report more readable and enables information to be found quickly.

The number of headings depends on the subject matter, but the structure should not be so complex that it is confusing. Headings themselves should be short and specific enough to give a clear indication of the content to follow.

Three different numbering styles are illustrated in Exhibit 9.2.

Exhibit 9.2 Headings and numbering

Traditional style	Decimal style	Bulleted style
1. ―――――――	1. ―――――――	1. ―――――――
(a) ―――――	1.1 ―――――	• ―――――
(b) ―――――	1.2 ―――――	• ―――――
(c) ―――――	1.3 ―――――	• ―――――
2. ―――――――	2. ―――――――	2. ―――――――
(a) ―――――	2.1 ―――――	• ―――――
(b) ―――――	2.2 ―――――	• ―――――

CONCLUSIONS

In this section the report writer assesses the evidence. This may involve making deductions from the facts, reiterating the most important points or making judgments. All conclusions should be reasonable, persuasive and consistent with the findings. They should not be influenced by personal interest or prejudice.

RECOMMENDATIONS

Recommendations are specific proposals for further action. They should never be confused with conclusions. Conclusions **identify** the problem; recommendations show how it can be **solved**. You should make them only if required to do so by your terms of reference. Otherwise, you are liable to give offence.

As a general rule, recommendations are listed and numbered in order of importance. They may be placed at the end of the report or after each chapter. They should always be expressed clearly and precisely so that the reader is left in no doubt as to your intentions. Recommendations often propose substantial expenditure or changes that impact significantly on people's work, so they cannot be ambiguous.

It is important to put them in the form of strong suggestions rather than orders. Thus they are often prefaced by such phrases as '*We advise . . . We recommend that . . . It is advised that . . .*'.

When deciding on your recommendations you should bear in mind the following points.

- You need to be objective. You cannot allow your own likes or dislikes to cloud your judgment.
- You should take as wide a view as possible. For example, you wish to recommend a change in work practices in your company. Management may be firmly in support of the idea – but what about staff? Clearly, their views must be canvassed and their likely response assessed before you can make a recommendation. In other words, you should be aware of the 'political' dimension of recommendations.
- At the same time, you should have courage in your convictions. If, having considered the matter, you believe that a certain course of action is right you should not be swayed from recommending it by the displeasure of one interest group or another.

APPENDICES

Material that cannot easily be reproduced in the main body of the report can be placed instead in the appendices. Examples of such material would be the following:

- tables of figures
- visuals such as graphs, charts, maps or diagrams
- references and bibliographies
- summaries of other reports
- copies of questionnaires or other research instruments
- transcripts of interviews.

However, if a set of statistics, map or diagram is crucial to an understanding of the report then it should appear in the main text as a Table or Figure.

Appendices should be labelled and there should be clear references to them in the text. Information provided in the appendices should always be justified. If it is of no use or interest to the reader then it should be omitted.

Exhibit 9.3   Short formal report (investigation)

REPORT ON HEALTH AND SAFETY AT INTERNATIONAL ENGINEERING (IRELAND) LTD, GLENEEN INDUSTRIAL ESTATE, GALWAY

1. Terms of reference

The purpose of this report is to give an overview of health and safety procedures and practices at the above plant and to make recommendations where appropriate.

The investigation was undertaken at the request of Mr H. Green, general manager, as part of a review of health and safety at all International Engineering facilities worldwide.

2. Procedure

Information for the report was obtained as follows.

2.1 Documents relating to health and safety, including the Procedures Manual and health and safety records, were examined.

2.2 Interviews were conducted with the human resources manager, the production manager, production supervisors and a number of operatives.

2.3 A one-day inspection of the shop floor was carried out on Tuesday, 19 May 20—.

3. Findings

3.1 Administration

Primary responsibility for the development of health and safety policy and procedure lies with the chief executive in consultation with the head of human resources. The head of production has responsibility for implementation of health and safety standards on the shop floor.

In accordance with government regulations, the company has set up a Safety Committee comprising the HR manager, two supervisors and four operatives. In general, the administrative arrangements appear to be satisfactory.

3.2 Education and training

All staff are given an hour-long presentation on health and safety as part of the induction process. All employees are trained in manual lifting and, where appropriate, operatives are trained in driving fork-lifts. However, no specific training is given on fire prevention or first aid.

While notices on safety are widely distributed around the plant these tend to be 'passive' methods of communication. No other formal mechanism for distributing information about health and safety is in operation.

3.3 Fire precautions

Detailed emergency procedures are set out in the Procedures Manual. Fire-fighting equipment is accessible and in good condition. A sprinkler system is in operation and fire doors are in place.

However, it was noted that the sprinkler system is fed by a single pump and tank and there is no back-up supply of water. It was also noted that a number of fire doors do not close properly.

3.4 Protective clothing

The wearing of protective clothing, e.g. safety glasses, heat-resistant gloves, is essential during certain manufacturing processes. It was noted that a small number of operatives were not wearing the appropriate clothing although it is available. There was some doubt as to who had responsibility for ensuring that procedures in this area were complied with.

3.5 Chemicals

Arrangements for the storage of chemicals were satisfactory, with drums and containers clearly labelled. However, there appeared to be an excess of stock in the chemical waste area. This represents an unnecessary fire hazard.

4. Conclusions

In general, there are no serious breaches of health and safety standards in the plant. However, improvements need to be made in training, education and communication. Some specific deficiencies with regard to fire prevention, protective clothing and management of chemicals should be rectified immediately.

5. Recommendations

The following recommendations are made.

5.1 All staff should be trained in fire prevention; production supervisors should be trained in first aid.

5.2 Periodic meetings should be held at which supervisors can brief operatives on health and safety issues. Awareness of health and safety issues could also be enhanced by occasional articles in the company newsletter.

5.3 All fire doors should be made fully operational immediately.

5.4 The existence of a single source of water is a concern. Consideration should be given to installing a second source, perhaps by taking water from the public mains.

5.5 All operatives should wear appropriate protective clothing. It should be the supervisors' responsibility to ensure this. Failure to wear the correct clothing should be regarded as a breach of discipline.

5.6 Old and unwanted chemical stock should be returned to the supplier or disposed of according to government guidelines.

Exhibit 9.4   Short informal report (information)

Teambuilding – a viable option?

Introduction

At the meeting of the board held on 5 February it was suggested that we consider the introduction of quality-focused teams at our Limerick and Athlone plants. This proposal is in line with our strategic objective of achieving world-class business excellence over all our activities. It was agreed that a summary report on teambuilding should be presented at our next meeting. Accordingly, the report below outlines the main features and benefits of the teamwork approach.

Information

The following appear to be the key elements in successful teams.

1. **Mission**

   Each team must have a clearly defined purpose. Objectives should be explicitly spelled out in a mission statement. If objectives are unclear, the team will be unfocused and waste its time in unproductive effort.

2. **Roles and responsibilities**

   A team must collectively decide on the role of each of its members. The division of authority and responsibility within the team must be clear. Team members can then be certain about who has responsibility for particular activities. However, there should be some flexibility: roles and responsibilities may change depending on a particular task.

3. **Team structure**

   There are three key individuals in team structure.

   - *Team sponsor*

     Every team should have a sponsor and his or her name should be known to each of the team members. A typical sponsor will be a department head or supervisor. The sponsor's role is to support the team, provide guidance and link with senior management. The sponsor will try to ensure that the team's activities are in line with company goals and that it has sufficient resources to meet its objectives.

   - *Team leader*

     The leader should be the person in the team with the most recognisable leadership skills. He/she should have good interpersonal and communication skills. The leader's role is to conduct meetings, motivate the team members and build consensus and morale.

   - *Team facilitator*

     The team facilitator's role is to help the team with process. The facilitator should remain neutral with regard to the issues discussed but should be skilled in group dynamics. For example, he or she should be able to prevent any member from either dominating or being overlooked.

4. **Support**

It is imperative that the introduction of teamworking has senior management's unqualified and sustained support. We also have to remember that for most of our employees teamworking will be a new and foreign concept. We will need to provide appropriate training before implementation and continuing advice and guidance thereafter.

5. **Recognition and reward**

It is important for the success of teams that they get recognition and reward for their efforts. Some forms of recognition we could consider are team photographs in the magazine, awards, team outings, etc.

Benefits

The evidence from companies I have looked at, both here and in the UK, is that teamworking can bring substantial benefits to the organisation.

Points that were specifically mentioned to me include the following.
* There is a noticeable improvement in employee involvement and morale.
* Employees are allowed to participate in the management of the organisation and get a broader perspective on their work.
* There is an increase in communication, particularly when problems arise.
* Quality is improved and fewer complaints are received from customers.
* Significant cost reductions are achieved and productivity increases. In one case, the introduction of teamworking led to a reduction in lead time from two months to three days.

Conclusion

There appear to be significant benefits to be gained from taking this route. Without exception, managers that I spoke to are enthusiastic about teamworking and sing its praises. However, they point out that the introduction of teamworking requires careful planning and top management support.

My view is that we should now move forward on this proposal, perhaps by setting up a subcommittee of the Business Excellence Forum to examine the proposal in greater detail.

Mick Lally
Head of Training and Development

PREPARING AND WRITING REPORTS ▄▄▄▄▄▄▄

NOTE Much of the advice given in this section can also be applied to the preparation of extended projects and theses.

Many reports are badly written because the writers have made inadequate or hasty preparation. When you come to write your own reports you will save yourself a great deal of time and effort if you set about the task in a systematic way. The five main stages in the production of a report are:

- preparation
- research
- analysis and evaluation
- writing and revision
- presentation.

These stages are replicated in the flow diagram in Exhibit 9.5.

Exhibit 9.5 Stages in report writing

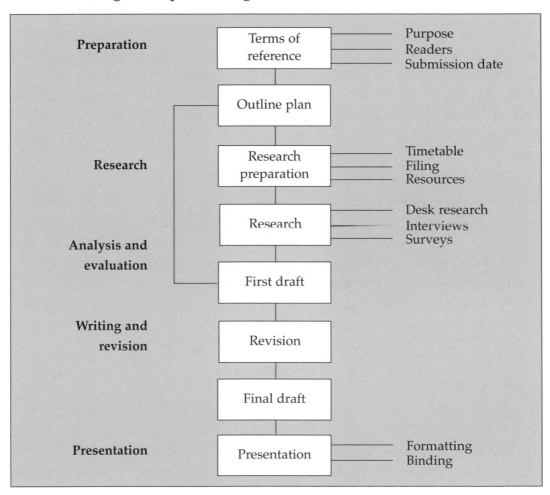

PREPARATION

Before you begin a report for a client you should be given clear instructions that set out the objectives and scope of your investigation. Technically, these instructions are known as your *terms of reference*. If you are writing the report on your own initiative you need to think out the terms of reference for yourself.

Unfortunately, terms of reference are sometimes vaguely or ambiguously expressed. Your boss may make a casual request such as, 'Oh, by the way, Peter, could you let me have a report sometime on that computer training course you attended last week?'

An instruction like this leaves too many unanswered questions. What is the purpose of this report? Is it merely for the record? Is it something the boss needs to have before she can deduct the cost of the course from her training budget? Or is she thinking of sending more staff on the course and wants to know how useful it has been? Other questions might be asked: what amount of detail is required? Should a particular format be used? What deadline is intended by the word 'sometime'?

If you have imprecise terms of reference you should always request a meeting with your client to remove doubts and ambiguities. Try to get the terms of reference put in writing and signed. If this is impossible, you can write down your own interpretation of the terms of reference and submit them for approval. One way or another you must seek clarification. If you do not, you may be criticised later on for pursuing irrelevant lines of enquiry and wasting your employer's time.

As a general rule, the following points should be covered.

- **The purpose of the report**
  As we have seen, report objectives can be stated in broad terms: to provide a record, to investigate a problem and so on. However, each report has its own unique purpose which needs to be spelled out. The great value of clearly defined objectives is that they help the writer decide:
  ‣ the contents of the report
  ‣ the best sequence of information
  ‣ the ideas that need to be given particular emphasis
  ‣ the most appropriate tone and style
  ‣ what response is required from the receiver.
  On the other hand, failure to define objectives may lead to a report that is incomplete, confusing or inappropriately worded.

- **The scope and limits of the report**
  Normally, you are not expected to research every aspect of the matter under

investigation. It is helpful to know what areas need to be looked at and what can be excluded.

- **The readers**
  You should know who your readers are and the level of knowledge and experience they have. This information will help you determine the scope of the report. It will also have an important bearing on the language you use. For example, if you are writing a report for fellow professionals then a highly technical vocabulary may be appropriate. If you are writing for laypersons then specialist terms may have to be avoided and simpler equivalents substituted.

- **Submission deadline**
  The terms of reference should always give a submission date. A short report may have to be submitted in a matter of days; a long report, on the other hand, may take several months.

- **Length and format**
  You should be able to judge the approximate length of the report from information given about its objectives, scope and so on. Most business reports are short, taking up at most ten pages.

  The format may vary depending on the receiver's status. Your department head may want quite a detailed report; the chief executive, on the other hand, may want a brief summary with key recommendations highlighted. If you have any doubts it is worth checking this out before you go ahead.

RESEARCH

Once the terms of reference have been clarified and recorded, the next stage is to organise research and assemble the required information. If you conduct your research in a systematic way you will not only ensure that the ground is covered but save yourself considerable time and energy.

Effective research for a report involves the following:
- making a plan of the areas to be investigated
- deciding on research methods and sources of information
- timetabling the research
- filing the material
- making sure resources are available.

- **The outline plan**
  The first step, even in short reports, is to map out the main areas to be covered. An outline plan at this stage has three principal advantages: first, it gives

direction to the research, second, it can help you get your filing system in order and third, it provides a skeleton structure for the report.

- **Research methods**

  Next, you will have to decide how to obtain the information you need. Some of the most commonly used research techniques are:
  - desk research, i.e. reading books, journals, other reports, etc.
  - interviews (face to face or by telephone)
  - questionnaires and surveys
  - first-hand observation
  - experiments and testing.

  When you have responsibility for designing your own research instruments you must ensure that they will provide you with relevant and accurate data. Great care must be taken with a questionnaire, for example. It must be precisely worded and the recipients carefully targeted. If possible, test the questionnaire on a small representative sample first. This will help you to fine-tune the questions and remove any ambiguities.

- **Timetabling**

  The benefit of a time plan is that it helps you keep control of the work as it proceeds. Of course, it is not needed when researching a short report that takes only a matter of days. However, it is essential when you are working on a long, complex project.

  A simple but effective timetable is shown in Exhibit 9.6. Always make sure to leave sufficient time at the end for writing, revising, printing and binding the report. Naturally, the plan needs some flexibility because some areas of research may take less or more time to complete than anticipated.

Exhibit 9.6   Timetable

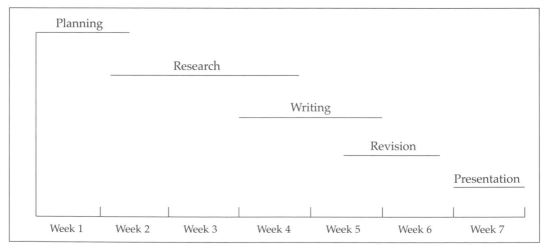

- **Filing**

  It is a good idea to think at the outset about how you will file information. An effective filing system prevents muddle later on and helps save time. The choice of system depends on the nature of the research and the resources at your disposal. Information can be stored on something as simple as a notebook or as sophisticated as a computer. However, folders, cards and binders are the most useful methods for all ordinary purposes.

  A set of labelled folders is probably best when the material collected is of different shapes and sizes, e.g. maps, reports, letters, newspaper cuttings, etc.

  However, a card file may be better if the research involves a great deal of note-taking. Each card should contain one item of information, together with a record of its source. All cards should be clearly numbered and headed. For ease of reference, tabbed guide cards can be used to separate one main section of material from the next.

  A loose-leaf binder can be used instead of a card system. It is not as flexible but has the advantage of being easily transportable.

- **Resources**

  All you may need to complete a short report may be a pen, paper and access to a computer. However, resources may become a more important issue if you are involved in a long and complex inquiry. For example, report writers sometimes need to have staff such as research assistants or secretaries seconded to them while the work is in progress. External consultants may have to be employed to provide technical expertise or to conduct market research. A budget may be needed to cover travelling expenses, library or database subscriptions, printing and binding. When everything is added together a major report can cost thousands of euro.

ANALYSIS AND EVALUATION

As the material comes in it has to be analysed and evaluated. This involves three main tasks, the first of which is to check data for accuracy and reliability. Be particularly careful when quoting the results of other people's research. It may be better to check back to primary sources rather than depend on secondary sources, which are not always reliable. The second task is to decide what material is relevant and what is not. Do not allow yourself to be sidetracked onto interesting but irrelevant lines of enquiry. The third task is to determine what weight should be given to material that is relevant and to discern what the most significant findings are.

In looking at data it is important to distinguish between **facts** and **opinions**.

With regard to facts, you might consider the following questions: what key facts are emerging? Can their accuracy be depended upon? Are they complete, or are they coming from a potentially biased source which might be presenting one side of the argument? Are there any unexpected facts which might cause you to think again?

An opinion is a statement of belief rather than something proven to be true. Some opinions are more valuable than others. An opinion expressed by an acknowledged expert will carry considerable weight. On the other hand, an opinion emanating from a self-interested source must obviously be treated with caution. As you conduct your research you will come across many opinions, all of which should be examined critically before you decide to use them.

You should try to keep an open mind at this stage. You should not suppress findings that conflict with your own views, but instead give them due prominence and change your ideas accordingly. You should also be prepared to follow up new or unexpected findings if they have a bearing on the investigation. The worth of your report will be seriously undermined if you allow personal prejudice to influence your handling of the material.

WRITING AND REVISING

Many report writers find this stage the most difficult part of the whole process. Yet if preparation has been thorough and the material has been properly sifted and evaluated, the actual writing of the report should be straightforward.

*   **A step-by-step approach**
    An effective way to proceed is to use the following step-by-step approach.
    1. Make sure you know what your conclusions and recommendations are going to be. These will determine how you organise and write the rest of the report.
    2. Plan the main body of the report. Arrange the main sections in a logical sequence and decide on suitable headings and subheadings. This task is easier if you have already devised an outline plan as part of your research.
    3. Next, working through a section at a time, set out the evidence in note form under each heading and subheading.
    4. Then, begin to write the report in the following order: *introduction, findings, conclusions, recommendations*. The 'outer structure' of *summary, appendices, table of contents* and *title page* should be left to the very end.

    The great advantage of this method is that by the time you come to the writing stage you already have a detailed picture of how the content is to be presented and you can give your whole attention to constructing coherent sentences and paragraphs.

- **Typing or keyboarding**

  Most writers now keyboard the report directly into a computer using a word-processing package. This kind of 'self-help' has many advantages. It enables you to edit and amend the text as you go along. Other features help you format the text, choose fonts and number pages. You can use the spell check tool to eliminate all or most spelling errors. You save time that would otherwise be spent paper-shuffling between yourself and the typist. (*By the way, all this highlights the importance of developing good typing skills!*)

- **Style**

  A report is an important document and the style should reflect this. The essential elements are the clear expression and orderly arrangement of ideas. Conciseness is also recommended, although it is not as important in reports as in some other forms of business writing. Jargon and pretentiousness should be avoided at all costs. There is no virtue in dazzling readers with a wide technical vocabulary or overwhelming them with pompous language. Aim instead for simple, direct expression with technical terms kept to a minimum.

- **Tone**

  Reports should be neutral and unemotional in tone. There should be a marked emphasis on logical argument and on supporting statements with evidence. However much you may wish to persuade your readers on a particular point of view or course of action, your method should be to let the facts speak for themselves. Impersonal constructions are often used to convey this sense of objectivity, e.g. *It was discovered that . . . The committee is of the opinion that . . . The results indicate . . .*. However, internal reports intended for colleagues at or near the same level in the organisation can be somewhat less reserved. In these, there is nothing wrong with using the first person singular (*I believe . . . My assessment is . . .*) provided that conclusions and recommendations are soundly based on the evidence and are not simply expressions of personal opinion.

- **Revision**

  Once the report has been completed, time should be set aside for a review. In carrying out the review you should look for aspects of argument and expression that need to be corrected or improved. Be particularly alert for mistakes in usage that might diminish an otherwise sound piece of work. It is always helpful to have a second opinion at this stage. A colleague might see errors or inadequacies in the report that you yourself have overlooked.

PRESENTATION

The final objective in producing a high-quality report is to ensure that it is easy to read and professionally presented. Some organisations have a house style for reports which sets out rules for layout, numbering and so on. This makes the writer's task a little easier. If there is no house style, however, you need to think about design issues at an early stage to ensure a consistent approach throughout the document.

- **Formatting**
  With ready access to computers it is common for the report writer to take full responsibility for formatting. This opens up new opportunities. For example, with computer graphics you can incorporate full-colour charts and diagrams. If you have desktop publishing facilities you can even produce reports to book-publishing standards. The main danger in all of this is that the report looks gimmicky at the end. Remember that a 'showcase' layout can never compensate for a poorly researched or badly written document.

- **Proofing**
  This is a necessary job that is often neglected. Always make a final check for figures left out, mistakes in language, etc.

- **Binding**
  Finally, you should choose a binding suited to the nature of the report and its readership. The alternatives are:
  ▸ *Stapling*: acceptable for short, internal reports.
  ▸ *Plastic comb binding* or *spiral binding*: cheap, sturdy and allows the report to lie flat.
  ▸ *Slide bars*: cheap, but pages tend to fall out of the plastic groove.
  ▸ *Print binding*: expensive; reports for government and semi-state bodies are usually printed and bound professionally.
  Whatever method is used, the finished report should have a pleasing appearance that enhances its contents.

ASSIGNMENTS

REVISION

1. Explain the difference between a routine and a special report. What problems can arise with routine reports?
2. What is the main purpose of each of the following types of report?
   - progress report
   - investigative report
   - disciplinary report
   - feasibility study
   - persuasive report.

3. What information appears on the title page?
4. Why is an executive summary often included with long reports?
5. Explain the difference between *conclusions* and *recommendations* in a report. Suggest some guidelines for writing recommendations.
6. What kind of information would you expect to find in the Appendices section?
7. 'The starting point of report writing is to obtain the terms of reference.' What are the terms of reference? Why does the report writer need to clarify them with the client?
8. Describe four key points that the terms of reference should cover.
9. List five common methods of conducting research.
10. What are the benefits of (a) a timetable and (b) a good filing system when researching a long report?
11. Comment briefly on the style of reports. Is it different in any way from the style of letters and memoranda?
12. How has the use of computers and word-processing packages changed the nature of report writing?

Exercises

1. Your college has just moved to a brand new building and the students' union has been given the use of three rooms on the ground floor. The college director has asked the union to submit a report setting out how it proposes to furnish and use these rooms. Write a short informal report setting out your ideas.
2. Ireland Overseas is a charity which carries out voluntary development work abroad. It needs to raise a substantial sum of money to support its activities. As development officer write a report for the board of trustees in which you make a number of fundraising suggestions.
3. You are safety officer on a large building site. Recently a serious accident occurred and you are required to report on the incident. Think up a plausible scenario and write a short report describing what happened.
4. Laura Cummins manages a branch of Excel Fashions Ltd, a group of clothes shops with outlets throughout Ireland. For the last two months her branch has traded at a loss. The area manager has asked her for a report explaining the reasons for this and suggesting how the situation can be improved.

   Laura is convinced she knows what is wrong. In her report she wants to highlight problems such as:
   • poor parking facilities near the shop
   • rapid turnover of young, inexperienced staff (it is group policy to employ school leavers and pay low rates)
   • the opening of a rival store in a better location and selling cut-price items
   • the slow response by the group to changing fashion trends.

Laura has also got good ideas about returning the branch to profitability. Write her report, inventing any details you think necessary.

5. Intertel (Ireland) Ltd is a Limerick-based computer company employing 120 people. In recent months, senior management has become increasingly concerned about security. You are the security officer and have been asked by the managing director to write a short report on the matter. In the course of your investigation you make the following notes.

> Staff careless with keys – spare keys often left in conspicuous places – lost keys not reported – handbags and wallets left unprotected while staff are absent from rooms – strangers can wander round the building without authorisation – callers left alone in offices – office equipment taken from the building without permission – some equipment missing and unaccounted for – windows and doors left open and unlocked at the end of work – blind spot at rear of premises not covered by security cameras.

Write your report using the above information and any other details you think fit. The report should be in a suitable format and should include recommendations.

6. Sean O'Grady manages a small garden centre on the outskirts of a town. He has built up a good trade, although the centre has limited space and no car parking. A timber-frame shed is used as a shop.

Now the owner has acquired an acre of land adjoining the centre and wants to expand and improve the business. She has asked Sean to write a report setting out his ideas on how the extra space could be most effectively used.

Sean wants to tackle the parking problem and get rid of the shed. He also thinks the centre should expand into garden ornaments, equipment and furniture. He has one or two other good ideas. Write Sean's report.

7. Fastfood Ltd, a food processing company, has recently located one of its factories in a new industrial estate on the outskirts of Dublin. Since operations in the factory began there has been a high turnover among operatives and junior office staff.

Assume you are the head of human resources. Write a short formal report for senior management in which you set out the reasons for the high turnover and suggest what action should be taken.

Reasons might include repetitive work, inadequate training, lack of opportunity for promotion or development, difficulty getting to and from the factory because of poor public transport, lack of facilities such as shops on the estate, etc. You may invent any other details you think necessary.

10 Other Written Forms

Apart from letters and reports there are several other forms of writing used in business. In this chapter we will consider five of these: the memorandum, notice, e-mail, sales letter and press release.

MEMORANDUM

The memorandum, or memo, is the main method used for transferring written messages within an organisation. Traditionally, the message is handwritten or typed on purposely designed stationery and then sent to the receiver via the internal mail system. However, it is increasingly common for memoranda to be attached to e-mails and sent via the company intranet.

Memoranda can be used for many purposes: to pass on information, to instruct, to direct or to make enquiries. Thus, memo messages can be as short as one or two sentences or as long as several pages. Most memos are typed in standard A4 format, and it is common for a copy of the message to be retained by the sender.

ELEMENTS OF THE MEMORANDUM

As can be seen from the examples below, the layout of a memorandum is simpler than that of a letter. The essential components are as follows.

- **Memorandum**: This word is printed at the top and usually centred.
- **To**: A space is provided for the receiver's name.
- **From**: This is followed by a space for the sender's name.
- **Date**: The date is usually given in full as in a letter.
- **Ref**: A reference may be provided for filing.
- **Subject**: Space is left for a brief statement of the topic.
- **Message**: The message is given under the subject heading. Depending on the topic, it may be set out as a series of paragraphs or in a more schematic form with subheads and numbers.

In addition, these headings may appear.

- **Company name and logo**: Many organisations print their name and logo on memorandum stationery. Although this is not strictly necessary it helps to establish a sense of corporate identity among staff.
- **Copy to** or **cc**: This is followed by a list of names if the memorandum is being sent to a restricted group.
- **Enclosure(s)** or **Encl.(s)**: As with a letter, these words indicate that other material is enclosed.
- **Signed**: Space may be provided for the writer's signature. Salutations and complimentary closes, familiar from business letters, are omitted.
- **Filing instructions**: These tell the recipient how to file the memorandum.

CONTENT

Memoranda usually convey official information on matters to do with the organisation (more personal issues are better dealt with by letter). They can be used for a great variety of messages and are particularly valuable where a record of the information needs to be kept.

Most commonly they are used for:

- requesting information, advice or help
- giving information, notifying, confirming, explaining
- setting out procedures or giving instructions
- putting forward proposals.

Exhibit 10.1   Making a request

MEMORANDUM

TO: *Tom Murphy*   DATE: *10 September 20—*
FROM: *Ann Moran*   REF:
SUBJECT: *ESRI Report*

Tom,
Could you please return the ESRI report on small businesses before Friday as I need to reread it for the seminar next week.
                                    Thanks,
                                    Ann

Hints

▸ List your questions or requests in order of priority.
▸ Write them clearly and simply to avoid confusion.
▸ Tell the receiver why you want the information.

Exhibit 10.2   Giving information

CEK INTERNATIONAL PLC

Head Office, Bedford Street, Belfast BT1 2GE

MEMORANDUM

To: All staff
From: Administration Dept.
Ref: AD/16
Date: —
Subject: **New Staff Canteen**

Due to the recent expansion in staff numbers our existing canteen on the ground floor is no longer capable of meeting our needs. You will be pleased to know that the senior management team has now decided to relocate the canteen on the penthouse floor while retaining the existing canteen as a staff common room. This decision was arrived at after a process of consultation with staff representatives.

1. New Canteen

    The new canteen will be located on the top floor, which will give us sufficient space to cater for current and projected usage. Construction is planned to begin on 15 April with completion by the end of August.

    We envisage that the new canteen will offer a comprehensive range of hot and cold dishes. A vegetarian menu will also be provided. The canteen will be open between 12:30 pm and 2:30 pm.

    As you know, the top floor gives superb views over the city and we anticipate that this will be an outstanding feature of the new canteen. We expect to begin discussion soon with the architects about furnishings and fittings. Our aim will be to ensure that these meet the highest standards of quality and design.

2. Existing Canteen

    When the new canteen is fully operational the existing canteen will be refitted as a staff common room. The kitchen will be removed and replaced with a small counter from which staff will be able to purchase tea or coffee and simple snacks.

    Visitors and clients accompanied by members of staff may also be admitted to the staff common room where appropriate.

We expect that there will be some disruption while the new canteen is under construction. However, we will try to keep noise etc. to a minimum and we ask for the forbearance of staff while work is in progress.

Eileen Digby
Head of Administration

Hints

▸ Tell the receiver **what, why, how, when** and **where** as needed.
▸ Make sure the information is factually correct.
▸ Do not forget to mention any qualifications or exceptions.
▸ Make sure all essential information is included.

Exhibit 10.3 Setting out procedures

Globus Engineering
MEMORANDUM

To:　　　　All staff
From:　　　Safety Officer
Ref:
Date:
Subject:　　**Fire Evacuation Drill**

The fire evacuation drill has been amended following a review of the fire practice held on —. The following procedures come into effect forthwith.

1. When a fire is discovered, the fire alarm should be sounded immediately by activating the nearest break glass unit.
2. On hearing the alarm all staff should immediately vacate the building and proceed to the assembly point in the car park.
3. Heads of department will collect staff lists from the porter's office and ensure that all staff are accounted for. They will inform security of any missing persons.
4. Visitors will assemble outside the main entrance and give their identity badges to security.
5. Responsibility for the fire should be surrendered to the fire brigade immediately on their arrival.
6. Staff should not re-enter the building until the all-clear is given.

Hints

▸ Set out procedures and instructions in a logical step-by-step sequence.
▸ Make sure they are described clearly and unambiguously.
▸ Check that they actually work by pretesting if necessary.

Exhibit 10.4   Putting forward a proposal

Globus Engineering

MEMORANDUM

To: Michael Tully
From: Jim Kennelly
Ref:
Date: —
Subject: Health and Safety Training

As agreed at the Safety Committee meeting held on 25 May I have made enquiries about the most effective way of providing health and safety training for our employees.

Having looked at various options I recommend that we opt for the multimedia solution and commission a custom-made CD-ROM. There are a number of reasons for taking this route, even though it may appear expensive at first glance.

1. The CD-ROM will allow each employee to learn at his or her own pace from a computer. Our people are accustomed to using PCs so they should have no problem with this.

2. As they watch and listen to the programme they have to answer questions. This ensures that they have seen and understood the safety procedures. At present, they are required only to read the safety manual and we have no way of ensuring they do so.

3. The programme will include video of the plant and personnel. This will make it more realistic for viewers.

4. At present, each employee spends approximately **fifteen hours** attending courses and seminars on health and safety. Using multimedia will cut down significantly on this time. It will also free up the safety personnel for other tasks.

5. The package can be used over and over again and can be adapted to meet new requirements.

I have had initial discussion with Janet Williamson at Image Interactive about developing a pilot. She tells me it would be possible to have the programme ready for inducting new employees in the autumn, but she needs to get the go-ahead fairly soon.

I suggest we put this down for decision at the next meeting of the Safety Committee.

Jim Kennelly
Training Officer

Hints

▸ Make sure your proposal is feasible.

▸ Explain it clearly and simply.

▸ Set out your arguments for it in a logical sequence and make sure the important points are emphasised.

▸ Provide supporting evidence.

▸ If necessary anticipate and counter likely objections.

LAYOUT OF MEMORANDA

The format of memoranda can vary considerably, as the examples above show. However, when the message is concerned with giving instructions, directives or complex information it is a good idea to use a schematic layout. Compare the two methods employed in Exhibits 10.5 and 10.6 below. The second is clearly more effective.

Exhibit 10.5   Memo without a schematic layout

MEMORANDUM

To: All staff   Date: 3 November 20—
From: M. Desmond (Administrative Officer)

Subject: **Internal Telephone System**

I hope you will find the following instructions for use of the telephone system helpful.

If you want to make an internal call lift the handset and dial the internal extension number required. To make an external call lift the handset and dial 0. If the busy tone is heard (series of rapid single pips) replace the handset and try again. If the dialling tone is heard dial the external number required. To make a call via the operator dial 9 and wait for a reply.

Etc.

Exhibit 10.6   Memo with a schematic layout

MEMORANDUM

To: All staff   Date: 3 November 20—

From: M. Desmond (Administrative Officer)

Subject: **Directions for using Internal Telephone System**

1. *To make an internal call*
   Lift handset and dial internal extension number required.
2. *To make an external call to a local number*
   Lift handset and dial 0. If you hear busy tone (series of rapid single pips) replace handset and try again. If you hear dialling tone dial the external number required.
3. *To make a call via the operator*
   Lift handset, dial 9 and wait for a reply.

Etc.

Students should note that it is nearly always advisable to use a schematic layout when writing a long memorandum in an examination.

STYLE

Effective memoranda should conform to the principles of good business writing set out in Chapters 6 and 7. However, there are some features of memo-writing style that require special comment.

- Short messages making requests or giving reminders – particularly those intended for one's peers – are usually informal in style. The message in Exhibit 10.1 above is an example. To use the more formal phrasing of a report or business letter would be inappropriate in this context.

- It is important to use an appropriate tone, especially in memos giving directives and instructions. Three different ways of conveying the same order are illustrated below. Compare the tone of each example.

   1. *You are required to assemble for fire drill in Section F at 4:30 pm sharp on Monday 19 May.*

      Note that attendance at fire drill is compulsory and absence will be considered a breach of company regulations.

   2. *Please note that fire drill will be held in Section F at 4:30 pm on Monday 19 May. We hope to be able to complete the drill by 5:00 pm so please assemble punctually.*

      All staff are advised that attendance at fire drill is obligatory under company regulations.

3. *Don't forget! Fire drill in Section F at 4:30 pm on Monday 19 May.*
    You have to attend this – see company regulations!
    Please be there on time. Your future safety could depend on it.

The tone of the first message is peremptory and might well antagonise the staff. A few small but significant changes make the second message more acceptable. The word 'please' is used; staff are 'advised' not 'required'; attendance is 'obligatory' rather than 'compulsory' and a reason is given for punctuality. Some people might consider the tone of the third message too casual, particularly when dealing with the important matter of staff safety. Nevertheless, given a different context, this style could be effective in a small organisation with a tradition of informal communication.

NOTICE

A notice or bulletin is an economical way of getting information to large numbers of people. Unlike a memorandum, which is sent directly to the individual and can be read at leisure, a notice is pinned to a noticeboard for all to see and often has to be read quickly. To be effective, therefore, it must attract attention and be written in a clear, concise style.

If the notice is informal (Exhibit 10.7) a variety of simple techniques can be used to make it more dramatic. Bright colours, bold lettering, staggered headlines, funny cartoons and sketches or a photograph all help to arouse the curiosity of potential readers.

Company notices (Exhibits 10.8 and 10.9) have to be more conventional in presentation but here also layout should be as attractive as possible. Even the most formal notices can be given visual appeal using short paragraphs, appropriate headings, bold or underscoring and some variation in colour, e.g. heading in blue, text in black.

The style of a notice should be simple and direct: this is so that it can be understood quickly by anyone reading it. Content should be short. Ideally, a notice should not be longer than one page.

Finally, all notices should give the date of issue. It is also a good idea to indicate the removal date, as is done in Exhibit 10.9.

Exhibit 10.7   Staff notice

STAFF INFORMATION
Staff basketball

Interested in a good workout once a week?

Then why not PLAY BASKETBALL!

We play every Thursday at 8 pm in St Enda's Hall

(opp. the Community School on Erinmore Rd).

Give your name to *Gráinne Walsh* (ext. 1209) or *Paul Fahy* (ext. 1134).

IT'S GOOD FUN – AND A GREAT WAY TO KEEP FIT.

Exhibit 10.8   Company notice (1)

MANAGEMENT NOTICE

Parking in Barrow Lane

Recently we have had a number of complaints from Mr H. Fox, proprietor of Barrow Body Repairs, about members of our staff parking cars in Barrow Lane. It seems that any vehicles parked along this very narrow lane cause a serious obstruction to customers trying to reach Mr Fox's garage.

We appreciate that there is a shortage of parking space near the factory. However, we may soon be able to provide more spaces on our own premises by opening up the old timber yard off Nore Road.

In the meantime, in the interests of good relations with our neighbours, **please do not park in Barrow Lane**.

14 April 20 —

Peter Mullen

General Manager

Exhibit 10.9   Company notice (2)

> # Globus Engineering
> ## Appointment of Human Resources Director
>
> I am pleased to announce the appointment of Margaret Moran as director of human resources. Margaret will take up her position in October and will report to me.
>
> Margaret joins us from MKP Group, Waterford, where she has worked as assistant head of personnel since 20—.
>
> She studied for a B.Comm. at University College, Dublin, where she also completed an MBA. She is a Fellow of the Institute of Personnel Practitioners in Ireland (IPPI).
>
> I am sure you will join with me in wishing Margaret every success in her new position.
>
> Signed: *Michael Tully*, CEO
> Issue date: 3/9/20—
> Removal date: 17/9/20—

E-MAIL

E-mail is increasingly replacing both conventional business letters and the telephone as a medium of communication. Indeed, it is not uncommon for co-workers sharing the same office to communicate with each other by e-mail when they could speak to each other more easily. Yet despite the extraordinary growth in e-mail usage, many companies underestimate the need for professionalism in writing and replying to e-mails and fail to provide employees with appropriate policies and guidelines.

Exhibit 10.10 below shows an example of an e-mail enquiry. This is followed by ten key rules that help towards the efficient, courteous use of e-mail in business.

Exhibit 10.10   E-mail

From:	Michael Murphy <mmurphy@globalnet.com>
To:	corkbks@eirenet.ie
Cc:	
Subject:	'Early Irish Watercolours': 1st ed.
Attachments:	

Hi Liam,

I have been trying to track down a first edition of Áine Wallace's 'Early Irish

Watercolours', which I believe was published by Irish Art Press in 1963.

So far I have had no luck, despite trying every bookshop in Dublin. Is there any chance you have a copy?

Kind regards,
Michael Murphy

NOTE:

The message has to be in plain text. This rules out underscoring, bold, italics, etc. Hence the book title is put in inverted commas.

E-MAIL ETIQUETTE

1. Use an effective heading in the subject line. Writing a general heading such as 'Message', 'Reply' or 'Product information' is unhelpful. Be as specific as you can – for example, name the particular product you have in mind.

2. Use an appropriate salutation. If you are e-mailing a client for the first time it may be advisable to use a formal style, e.g. 'Dear Mr', 'Dear Ms'. However, when the person is known to you, such as a co-worker or regular customer, a more personal approach is appropriate, e.g. 'Hi John' or simply 'John'.

3. Formatting should be as plain as possible. Any attempt to enliven the message by using colour or unusual fonts or formats is likely to end in disaster. Avoid typing in upper case as this makes the message shout at the receiver. Be careful, too, about overusing exclamation marks for emphasis.

4. Keep your message concise and to the point. After all, one of the benefits of e-mail is speed, and you lose this advantage if you write long-winded and repetitious messages. You will also help the recipient if you construct your message in short, logical paragraphs. Always reread the message before sending it.

5. As with all forms of communication, provide enough information to enable the receiver to deal efficiently with your enquiry. For example, type order or invoice numbers, serial numbers, relevant dates, times and so on. If making a request, remember to say please.

6. Use a writing style appropriate to the context. If the relationship with your recipient is formal then use Standard English and avoid slang or idiomatic expressions. A more relaxed style can be used with people you know well.

E-mail abbreviations, e.g. 'Rgds' for 'Regards', are acceptable when time is at a premium and the recipient understands what is intended. Grammar mistakes and misspellings should be avoided, as in any written form.

7. A formal e-mail may be closed with the conventional 'Yours sincerely', but in most circumstances expressions such as 'Best wishes' or 'Kind regards' are preferred.

8. It is good manners (as well as more efficient) to reply to e-mails promptly. This points to an important difference between e-mails and the telephone. The telephone is an interactive medium designed to facilitate an immediate response. E-mail is not interactive in this way. It does not guarantee a reply, or even that the message sent will be read.

9. Do not send confidential information by e-mail as this medium is notoriously insecure. You may inadvertently send a message to the wrong address, thereby revealing information that is embarrassing to yourself or the intended receiver. Be aware that some companies regularly monitor messages sent by employees in an effort to reduce nonbusiness conversations.

10. Finally, treat your e-mail facility with caution as it is particularly open to abuse. Delete unsolicited advertising messages immediately and take care not to forward chain letters, viruses or other e-mail nuisances.

SALES LETTER

In general, business students do not need to know the highly specialised skills of the advertising copywriter and visualiser. However, you should know the basic principles involved in writing copy for simple advertisements. A considerable amount of relatively cheap, small-scale commercial advertising is carried on without the help of advertising agencies. The main advertisers here are small shops and businesses. The types of advertisements used include small classified or display ads in the press, sales letters, leaflets, posters and bills. Copy for these advertisements is usually written by the advertisers themselves, and you may be called on to write such copy when you take up employment. Many of the characteristics of this form of writing are illustrated in the sales letter in Exhibit 10.11.

Like all advertisements a sales letter needs to fulfil three broad functions. First, it needs to attract the receiver's attention and interest. Second, it needs to create a desire for the product or service and third, it needs to encourage the receiver to take the next step towards purchase.

GETTING ATTENTION AND INTEREST

A sales letter usually begins with an eye-catching opening which, it is hoped, will persuade the recipient to read further. This could be a question designed to excite curiosity, such as that used in the sample letter. Alternatively, it could be an intriguing claim:

> *Let us tell you how Superfuel can reduce your home heating bills by as much as thirty per cent.*

or a flattering remark:

> *As one of our most valued customers we thought you would like to know about our new Saveplan policy.*

or a command:

> *Buy* Irish Moneymaker *now! – Ireland's newest and brightest business magazine.*

Very often the opening draws attention to some special offer. This could be a free gift, a discount, a trial offer or a money-back guarantee.

CREATING DESIRE FOR THE PRODUCT

The next stage is to persuade readers that the product or service can be beneficial to them. Selling points have to be selected with care. Depending on what is being advertised, a benefit could be ease of use, quality, value for money, newness, prompt delivery, good back-up service and so on. In deciding which benefits to advertise, the writer should aim to satisfy the particular wants and needs of potential customers. Favourable testimony from an existing customer (as in Exhibit 10.11) can be used to reinforce the sales appeal.

PROMOTING ACTION

The last stage is to encourage readers to take follow-up action. For example, the letter could invite recipients to send off for a brochure or free sample, to enter a free competition or visit a showroom.

Any device that makes it easier for readers to respond should be used. Enclose a reply-paid envelope or card if a written reply is required. Include a map if you are inviting visits to your shop or showroom. Even the simple device of locating your premises by reference to a well-known local landmark can be helpful:

> *Call in to see us any time. We are just beside the National Bank on Main Street.*

STYLE

In general, sales letters should be written in a brisk, lively style. Both sentences and paragraphs should be very short. Often, an informal, even ungrammatical style is acceptable.

Choose from more than a hundred patterns. In a wide range of colours. And we'll be happy to measure up for you. Free of charge!

Even when the subject requires a more dignified approach the style should not be too solemn.

A sales letter should also be visually appealing. The most important selling points can be highlighted by bold, underscoring, some variation in fonts or different colours. Headings can be used to lead the reader through the text. The letter should be carefully printed and only good-quality stationery with an attractive letterhead should be used.

Exhibit 10.11 Sales letter

VisionCom Ltd
19 Lr Dorset Street
Dublin 3
Tel: 01 855 3456
Fax: 01 855 6543
E-mail: sales@visioncom.ie
Web: www.visioncom.ie

Mr R. Woods
Sales Manager
Commercial Enterprises Ltd
Santry
Dublin 9

Dear Mr Woods,

Are you getting the most out of your sales team?

Perhaps you haven't the resources to provide full training for new sales staff. Or perhaps it's time to think about putting your experienced sales personnel in touch with the very latest selling techniques.

Our new training video, '**Selling Success**', could be the answer you are looking for.

This lively, informative course in selling methods will show your sales team how to:

▸ identify the selling points in their products
▸ deal with many different types of customers
▸ build an effective sales presentation
▸ break down resistance to buying.

The full two-hour programme is set out in four easy-to-complete modules. There is an accompanying manual which contains interesting case studies and assignments, so your sales staff can *immediately* put into practice what they have learned.

Here is what Mr Jim Powell, sales executive with International Merchants Ltd, has to say about 'Selling Success':

This is the best training programme I have seen in years. What I like about it is the absence of gimmicks. Sound, practical advice is given throughout. We found that our sales increased significantly after all our salespeople had completed the programme. I would recommend it to any salesperson who wants to improve selling technique.

If you would like to judge 'Selling Success' for yourself, why not come to one of our previews? These are now being held at evening receptions in Dublin, Cork, Limerick and Galway.

Just return the enclosed reply-paid card indicating your choice of venue and we will send your invitations by return.

We look forward to meeting you.

Yours sincerely,

Ms Diana O'Neill

Managing Director

PRESS RELEASE

The press release is the principal form of written communication used by businesses to convey information to the media. Usually, it contains a news story intended for publication. The story could be about:

- a new investment programme
- the launching of a new product
- the opening of a new factory
- sponsorship of a local or national event
- the promotion of a senior member of staff
- any other aspect of the company's activities that has news value. A typical example is given in Exhibit 10.12.

Releases are useful to the press because they help fill up space and save on journalists' time. Yet despite these advantages, many of them are discarded as soon as they reach the editor's desk. Either they contain nothing of interest or they are presented in an unprofessional manner. A press officer's job, therefore, is to ensure that all releases sent out from the organisation meet press requirements in terms of both content and layout. Otherwise, they are simply a waste of paper.

Exhibit 10.12   Press release

Plastico Ltd
Newry Road, Dundalk, Ireland
Tel: 047-8331
Fax: 047-8462
E-mail: info@plastico.com
Web: www.plastico.com

Press Release
Date: 8 May 20—

For immediate release

€3.5 MILLION EXPANSION AT DUNDALK PLANT

Mr Tony Wall, chief executive of Plastico Ltd, announced today that the company is to invest €3.5 million in its Dundalk plant over the next two years. This injection of capital will enable the plant to manufacture a new range of plastic moulded products for the European and Pacific markets.

Launching the expansion programme, Mr Wall said that factory floor space would be increased by 1,000 m² and a new, fully automated production line installed. The project would provide twenty-five additional jobs in its first year with the prospect of a further fifty jobs by the end of the third year.

'This development marks another important stage in the remarkable progress of Plastico,' Mr Wall said. 'The company began in Dundalk in 1985 with only twelve workers. Today, with a workforce of 240, it is one of the largest industrial employers in the northeast.'

The new product range will consist mainly of components for computers and computer-related machines. The market for these components has grown substantially in recent years. Wherever possible, raw materials and other requirements will be purchased in Ireland.

Mr Wall also reaffirmed Plastico's commitment to research and development. 'We are very conscious that continued investment in research is vital to the future success of the company,' he said.

Ends

For further information contact: John Conlon, Press Officer, Plastico Ltd
Tel: 047-8331 Fax: 047-8462 Mobile: 087-654456

CONTENT

The main points to bear in mind are as follows.

- The release should be relevant and useful to the publication that receives it. Common sense plays a large part here. The new liquid chromatograph your company is introducing to the market may be of interest to a magazine like *Technology Ireland* and your sponsorship of a local football tournament may be worth a mention in a provincial newspaper, but neither of these two stories is likely to be of much value to the news editor of a national daily.
- It is common practice to state at the outset whether the content of a release is **embargoed** or to be **published immediately**. An embargo, e.g. *not to be published before 7 pm 15 May*, means that the information in the release cannot be used until after the date and time specified. It is a useful device if, for example, you want to let the press know about an event before it actually happens.
- The release should begin with a **headline**. This helps the editor or journalist decide whether the story deserves attention. The headline should give a short, simple description of the content.
- The essential details of the story should be set out in the first paragraph, e.g. what happened? Who was involved? When? Where? Why?
- The remaining paragraphs should expand on this information in descending order of importance. Then, if the subeditor wants to shorten the story he can prune back from the last paragraph. (The subeditor prepares copy for print by cutting or altering it as required.)
- There should be a strong emphasis on **factual** information. Exaggerated or unsubstantiated claims of the type sometimes found in advertising should be strictly avoided.
- The style should be plain and concise.
- It possible, **direct quotes** should be included. These are popular with journalists because they add colour and interest to the story.
- The name and telephone number of a contact should be given at the end.
- The release should always be dated.

LAYOUT

It is important that a press release be set out in a form that a journalist finds easy to edit. This greatly increases its chances of being published. The main points to watch out for are these.

- Ideally, a company release should be set out on preprinted stationery bearing the company name and address, etc. and the heading *News Release* or equivalent.

- Plenty of white space should be left for the subeditor's markings. It helps if the release is double spaced and has fairly wide margins. Only one side of the paper should be used.
- All pages should be numbered and all except the last one should have **more follows** or **m.f.** at the bottom.
- Each continuation page should have a catchline, i.e. a two- or three-word subject heading, at the top.
- Each page should end with a complete paragraph. All this is to help journalists in case the pages become separated in a busy newsroom.
- The end of the release is marked with the word **ends**.

ASSIGNMENTS

REVISION

1. What is a memorandum? What kind of message does it usually convey?
2. List and comment briefly on the main components of the memorandum format.
3. In your opinion, what are the advantages of using a schematic layout in long memoranda?
4. Why is it important to have the right tone in memoranda?
5. Why must a notice attract attention? Describe some techniques that can be used to give notices greater visibility.
6. What guidelines are recommended for using e-mail in a professional manner?
7. What techniques are used in a sales letter to:
   - get the reader interested
   - create desire for the product
   - promote action?
8. How does the style of a sales letter differ from that of other business letters?
9. It is estimated that ninety-five per cent of all press releases end up in the journalist's bin. How should you write a press release to ensure that it conforms to the journalist's expectations? Consider both content and layout in your answer.

ACTIVITIES

1. Collect as many samples of memos, notices, sales letters and press releases as you can. (Voluntary organisations can be good sources of press releases.)

   With each form, compare layout and style. What similarities do you notice? Are there differences that stand out? Which examples are most effective and why?

2. Collect and compare examples of other types of sales literature such as brochures, leaflets, etc. Samples of these are easy to find – they come with every telephone, electricity or gas bill, for example. Discuss the effectiveness of this type of sales literature. What selling techniques are employed? How are design elements used to make the material colourful and attractive? What do you notice about the copy, that is, headings and text?

EXERCISES

1. You are head of training at Tradeco, which has two DIY superstores located in Dublin. You have arranged a special two-day course to train recently recruited staff in 'Meeting Customer Needs'. The course is to be held at the head office and the company will pay all expenses.

   Write a memo to staff giving details of the course. Point out that staff who wish to apply should give their names to their staff training officer by the following Friday at the latest. Places on the course are limited to fifteen.

2. At a recent staff/management meeting in your organisation it was decided to ban smoking in almost all areas of the building for a trial period of one month. This followed several complaints from nonsmoking staff.

   Two areas are to be reserved for smokers: a small partitioned-off area of the canteen and a smoking room on the second floor in which there will be a drinks dispenser.

   At the end of the trial period a final decision on smoking policy will be made.

   As office manager write a memo to all staff advising them of these new arrangements and asking for their co-operation.

3. The private car park at Tradeco's headquarters has space for forty cars. During a rebuilding programme which is expected to last for three months starting on 1 September the number of spaces will be unavoidably reduced to twenty-five.

   While this disturbance lasts, the company has made provisions for staff to park at a reasonable rate in a nearby surface car park operated by Take Your Chances Carparks Ltd.

   Write a memo to all staff explaining the situation.

4. The marketing department at Wing 'n' a Prayer Airlines has decided to enter a team in a national talent competition, the finalists of which will appear on a special pre-Christmas television spectacular.

   Write a notice encouraging staff with musical, comic or other talent to get involved. Anyone interested is invited to an initial meeting in the press room at 1:30 pm on Wednesday 14 June.

5. You are a supervisor in a small light engineering factory. Recently there have

been a number of accidents, mainly involving young apprentices. You decide to draft a notice pointing out the need for greater care on the shop floor.

You might refer to the need to keep guards on machines, switch off machines during maintenance, wear eye protectors, mop up oil spills immediately and so on.

Write the notice.

6. You are general manager at Foxworth Ireland, a subsidiary of Foxworth International, a Boston-based multinational. The chief executive of Foxworth, Mr James Dean, is to visit the Irish facility for one day on Wednesday 9 May.

Write an e-mail to your senior managers only informing them about this visit. It is expected that Mr Dean will arrive at approximately 10:00 am. He will meet the senior management team first and then will be taken on a tour of the plant. After lunch in the Bell Tower restaurant, the CEO will address all staff and then hold a further meeting with senior managers, at which he will hear presentations. He is expected to leave at approximately 4:30 pm.

Stress the importance of this meeting and the need for the senior management team to be fully prepared.

7. Your company, Spareparts Motors Ltd, is opening a new branch in an expanding city suburb. The new garage will offer a range of on-the-spot services (new tyres, wheel balancing, etc.) and will have a motor accessory shop attached. Write a sales letter advertising the garage and intended for distribution to local householders.

8. Country Gardens, established ten years ago, provides a garden landscaping, maintenance and clearing service. It has just won a prestigious Gold Medal award for garden design at the Glasgow Garden Festival. Write a sales letter for distribution to local householders advertising the firm.

9. Threads Fashions Ltd imports and distributes a wide range of garments for women and teenagers. It is sole agent for a number of top international brands, including FunWear, Camilla, B-Line and Toughguy Jeans. Established for fifteen years, the firm guarantees to stock the very latest fashion at highly competitive rates.

Design an advertising leaflet for Threads for distribution to selected retail outlets nationwide.

10. As manager of a small coach company you have decided to send a sales letter to local businesses, schools and colleges advertising the use of your coaches for outings and excursions. Write the appropriate letter.

11. You have recently opened a small shop, e.g. florist, dry cleaning, fashion outlet, in a suburban shopping centre. Write a sales leaflet for door-to-door distribution advertising the shop.

12. Your firm has been engaged as a letting agent for a new shopping precinct in the city centre. Write a suitable press release for insertion in the property pages of the national newspapers to announce this development.

13. The marketing manager of your organisation has become president of a professional association. Write a press release to announce this. The release is intended for publication in the business section of the national press.

14. Your managing director has a long association with a local sports club. At a reception held in a nearby hotel, he presents a trophy to the club's outstanding sportsperson of the year. Write a press release describing the occasion and aimed at the local newspaper.

15. Donegal Milk has recently reached agreement with a German firm to manufacture a new range of cheeses and yoghurts under licence. These products are intended for both the home and export markets. New equipment will have to be installed and it is expected the workforce will have to be increased.

    Write a press release announcing the development. Invent whatever details you think necessary.

16. Freeway PLC, a large Irish company specialising in the manufacture of building materials, has recently purchased the Ohio Asphalt Company, a US-based company with headquarters in Dry Gulch, Ohio. The cost of the acquisition is US$45 million.

    The Ohio Asphalt Company is a substantial group involved in asphalt, ready-mixed concrete, road building and haulage. It has sites and plants in several Midwestern states.

    The acquisition of the company fits neatly into Freeway's existing US operations. In the coming year it is expected to make a contribution to group profits of not less than US$8 million.

    Write a press release announcing this acquisition. Invent any other details you think fit.

PART 4

Oral, Visual and Nonverbal Communication

Nonverbal Communication

Nonverbal communication (NVC) is a broad term that encompasses all the ways we communicate by our behaviour rather than words. It is primarily applied to four areas:

- body language such as gestures, facial expressions and head nods, etc.
- our use of space and territory
- how we dress and present ourselves
- qualities of the voice such as pitch, tone and volume. (This is referred to as *paralanguage* and is discussed in the next chapter.)

However, the meaning of the term extends well beyond these boundaries. Researchers have looked at much less obvious forms of nonverbal communication (how we decorate our homes, for example, or how we interpret and use time). In fact, *any* nonverbal behaviour that sends a message may be regarded as a part of NVC.

It has been estimated that in a typical encounter between two people, two-thirds of information is conveyed nonverbally and only one-third verbally. Nonverbal signals give important clues to personality, relationships, status and so on. Indeed, when there is a discrepancy between verbal and nonverbal messages (as when someone grits his teeth while denying that he is angry) it is the nonverbal message that is believed.

The power of nonverbal behaviour to convey meaning is something storytellers have always known and exploited. For example, here is how Emily Brontë introduces Heathcliff in the first paragraph of *Wuthering Heights*. Notice how she uses three telling details of body language to reveal the reserved and deeply troubled nature of her hero.

> A capital fellow! He little imagined how my heart warmed towards him when I beheld his black eyes withdraw so suspiciously under his brows, as I rode up, and when his fingers sheltered themselves, with a jealous resolution, still further in his waistcoat, as I announced my name.
> 'Mr Heathcliff?' I said.
> A nod was the answer.

Nonverbal communication is not just the preserve of novelists and their readers, however. It is also an important aspect of business communication. One can think of many situations where NVC can have a significant effect: the first few moments of an interview or presentation, for example, or the opening exchanges between a shop assistant and a customer. It is claimed that first impressions, which are mainly based on appearance, can disproportionately influence the outcome of a job interview. And customers know that a pleasant, smiling assistant will encourage them to buy whereas a grim-looking or 'snooty' assistant will not, so nonverbal communication matters in business and professional life. We may never control it completely, but we can become better communicators by understanding its effects and learning to use it purposefully.

THE FUNCTIONS OF NONVERBAL COMMUNICATION

This section gives an overview of the purpose of nonverbal communication before we move on to look at particular forms. Broadly speaking, the following six functions can be distinguished.

1. **Expressing emotions**

    This is one of the most obvious functions of nonverbal communication. From an early age we learn to read the nonverbal signs of emotional states: pursed lips and foot-stamping for anger, tears and a drooping posture for sadness, a broad smile for happiness or tense, nervous movements for anxiety.

2. **Supporting speech**

    Nonverbal communication may support speech in various ways. First, it can repeat and reinforce what is said. For example, a person may say, 'There are three points I want to make' and then count these out on his fingers. Second, it can be used to illustrate the size, shape or appearance of something, e.g. holding the hand horizontally to show a person's height. Third, it can give additional emphasis to speech. This can be done by using emphatic gestures, for example, or by changing the pattern of the voice.

3. **Replacing speech**

    There are many instances where nonverbal symbols are used as an alternative to words. Sign language, for example, is a nonverbal code used by the deaf. In addition, many people work in environments where the use of nonverbal signs is essential, either because the voice will not carry or because speech is too slow. For example, think of a policeman directing traffic at a busy junction or a broker dealing on the floor of the stock exchange. Sometimes isolated nonverbal signs are used because they are more dramatic than words – for example, raising one's fist in triumph after a success in sport.

4. **Indicating relationships**

Nonverbal cues are important indicators of relationships. First, they may indicate degrees of attraction or liking. For example, we recognise an intimate relationship when two people stand or sit close together, touch each other affectionately and have a high level of mutual eye contact. Second, they may communicate degrees of dominance or submission. A wide range of nonverbal signs – dress, posture, use of space, eye gaze, etc. – enables us to draw conclusions about the status and power of individuals. A television presenter may sit on a slightly higher seat than his guests, the boss at work is likely to have the biggest office, the most influential person in a meeting will get most eye contact and so on.

However, it is important to remember that nonverbal signs can be used deliberately to communicate more equal relationships, for example, changing seating arrangements at a meeting so no one has a dominant position.

5. **Regulating conversation**

Turn taking in conversation is something that occurs naturally and without much thought. We become aware of it only when it breaks down and we have to make a verbal adjustment: 'You were going to say . . .', 'No, you finish first', 'It's OK, you go ahead.' Normally, we do not need words to manage the changeover. Instead, we use a number of subtle nonverbal cues. The person yielding a turn indicates this by changing eye contact and the pitch and volume of his voice. The person seeking a turn may lean forward and perhaps raise a finger. Shifting position or looking at one's watch can signal a desire to end the conversation altogether.

6. **Getting feedback**

Finally, nonverbal communication is an important source of feedback. This point was made in Chapter 1 and will be emphasised again in Chapter 13. In any interaction, we should always be alert to the unspoken cues sent to us by the receiver. Positive feedback (good eye contact, nods of support or more overt signs of approval such as clapping) can give an important psychological boost to the communicator. Negative feedback (signs of boredom or discomfort) may give a strong indication that the communicator should alter his approach or style.

Before we conclude this section and turn to the main forms of NVC, a word of caution may be necessary. Some nonverbal signs have a definite and unvarying meaning, e.g. thumbing a lift, but others are more ambiguous. For example, what does folding the arms across the chest mean? Is it a defensive gesture, as some suggest, or merely a way of 'parking' the arms while listening? We should always be careful in how we interpret nonverbal communication. Usually a cluster of signs needs to be looked at before we can come to any decision about what they reveal.

KINESICS

The word *kinesics* comes from the Greek *kinçsis*, meaning 'motion', so it is no surprise to find that this heading includes all the various movements of the body: gestures, facial expression, eye behaviour, posture and so on. This is the area of nonverbal communication that has received most attention in research and that appears to carry most nonverbal information.

GESTURES

Each of us uses a wide repertoire of gestures, some of which are conscious, some unconscious. The most obvious gestures are made by the upper body (head, shoulders, hands) but we often convey more covert messages with our lower body, e.g. shuffling our legs or toe-tapping under the table. Some cultures make more expansive gestures than others, and sometimes this is used as a crude form of ethnic stereotyping: the wildly gesticulating Italian contrasted with the self-controlled and undemonstrative Englishman.

There are three basic types of gestures. **Emblems** are those we use instead of speech, for example, nodding the head in agreement, thumbs up for success, waving to say goodbye or finger to lips for silence. There are several reasons for using gestures in this way. They are faster than speech, they are silent and can be used surreptitiously, they can be used in a noisy background such as a factory or the stock exchange and they can be seen over distance (an invaluable aid to the tick-tack men at racecourses).

Emblems are well-understood signs within a particular culture. However, they can mean something else, or even give offence, in another culture. A story is told that on one occasion a Russian premier visiting the US clenched his hands above his head on emerging from the plane. His gesture was intended to show his delight at being so well received, but his American audience thought it was a sign of arrogance.

A second use of gestures is as **illustrators**. This is when we use them to support or reinforce speech. For example, we regularly point when giving directions, extend our arms to show shape or size and make urgent movements with our hands to emphasise what we are saying. Gestures are also used to regulate conversation. One of the signs that a speaker is concluding is when his hand movements come to an end.

Finally, **adaptors** are those gestures that are taken to reveal emotional states. Communicators need to be aware of these because they sometimes 'leak' undesirable information. A public speaker or interviewee may unwittingly betray lack of confidence by hand-wringing, covering his mouth, toying nervously with a pen, etc.

FACIAL EXPRESSION

The human face is capable of thousands of different expressions. However, most of these involve such minute changes that we do not recognise them. Those that we do recognise are a rich source of information about moods and feelings – indeed, it is thought the face is the second-most important medium of human communication after language. Some facial expressions lie within our control, e.g. the deliberately raised eyebrow to signify scepticism, while others, such as blushing, are involuntary. Sometimes, too, the face can be used to disguise rather than reveal, e.g. the notorious poker face of the professional gambler.

Perhaps the most influential facial expression is the human smile. It is difficult not to respond positively to a smile, although we make a distinction between a 'real smile' of genuine pleasure and the 'fixed smile' of the well-trained waiter. In fact, so powerful is the smile that telephone users are advised to 'smile into the phone', as this carries over positively into their voice and telephone manner.

How do you feel today?

Happy? Sad? Optimistic? Frustrated? Determined?

Recent research indicates that humans experience over 400 different emotions. We recognise these by changes in facial expression and they appear to be common to all cultures.

Researchers at the University of California are building a database of how the face moves in every emotion. It appears that the face can make forty-three distinct muscle movements and these can be combined into over 10,000 configurations. Some of the movements are so rapid that they last only for microseconds.

Researchers also believe that it is difficult to fake emotions because they start prior to consciousness. According to Professor Paul Ekman at the University of California, 'Decisions and evaluations in our brain happen so quickly we don't know we're having an emotion until it has started happening. We can't decide to be happy or sad: it simply happens to us.'

One of the most difficult expressions to fake is the smile. This may explain our ability to distinguish smiles of genuine pleasure and smiles that are forced or false.

Source: *The Guardian*, 3 September 2002

THE EYES

Of all our facial features, the eyes are the most important and get the most attention in social interactions. Many cultures intuitively acknowledge this by highlighting the eyes with some form of eye decoration. We can control the 'look' of our eyes by altering facial muscles – narrowing our eyes, for example, or making them 'laugh'. However, there is one aspect of the eyes that cannot be consciously changed – the size of the pupil.

What does eye behaviour (making and breaking eye contact, gazing and blinking) tell us?

- First, it tells us something about **attitudes**. Compare the soft gaze of lovers with the intense, aggressive stare of boxers facing off before a fight.
- It is a measure of **attraction**. Our pupils dilate involuntarily and we look more at someone or something we like.
- It may reveal **personality types**. Gaze levels are higher in those who are extroverted, dominant, assertive and socially skilled.
- It may reveal **moods and feeling**. For example, we look away when we feel shy, annoyed or anxious.
- Finally, it is a key mechanism for **regulating conversation**. A person beginning to speak makes eye contact with the receiver, then breaks contact intermittently as he proceeds and finally makes eye contact again just before he concludes. The receiver, meanwhile, maintains a fairly steady gaze. This ritual dance of the eyes continues throughout the exchange.

POSTURE

Posture is the way we move our whole body when we stand, sit or move. Like other forms of NVC this can convey a variety of meanings.

To begin with, posture is often read as an indicator of *mood* or *physical state*. An athlete who has just finished a demanding race may spend several seconds bent over with exhaustion. If he has lost he may then walk away from the arena with lowered head and drooping shoulders.

Posture is also an indicator of *status differentials*. For example, in a conversation between boss and employee, the superior is likely to have a more relaxed posture, while the subordinate will sit or stand in a more rigid, upright position.

On the other hand, when the relationship between people is equal, they tend to *mirror* each other's posture. Watch two friends in close conversation across a table in a restaurant. There is likely to be a noticeable similarity in posture, both leaning on the same elbow, both changing position at the same time, both, perhaps, lifting their coffee cups at almost the same moment. This congruence has been called *postural echo*.

PROXEMICS

Proxemics (from the Latin *proximus*, meaning 'nearest') is the study of the way humans use space to convey messages. It has three distinct aspects: proximity, territoriality and orientation.

PROXIMITY

Proximity refers to the distances we maintain between ourselves and those around us. Each of us carries around a 'bubble' of personal space which expands or contracts into four different zones, as shown in Exhibit 11.1.

- **Intimate zone**: The distance we allow between ourselves and those who are very close to us (parent, child, lover).
- **Personal zone**: The somewhat greater distance we maintain with personal friends.
- **Social zone**: This is the professional distance that would be maintained, for example, between counsellor and client.
- **Public zone**: The distance between a speaker and the audience.

Exhibit 11.1 Personal space

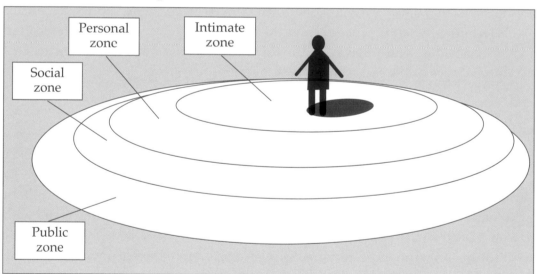

Sometimes, of course, the 'rules' of proximity have to be broken. A doctor or dentist, for example, has to approach very close to or touch a patient in order to make an examination. Similarly, when we enter a crowded lift or bus we accept that our personal space will be severely restricted. Normally, such restriction would make people feel uncomfortable so they use various adaptive behaviours to compensate. For instance, notice how people behave in a lift. They take up rather frozen positions, all facing in the same direction and avoiding eye contact. The light moving up and down the floor indicator becomes the centre of attention.

Sense of personal space varies somewhat with personality, gender, culture and status. Extroverts stand more closely than introverts, women more closely to each other than men and southern Europeans more closely than northern Europeans. Individuals with high status or authority usually feel freer to invade personal space than those with lower status. A teacher, for example, will more freely approach a pupil than the reverse; the same applies to boss and employee.

TERRITORIALITY

While personal space is the area around our body, territory is a much wider area to which we lay claim. It may include not only our home or car, but space at work, in the classroom or in the pub (the seat with the cushion where old Mr Mulligan always sits). Markers of territory can take many forms: the 'do not enter' sign outside the bedroom, the jacket draped across the restaurant seat, the towel on the beach, nameplates on office doors or the large desk that takes up half the room.

Our sense of territory is so strong that we take elaborate precautions to avoid invading that of others. Few people would claim an empty chair without asking permission first, sometimes with the rather illogical question, 'Is anyone sitting here?' If we have to pass through someone else's territory, e.g. through a conversing group at a crowded party, we apologise profusely and make ourselves as small and narrow as possible. Even with an 'open door' policy most people would knock on the boss's door before entering.

If our own territory is invaded without these ritualistic permissions, we can become upset and sometimes even angry or violent. Some of the more extreme examples of this are seen at football matches when the supporters of one team cross into the traditional territory of the other.

ORIENTATION

This is related to proximity and refers to the angle at which people interact with each other. As shown in Exhibit 11.2 different orientations convey different meanings and are suited to different situations. Generally, people sit side by side when co-operating and face to face when in competition. A ninety-degree orientation suits conversation and more informal interviews. Finally, people sit at a distance from each other when travelling or working alone.

Special arrangements also have a strong influence on group communication. For example, a circular seating pattern is more conducive to participation than sitting in rows. Even the positions people take up at a table affect the interaction. The group leader will automatically go to the head of the table and those who sit closest to him are more likely to give support. Those who sit further away tend to take less part in the discussion.

Exhibit 11.2 Orientation

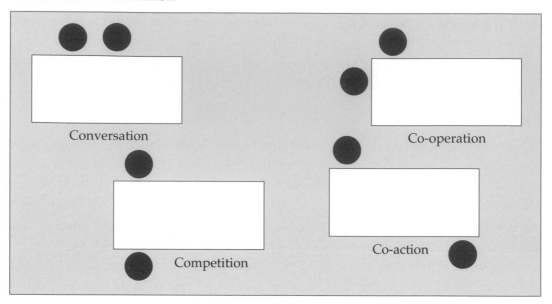

PHYSICAL CONTACT

Touch is the most intimate form of nonverbal communication and fulfils deep psychological needs in humans. Perhaps the most natural and uninhibited physical contact occurs between young children and their parents. However, as children grow into adults they learn that touch is overlaid with many restrictions and taboos. In organisations there are specific social and cultural rules regarding the contexts in which physical contact is acceptable and what kinds of touch can be used.

The three forms of physical contact that are most relevant to professional relationships are:

- **Functional touching**: Many professionals are required to touch their clients as part of their work, e.g. doctors, dentists, physiotherapists, etc.
- **Ritual touching**: Different forms of physical contact are used to begin and end social encounters. These vary from culture to culture and include the handshake, kissing on the cheek, embracing, etc.
- **Playful/supportive touching**: This includes touching on the hand or arm or patting on the back. It may be used as a sign of affection or sympathy, to lend support or to encourage.

The last of these three is the form of touching most open to misinterpretation in the workplace. Playful or supportive touching can have positive effects. It can convey a feeling of warmth and comradeship and it can make people more open and more willing to comply with requests. Sometimes, however, it may not be welcome because it is regarded as patronising or an invasion of personal space.

PHYSICAL APPEARANCE

Physical appearance may refer either to actual body shape or to the way we enhance appearance with body decorations, dress and accessories.

Researchers have identified three main body shapes:

- the **endomorph** is fat, round and soft
- the **mesomorph** is bony, muscular and athletic
- the **ectomorph** is tall, thin and fragile.

Certain characteristics are associated with each body type. Endomorphs are thought to be relaxed, happy and lazy. Mesomorphs are regarded as cheerful, optimistic and confident. Ectomorphs are serious, sensitive and tactful, but also cautious and suspicious. Caesar is undoubtedly describing an ectomorph when he confides to his friend Antony in Shakespeare's great political drama, *Julius Caesar*:

> Yond Cassius has a lean and hungry look;
> He thinks too much; such men are dangerous.

There is much evidence that humans attach both positive and negative meanings to body shape and some evidence from research in the US that shape can be the basis of discrimination in jobs and promotion. Those who are uncomfortable with their body shape will sometimes go to great lengths to change it, as witnessed by the growth in cosmetic surgery and the ready availability of slimming products, body-building machines, etc. Clothes can also be used to change body shape: wearing high heels to give extra height, for example, or tight-fitting clothes to give a narrower figure. Many of these practices have been attacked by feminist writers who object strongly to the pressure the beauty industry exerts on women in particular to conform to an ideal body shape.

Clothes and accessories are the form of nonverbal communication that can be most easily altered. There are various reasons for choosing a particular form of dress:

- to enhance physical attractiveness
- to conform to a role, e.g. uniforms and working clothes
- to conform to social norms, e.g. ties, dinner jackets
- to display attitudes or beliefs, e.g. deliberately wearing casual clothes on a formal occasion
- to show membership of a group, e.g. band uniforms, sashes, etc.

Fashion in clothes changes regularly. There are many cultural differences, but it is noticeable that these are being reduced with the growth in global travel and communication. Young people wear much the same clothes whether they are in New York, Moscow or Dublin. A photograph of almost any group of international businesspeople will show a remarkable uniformity in dress.

The fashion business

Fashion is as old as human history. From earliest times, men and women have attached meaning to dress and adornment. No age has been free from eccentric notions about what people should wear.

▸ Cosmetics were known and used by the ancient Egyptians. Eyeliners, eye shadow, face masks and ointments were all part of an upper-class Egyptian lady's make-up box. Lipstick, far from being a modern invention, is at least 5,000 years old.

▸ In fourteenth-century England dress was so important an indicator of social position that laws were laid down regulating what each rank could wear. A person who broke the rules could be heavily fined.

▸ Black spots were a seventeenth-century craze. These were small patches initially used to cover scars and spots. Before long, however, they had acquired a social meaning. In London, the right-wing Whigs wore them on the right cheek and the left-wing Tories wore them on the left cheek.

▸ In eighteenth-century Europe wigs, which were worn by both men and women, reached new heights – literally. In some cases, doorways had to be raised to let the wearer through. Only the wealthy could afford the largest wigs – hence the expression *bigwig*.

Source: Morris, 2002

Two aspects of clothes are particularly relevant in the workplace. First, a certain type of dress may be essential because of the nature of the work. For example, there are usually strict requirements for operatives to wear protective clothing when working in a hazardous environment. Second, even where a particular form of dress is not essential it may be required by the norms of the organisation. Bank employees, for example, are expected to conform to a rather formal dress code that is strictly applied. In small organisations the dress code may be more relaxed. Some organisations make a deliberate attempt to reduce status differentials by insisting that every employee, whether management or staff, wears exactly the same uniform.

NONVERBAL COMMUNICATION IN PRACTICE

It is important to have a balanced attitude to nonverbal communication. On the one hand, it is foolish to think that we must always be conscious of our nonverbal behaviour. Most of the time we manage social encounters perfectly well without wondering whether we are sitting in the right way, maintaining eye contact and so on. Indeed, we would communicate less effectively if we worried too much about NVC.

On the other hand, it is equally foolish to think that nonverbal communication is of no consequence whatsoever. The evidence suggests that it can make a significant difference in encounters that may mean a great deal to us – meetings, interviews and sales presentations, to name but a few.

Here are ten practical tips on how to use nonverbal communication to advantage in a business context – without becoming too self-conscious about it.

1. The handshake is the ritual way of beginning and ending business meetings. Shake hands firmly – this conveys confidence and control.
2. Good eye contact is essential in all kinds of business interactions. If giving a presentation, look around your audience to show confidence and gain feedback. In an interview, look at the interviewer when you first meet and smile.
3. At a meeting, watch for turn-taking cues and indicate in good time that you want to speak. If you miss your turn, the discussion may move forward and the opportunity to contribute is lost.
4. Give other people positive feedback by looking with interest and nodding in support. They in turn will have a more positive attitude towards you.
5. Use gestures in a controlled way. Be alert for 'leakage', those nonverbal signs that betray anxiety or nervousness.
6. In interviews, adopt an upright posture, leaning slightly towards the interviewer. If the interviewer adopts a relaxed pose, do not make the mistake of mirroring him.
7. Use space effectively. If you are organising a meeting you can create a more formal or informal atmosphere by changing seating arrangements or altering the ambience of a room.
8. Respect other people's space.
9. Be aware of the importance of dress codes. Formal dress is almost always required for an interview or business presentation. Being well dressed and groomed – and taking particular care with the details – makes a positive impression.
10. And finally, *relax*! Most nonverbal skills come naturally, so 'be yourself' is often the best advice.

ASSIGNMENTS

REVISION

1. How would you define nonverbal behaviour?
2. Briefly outline the six functions of nonverbal behaviour described at the beginning of the chapter.
3. What forms of nonverbal communication are included in the study of kinesics?
4. Distinguish clearly between gestures used as (a) emblems (b) illustrators and (c) adaptors. Give examples of each.
5. What kinds of information can be conveyed by eye behaviour (making eye contact, gazing, blinking, etc.)?
6. Give examples of how posture can indicate moods, status and relationships.
7. What is meant by the term *personal space*?
8. Describe some ways in which humans mark out territory. What is the effect on us if we feel 'our' territory is being invaded?
9. What is meant by *orientation*? Show with the aid of a simple sketch two seating arrangements that facilitate co-operation in meetings and interviews.
10. Group the following forms of touching under the two headings 'Ritual' and 'Playful/supportive'. Is there any form that does not fit under either of these headings?

holding hands	patting on the back
shaking hands	putting arm round waist
linking arms	kissing on cheek
full embrace	mock fighting
patting on the head	pushing

11. Which body shape is indicated by the terms (a) endomorph (b) ectomorph (c) mesomorph?
12. Describe some of the ways in which nonverbal communication can be significant in business encounters and relationships.

ACTIVITIES AND DISCUSSION POINTS

1. In small groups, discuss the kind of assumptions we might make about a person who:
    *   evades eye contact
    *   stands very close
    *   has slurred speech
    *   has hair dyed bright green
    *   wears a conservative suit and tie
    *   has a limp handshake

- yawns during a meeting
- stammers during an interview.

What mistakes can arise from these assumptions?

2. Think of an occasion when you misread a nonverbal signal. Collect examples in your group.
3. In your group, have each person list and give the meaning of six distinctive gestures under each of the following headings:
   - emblems
   - illustrators
   - adaptors.

   Does anyone come up with an unusual example?
4. In small groups, collect photographs from newspapers and magazines of different facial expressions. What does each person's face reveal? What are the visual clues? Is it possible to be certain about meaning in each case?
5. Write a set of cards, each with a word describing a mood or emotion, e.g. happy, excited, angry, depressed, exhausted, in love. Invite volunteers to display these feelings nonverbally through posture, facial expression and gesture. Can the rest of the group guess which feeling is being displayed?
6. Think about how your group has arranged itself in the classroom. Does everyone always go to the same seat? Have males and females grouped themselves separately or are they mixed? Do some always go to the back and some to the front? If so, does this have any significance?
7. Consider how physical environment might help or hinder communication. Look at your classroom or lecture theatre, for example. How is it laid out? (How many seats? Tiered or flat?) Where are the windows positioned? What colour scheme is used? Is the room pleasant to work in or not? Have you any suggestions for improving it?
8. Many trainers use physically active games as a way of releasing tensions and inhibitions before or during training sessions. You could try the following, both of which involve some physical contact.
   (a) *The snake*: Everyone joins hands and then the 'head' of the snake weaves its way in and out through the 'body' until further movement is impossible. Then, the snake disentangles.
   (b) *Musical chairs*: The group runs around a diminishing number of chairs (mats, sheets of newspaper, etc.). Each time the music stops, participants rush to occupy the remaining places.
9. Use a variety of materials (wool, bits of fabric, paints, markers, soft drink straws, glue, cut-outs from magazines) to build up a nonverbal montage of 'you'.

10. Spend some time discussing the following observations about nonverbal communication.
    - 'Women are much more perceptive than men when it comes to nonverbal communication.'
    - 'It is impossible to wear clothes without transmitting social signals.'
    - 'There is no art to find the mind's construction in the face.'
    - 'To succeed in business, women need to behave more like men.'
    - 'We are far more relaxed about dress codes today than they were fifty years ago.'
    - 'Body language never lies.'

12 Oral and Aural Communication

In our ordinary life we speak and listen far more than we read and write. According to one estimate speaking/listening takes up seventy-five per cent of our communication time, while reading/writing takes up only twenty-five per cent. Yet the second pair of basic communication skills is given much more attention in schools. We seem to assume that speaking and listening come naturally and therefore require no special training.

	Listening	Speaking	Reading	Writing
Learned	First	Second	Third	Fourth
Used	45%	30%	16%	9%
Taught	Least	Next least	Next most	Most

It is only when we move into a business or professional environment that we realise how important effective speaking and listening skills can be. We may find that we have to master a new 'language': the rather formal and dignified register used in meetings, interviews and presentations. We may also find that we have to listen with far greater care and precision than before.

CHARACTERISTICS OF SPEECH

Some of the main characteristics of speech can be illustrated by a simple example.

Tom has received an e-mail from Ann asking for an urgent meeting. However, he is very busy and cannot find time for the meeting until the following day at the earliest. First, he writes another e-mail in reply.

Hi Ann,

I'm afraid I will not be able to arrange a meeting for today because we are very busy here with stocktaking. Could you let me know if 10:30 am tomorrow would suit?

Regards,
Tom

Then he has second thoughts and decides instead to talk to Ann on the telephone. Only his part of the ensuing conversation is recorded below.

> Oh, hello Ann, how are you? . . . About that meeting . . . Yes, I got your note . . . Yes, that's right, I appreciate that . . . Look, could we leave it until tomorrow? It's just that there's a bit of a rush on downstairs at the moment, stocktaking, you know the usual . . . Well, what about 10:30, how would that suit? OK . . . Certainly I can ask Jim Smith to sit in on it, no problem . . . In fact, I know he'll be interested in this . . . So, 10:30 it is then . . .

THE USE OF LANGUAGE

The first thing to notice is that the language of speech (vocabulary, syntax, etc.) is more informal than that of writing. This shows itself in various ways.

- Colloquialisms are more acceptable in speech – *there's a bit of a rush on, you know the usual, no problem*.
- Contractions are used frequently – *that's, it's, there's, he'll*.
- Both verbal and nonverbal fillers occur regularly – *oh, look, well, y'know, sort of*.
- There is a good deal of repetition and redundancy – *Well, what about 10:30, how would that suit* is an example.
- In general, speech appears to be disjointed and fragmented when compared with writing. This leads many people to think that speech is ungrammatical. In fact, the grammars of speech and writing are quite different.
- There are no sentences or paragraphs in speech. Instead, a speech sample consists of a series of short information units which are marked by changes in intonation.
- Speech often contains hesitations, abandoned thoughts and new starts. This is because it is a form of thinking aloud in which the speaker is editing her thoughts as she goes along. The same editing occurs during the process of writing but is hidden in the final draft.

Of course, the degree of formality of speech varies depending on the context in which it is used. Prepared speech can be close to writing. Listen carefully to a television or radio newscast and you will find that most of the informal elements of speech have been edited out. The same rule applies to spoken presentations in business, where using too informal a style would undermine the speaker's credibility.

PARALANGUAGE

Another important feature of speech is that the speaker can use qualities of the voice to give colour and intensity to what she is saying. These voice qualities are collectively known as paralanguage, a form of nonverbal communication mentioned briefly in the previous chapter.

Paralinguistic elements include the following.

- **Volume**: How loudly or quietly a person speaks.
- **Pace**: The rate or speed of speech.
- **Pitch**: Whether the voice is high or low. We use words like *shrill* or *piercing* to describe a high-pitched voice, *gruff* or *throaty* to describe a low-pitched voice.
- **Stress**: Changes in volume, pitch, etc. that denote emphasis. For example, 'Can I have fifteen please?' 'Did you say fifty?' 'No, fif*teen*.'
- **Pauses/silences**: Common features of speech that may indicate that the speaker is gathering her thoughts or moving on to a new topic. Long silences, however, are uncomfortable and someone will usually try to fill them.
- **Accent**: The quality of speech that indicates place of origin, class background, etc. However, many people change their accents when they move to a new country or region or when their lifestyle changes.
- **Pattern and rhythm**: The overall impression that the speaker gives when all the elements above are combined. A good speaker varies pattern and rhythm to stimulate the interest of her listeners.

FEEDBACK

A third significant feature of speech is that in all but a few cases, e.g. recorded messages, there is immediate feedback from the receiver. Nonverbal feedback can be even more important than verbal feedback. In face-to-face communication it is possible to tell from a look or gesture whether the listener is interested or bored, pleased or offended, convinced or sceptical. Over the telephone, valuable clues can be gleaned from the listener's voice as well as words. Perhaps the speaker notices a pause that suggests surprise or a hesitancy that indicates doubt and can alter the message accordingly.

In summary, it can be seen that speech is a rich medium of communication. The speaker has greater freedom to use informal words and constructions than the writer. In addition, she can draw on a vast repertoire of nonverbal signs, both paralinguistic signs and all the other nonverbal signs discussed in the previous chapter. In comparison, writing is actually a more restricted form of communication which uses a narrower range of linguistic and nonverbal devices.

Some weaknesses

If we were able to fulfil every communication task perfectly through speech, nobody would bother writing. However, we know there are occasions when speech is inadequate and writing, despite its limitations, is the more effective medium. So what kinds of problems can arise during oral communication?

1. The informality of speech can be a trap. The communicator may express herself so carelessly that she cannot be understood.
2. The directness of speech can occasionally be a disadvantage. The communicator may not want an immediate response. This is particularly the case when the message contains bad news.
3. Oral communication is generally unsuitable for detailed or complex messages that require careful study. These should be put in writing.
4. Even with short messages, speakers too often prepare poorly. For instance, it is estimated that, on average, as much as half the content of a telephone call in business is irrelevant. This loss in efficiency could be reduced if calls were planned before being made.
5. Usually, no verbatim record is kept of an oral message. Consequently, there is always the possibility that the content of the message could be disputed afterwards.
6. Finally, effective oral communication depends on good listening, yet most of us listen very inefficiently (see below).

In general, however, the strengths of oral communication are considerable. It is fast, informal and direct, it permits an immediate response and it conveys subtleties of meaning that are not available in writing. At every level of business it is by far the most important means of transferring information.

FACE-TO-FACE COMMUNICATION

Most communication in business is face to face, that is, direct, spoken communication between individuals. Much of this takes the form of casual conversation between colleagues on topics of personal rather than professional interest. There are many contexts, however, in which the relationship between the communicators is a professional one:

- receptionist dealing with visitor
- interviewer talking to job applicant
- plant manager briefing supervisors
- salesperson meeting customer
- business meetings over lunch.

It is in these situations that we need to be particularly careful. Face-to-face contact is often the prelude to important decisions: selling a product, hiring an employee, signing a contract, etc. The customer or client will judge us by how successfully we manage the encounter. It is with this in mind that the guidelines below are set out.

Managing face-to-face communication

Planning	If possible, plan face-to-face encounters in advance. Think out what you want to say, but be flexible because the exchanges may take an unexpected turn.
Speaking	Develop a clear, pleasant voice that conveys enthusiasm for your work and interest in the needs of the other person. Avoid speaking too quickly to be understood, slurring words or using the wrong tone.
Language	Adapt language to context. Avoid words that are too difficult or specialised for the listener – this is most important when talking to customers who are not as knowledgeable about your products as you are. Equally, avoid slangy or colloquial expressions that may suggest to the listener that you are not to be taken seriously.
Manner	Be polite, good-humoured and efficient. Show respect for others without being too deferential. Don't be overfamiliar, particularly with people you are meeting for the first time.
Dress	Take care with dress and grooming. In face-to-face communication you will be judged not only on your voice and manner but on your appearance. A smart, well-groomed look is always impressive.
Listening	Face-to-face communication is a two-way process, so be sensitive to the spoken and unspoken reactions of the listener. Don't try to dominate. Give the other person plenty of opportunity to speak and listen attentively.
Responding	Help the speaker by giving verbal and nonverbal feedback. Respond to the points that are made: don't just ignore them. Look at the other person and show by nods etc. that you are following.

ABOUT CONVERSATION

There are many occasions in business where social and professional roles overlap, such as when you have lunch with a client or mingle with visitors to your exhibition or reception. On these occasions, be prepared to talk about a range of topics and to take the initiative if the conversation shows signs of flagging.

If you find conversation difficult – not everyone has a natural gift for it – remember that a good conversation requires effort. You cannot expect others to be interested in you when you have nothing interesting to say, so to begin with, make sure that you are well informed both about your own organisation and about the wider concerns of the business, industry or profession in which you work. Keep up to date with current affairs through your reading and television viewing. Build a fund of anecdotes and stories that you can use. And remember that conversation topics do not have to be extraordinary to be worth introducing. Many a lively conversation has centred on hobbies, holidays or a recent visit to the cinema. Even the most mundane topics can be made interesting if discussed with animation and verve.

THE TELEPHONE

When Alexander Graham Bell invented the telephone in 1876 he began a revolution in spoken communication. For the first time it became possible to transmit the voice over a long distance. Since then the telephone network has been enormously extended and refined. It is now almost as easy to speak to someone thousands of miles away as it is to speak to someone in the office next door.

As we saw in Chapter 4, a modern telephone system is a flexible network which can carry speech, text, data and images. In this section, however, we are concerned solely with the telephone as a medium of voice communication. As such, it has always had an important role in business. For many organisations, it is often the first and sometimes the only point of contact with customers, suppliers or clients. It is also a quick, convenient channel for internal messaging. Exhibit 12.1 outlines some of the add-on features which can make it even more efficient as a communication tool.

Exhibit 12.1 Special telephone features

FEATURE	YOU CAN
Call answering	Record messages when you are away from your desk or busy with another call. Listen to recorded calls whenever you like, using your own phone or any touch-tone phone, including public payphones.
Call waiting	Deal with two calls at the same time by switching from one to the other at the press of a button.
Call forwarding	Programme your phone to transfer incoming calls to another number.
Abbreviated calling	Programme the phone to dial the numbers you use most often by dialling a simple code.
Alarm call	Use your phone as an alarm clock – for important appointments and early morning meetings!

There are also drawbacks with the telephone, however. The very convenience of the phone can in itself be a problem. Because picking up the handset and dialling a number is so easy (even more so with the increasing use of mobile phones), many business callers make little or no preparation. Consequently, they:

- make calls that are not needed
- fail to think out what they want to say
- express themselves badly during calls
- spend much longer on the line than is necessary.

All this adds up to a considerable waste of time and money.

In addition, callers sometimes fail to take account of the fact that the telephone transmits the voice only. They forget that the person at the other end cannot see their facial expression and other nonverbal signals. They overlook the need to convey friendliness and interest in the voice and perhaps sound surly or bored even though they do not intend to give that impression.

In light of these problems, a number of suggestions for improving the quality of business calls are given below.

Making effective business calls

▸ **General rules**
1. Speak clearly into the mouthpiece.
2. Use a friendly and helpful tone.
3. Avoid loose expressions that might give an impression of familiarity or rudeness, e.g. *just a sec, who's that, hold on a tick*.
4. Have pen and paper handy.
5. Keep a list of phone numbers that you use regularly.

▸ **Making a call**
1. First, decide the purpose of your call. It is estimated that more than one-third of all telephone calls in business are unnecessary.
2. If you have several points to make or questions to ask, jot them down. Then you will not forget them while the call is in progress.
3. If you need to refer to any documents make sure they are to hand.
4. Check that you have the right telephone number and dial it carefully.
5. Try to get routed through as quickly as possible to the person or department you want. Modern telephone systems make it possible for each member of staff to have an individual number, so you may be able to phone the person directly without going through the switch.
6. If you are uncertain who you want, the receptionist may be able to help. Common sense is often a good guide. For example, if you are looking for

information for a project, you will probably need to contact either the public relations or the marketing department. If you are enquiring about a job, the personnel department is the obvious place to go.

7. When you have been put through, check that you are speaking to the right person. Then give your name and, if appropriate, the name of your company or organisation.

8. Explain clearly and precisely what you want. Refer to your notes if necessary.

9. At the end, thank your respondent.

▶ **Receiving a call**

1. Answer promptly. Pick up the phone within four rings. The longer the caller waits for you to respond the more irritated she is likely to be.

2. Identify yourself by giving your name and, if appropriate, the name of your department or organisation. Remember that it takes a caller several words to adjust. Start with a greeting, e.g. *Good morning, this is . . .*

3. Listen carefully. Repeat numbers, dates, times, etc. so that there is no doubt about them.

4. Take messages with care. It is helpful to have a telephone message pad on your desk for this purpose (see Exhibit 12.2). Make sure you find out the caller's name and address or telephone number so that a reply can be sent.

5. Do not leave the caller unattended. If you think it will take a long time to find the information requested, either give the caller the option of holding or, better still, offer to call back. If the caller decides to hold, return periodically to assure the person you are still there.

6. Be patient and polite with difficult callers, e.g. those who are angry, long winded or unsure what they want.

7. Know how to reroute a call that has been put through to you in error. A list of extension numbers for all departments should be beside your phone.

8. Keep yourself well informed about the movements of people in your office. Telling a caller, 'Mr Smith has gone down to our other branch this morning. He should be back at 2:30 if you would like to ring then' is much better than muttering noncommittally, 'Mr Smith is out at the moment. . . No, I'm afraid he didn't say when he'd be back. Perhaps you could try again sometime this afternoon.'

USING ANSWERING MACHINES OR VOICE MAIL

Many telephone users are quite uncomfortable when invited to leave a voice mail message. The likely reason is that we depend heavily on feedback from the receiver to complete what we want to say. It is disconcerting to find that the two-way transaction we expect is changed suddenly into a one-way transaction with a machine, so we put the receiver down like a hot coal!

However, answering machines and voice mail are now common in business – so much so that you are likely to hear a recorded greeting as often as you hear the person herself when you ring, so it is well worth preparing a suitable message just in case. Here are two simple examples that can be adapted to many different situations:

> Hello, Tom. This is Ann Moran calling you at about 11:30 on Tuesday. I wanted to ask you about . . . Could you ring me back when you get a chance? My extension is 3456. Thanks. Cheerio.

or more formally:

> Good afternoon, Mr Smith. My name is John Dwyer and I am calling at 3:30 pm on Tuesday. I am interested in the . . . you advertised recently in the press and would like some further information. My telephone number is 3456789 and I will be here until about six this evening if you wish to contact me. Otherwise, I'll ring you again at 10:30 tomorrow morning. Thank you. Goodbye.

A few more tips!
- Sometimes there is a long gap between the end of the greeting and the signal to begin speaking. Remember – wait for the beep!
- Give the date and time of your call – this may seem a bit pedantic, but it helps the receiver.
- Give your telephone number slowly, breaking it into groups of three or four numbers. This makes it easier to take down.
- Speak as if the receiver really *is* listening.

In conclusion, it should be said that almost all organisations recognise the importance of the telephone in their business nowadays and this has led to a significant and welcome improvement in telephone behaviour. It is now the rule rather than the exception to find telephone enquiries dealt with in a pleasant and efficient manner.

Exhibit 12.2 Telephone message

TELEPHONE MESSAGE

For: *Jim Donnelly*

From: *V. McAvoy*

Company: *Icefoods*

Telephone: *01-4564567*

Date: *21/3*

Time: *11:00 am*

Mr McAvoy would like further information on the Aercal condensing unit. Could you please ring him between four and five this afternoon.

Taken by: *Jane Wright*

Spotlight on Irish Business – Superquinn

Listening to customers

Marketing is about meeting the needs of customers in a profitable way, so by definition the better a company knows its customers the more likely it is to be successful. Hence the key role of market research and of carefully studying sales figures.

However, Senator Feargal Quinn, executive chairman of Superquinn, argues that these techniques, vital though they are, are not enough to get you close to your customers. To do that properly, you also need to physically *listen* to them.

Why?

First of all, because there is a dimension to meeting a customer face to face that you can never get from looking at a page of figures. Only by listening to a customer speak can you get a real sense of how intensely they feel on a subject. Reading that one per cent of your customers are dissatisfied is unlikely to spur you into action, certainly not in the same way as when you directly face the wrath of that one per cent (or even that of a single individual). Perhaps this is one reason people are often reluctant to listen to customers: it can be an uncomfortable experience.

But more fundamentally, there is a crucial difference between looking at any situation from the top down (which inevitably is the position of anyone providing a product or service) and looking at the same situation from the bottom up (which is the position of the person buying the product or service). You can attempt to bridge that difference by imagining yourself in the customers' shoes (or even literally, by becoming an actual customer of your own business), but to get the real picture of the customers' needs you simply cannot beat actually listening to them.

A key characteristic of customers' needs is that, over time, they change. When Feargal Quinn became chairman of what later became An Post in 1979, he insisted that the top management regularly take their turn at serving the public at post office counters. At first some of them were reluctant, arguing that since they had come up through the business they knew all there was to know about their customers. But running a business on the customer needs of yesterday can be just as bad as ignoring their needs altogether.

For almost thirty years now, Superquinn has held customer panels on a weekly basis in one or another of its shops. 'In all that time,' says Feargal Quinn, 'I have never come away from one without learning something new. Sometimes what you learn is a tiny thing about the nuts and bolts of your business; other times, listening to customers can alert you to a sea-change in customer needs that allows you to gain competitive advantage by responding quickly.'

EFFECTIVE LISTENING

The importance of listening in interpersonal communication is seldom properly appreciated. We spend more time listening than speaking, yet most of us listen inefficiently. Poor aural comprehension is obviously a handicap for students who spend up to seventy per cent of classroom time listening to lecturers or tutors, but it is no less of a handicap in business. In fact, many managers now recognise how costly listening mistakes can be at every level of the organisation. A receptionist mishears part of a telephone message and consequently an order is sent to the wrong destination. An operative misunderstands an instruction from her supervisor and an accident results. An interviewer half-listens to an interviewee's remarks and misses important clues about her ability to perform the job. To overcome problems like these many companies now consider it worthwhile to provide special courses in listening skills for their employees.

WHAT IS LISTENING?

Listening consists of three components: hearing, understanding and retaining.
- *Hearing* is the physical ability to receive sounds. Even when we are asleep we hear every sound within hearing distance. However, we attend only to those sounds that interest us or that intrude upon our consciousness.
- *Understanding* is the ability to make sense of what we hear. Comprehension will be difficult or impossible if the speaker is using an unfamiliar language or

the receiver has a limited vocabulary. Other factors that may affect understanding are the clarity of the message, the effectiveness of delivery and the level of the receiver's concentration.

- *Retaining* is the third component of listening. Clearly this is an essential ability for students who need to recall information for examinations. Managers also need to retain information that they have heard at meetings and elsewhere. This is where a good memory and effective note-taking skills become important.

IMPROVING LISTENING SKILLS

The first step towards improving listening skills is to recognise the common barriers to listening and then make a conscious effort to overcome these problems. Here are a number of suggestions that will help you to improve your own listening ability.

The bad listener . . .

1. Allows stimuli in the listening environment to distract them, e.g. background noise, stuffy room, sun shining through a window.
2. Fails to concentrate. Daydreams, doodles, gazes out the window, fakes attention. Makes no effort to listen.
3. Is poorly motivated. Finds it hard to stay interested.
4. Tunes out when the material is difficult.
5. Allows the speaker's personality or delivery to influence listening. Is put off when the speaker is dull or unable to get the information across clearly.
6. Reacts emotionally. Allows prejudice or strong feeling to cloud the message.
7. Gets lost in detail. Cannot see 'the wood for the trees'.
8. Accepts information passively. Fails to take notes.

The good listener . . .

1. Removes or ignores distracting stimuli, e.g. closes a window to shut out traffic noise, pulls down a blind.
2. Listens actively. Realises that listening requires effort. Sits up, looks at the speaker, stays alert.
3. Reminds herself about examination or career goals. Remembers that the information may be needed later on.
4. Recognises that new concepts and ideas have to be learned. Reads around the subject and asks others for advice. Fills knowledge gaps.
5. Compensates for the speaker's deficiencies. Encourages the speaker by giving verbal and nonverbal feedback.

6. Keeps an open mind. Pays attention to what is said and is not unduly influenced by who is saying it.
7. Ignores unimportant detail. Instead, listens for broad themes and key ideas.
8. Listens critically. Weighs the information. Takes notes of key points.

BE OBJECTIVE!

A significant barrier to effective listening is the tendency that exists in all of us to allow the personality or allegiances of the speaker to become more important than the message. We find it easy to misunderstand, distort or reject the words of someone we dislike or whose views we disagree with and we find it no less easy to uncritically accept the words of someone who has our approval. This lack of objectivity becomes more pronounced when we are part of a hostile or approving crowd and the speaker is surrounded by the symbols of allegiance (flags, banners, etc.).

There is perhaps no quality of effective listening more difficult to achieve than objectivity, yet the effort should be made. When we set aside our prejudices we often find much that is worthwhile in the other person's point of view. We may also recognise the need to change our own attitudes and beliefs. Listening with an open mind to the opposing side can be a valuable form of learning.

NOTE-TAKING

TIPS ON NOTE-TAKING IN CLASS

- Always write the *date* and *subject/topic* first.
- Set out notes in schematic form, i.e. using headings, indents and numbers to show the relative importance of items (see Exhibit 12.3).
- Avoid summary notes, i.e. notes written in continuous prose. These take longer to complete than outline notes and are more difficult to revise.
- Write in short sentences or phrases.
- Try to write legibly – ask yourself if your notes will still make sense in six months' time.
- If it helps, supplement notes with explanatory diagrams, e.g. a flow diagram to show steps in sequence, tree or spider diagram to show how ideas relate to a central theme.
- To save time use common abbreviations or invent some of your own. Do not repeat them in examinations, however. Examples of useful abbreviations are:

chap	chapter
comm	communication
e.g.	for example

i.e.	that is
info	information
mgt	management
n.b.	this is important
org	organisation

- Keep notes in good order. Use an A4 loose-leaf file instead of a jotter or exercise book. Use coloured dividers to separate one set of notes from another.

Exhibit 12.3 Sample notes

Subject: Communications
Date: 24/10
Topic: Internal communication media
Note: Read Ch 2 — possible exam question
1. Memos
    Advs   — ensure message received (compare notices)
                — ensure record of message kept
                — suitable for detailed/complex info
                — formal, carry authority
    Disadvs   — relatively slow
                — not suitable for comm to shop floor
2. Meetings
    Advs   — everyone has a say
                — quests can be asked
                — decisions more acceptable

ASSIGNMENTS

REVISION

1. Outline five ways in which the language of speech differs from the language of formal writing.
2. Briefly describe the following paralinguistic elements of speech: (a) volume (b) pace (c) pitch (d) stress (e) accent.
3. Write a short commentary on the limitations of speech as a communication medium.
4. What advice would you give to those involved in face-to-face communication in a professional context?
5. What are the advantages and disadvantages of the telephone as a business medium?

6. Set out in point form guidelines for (a) making (b) receiving telephone calls.
7. What are the three components of listening?
8. How would you identify a good listener?

FOR DISCUSSION

1. What mistakes can you find in the following telephone conversation?

Joe:	Hello.
Caller:	Hello?
Joe:	Hello.
Caller:	Is that Murphy's Appliances?
Joe:	It is indeed. What can I do you for?
Caller:	Who am I speaking to?
Joe:	Joe Murphy . . . Junior, that is.
Caller:	Well, I have a problem with my fridge. You see, the light's coming on when I open the door but the fridge isn't getting cold. Would you have any idea what's wrong?
Joe:	I'm afraid there's no point in asking me. I'm just in here tidying the place up.
Caller:	Well, is there anyone there who could help me?
Joe:	Hold on. I'll see if Mick is still around. (*Sound of phone being put down and loud voice calling 'Hi, Mick', then a door banging. Several minutes later . . .*) No, I'm afraid Mick must have gone out on a job and my dad isn't around either.
Caller:	Well, when do you think they'll be back?
Joe:	Haven't a clue really. Usually when they go out, they're out for the afternoon.
Caller:	Well, that's a nuisance. I need this fridge fixed before the weekend.
Joe:	(*After a long pause*) Maybe I could take a message . . . or something.
Caller:	I really need this fixed as soon as possible. I've tried everywhere else. Anyway, I'll give you my phone number. It's . . .

Joe:	Sorry, can you hold on while I get a pen? (*Pause. Sound of paper rustling.*) OK, fire away, then.
Caller:	It's 49464.
Joe:	4946 . . . 4 was it?
Caller:	Yes (*getting irate*), 49464!
Joe:	Right, got that. I'll get my dad to ring as soon as he gets back.
Caller:	Yes . . . and . . .
Joe:	(*Brightly*) OK, Bob's your uncle. I'll do that for you, no problem. OK, cheerio then.
Caller:	(*Spluttering.*)
Joe:	(*Puts phone down.*)

ACTIVITIES AND EXERCISES

1. Write a *short report* on the aims and activities of an organisation of your choice, e.g. An Taisce, ECO, ICA, Greenpeace. Part of your research should include a *face-to-face meeting* with a representative of the organisation. Remember to have a list of questions prepared. Your report should include a transcript or summary of the meeting.

2. Write *scripts* for the following telephone conversations and then choose group members to play the various roles.

   (a) VisionCom Ltd sells or hires training videos. It has recently acquired a new twenty-minute video on listening skills which features two well-known actors. The receptionist receives a telephone call from a teacher who has heard about the video and wants to hire it for two days.

   (b) A householder has his central heating system converted to natural gas. Since the conversion the system has not worked effectively. Service engineers have called on two occasions. On the most recent visit they installed a new thermostat, but this has still not rectified the problem. Angrily, the householder rings the customer service department at the gas company's headquarters.

   (c) Infaray, a manufacturer of electrical goods, has inadvertently sent out a batch of defective heaters to a number of retail outlets. These heaters are dangerous and the company has asked for them to be recalled. A local radio chat-show host rings the company to find out what has happened. The marketing manager takes the call.

3. Write a *leaflet* on good listening and note-taking skills suitable for distributing to first-year students in a college.
4. Using the listening guidelines above, design a *questionnaire* in which you try to discover the level of listening skills in your group. For example, you could set out questions as follows.

Questionnaire

Do you:

-   Give the appearance of listening even when you aren't? (a) often (b) sometimes (c) never
-   Tune out when the other person says something you disagree with? (a) often (b) sometimes (c) never
-   Daydream while the person is talking? (a) often (b) sometimes (c) never

---

Decide on a rating scheme and distribute the questionnaire to the group.
5. Two people sit facing each other. One tells a short story about a subject of his or her choice (summer holiday, recent shopping trip, etc.). The other pretends not to listen. Then repeat the exercise, but this time with the listener appearing to listen carefully. Talk about the different behaviours that were used and how they affected the speaker.
6. The group sits in a circle. The tutor introduces a discussion topic and hands a stick to one person. The person holding the stick talks for a few moments and then passes the stick to someone else. The person receiving the stick must repeat the *last two sentences* of the previous speaker. If he or she cannot, then the right to speak is forfeited. This is a good exercise for demonstrating how difficult it is to listen continuously and carefully.

13 Giving Talks and Presentations

I t is virtually certain that at some time in your career you will have to make a speech or give a presentation to an audience. The occasions when you may be called on to speak – conferences, training courses, receptions, social events, etc. – are too numerous to list in full. Yet the thought of having to stand up in front of a group of listeners fills many people with apprehension or dread. It need not be so. Despite initial nervousness, even inexperienced speakers can give a good account of themselves if they approach the task in the right way.

Credibility lies at the heart of effective speaking in business. Members of your audience will not be actively hostile as they might be if you were addressing a public meeting or a political rally, but they will often be watchful and critical. You must establish credibility quickly in your talk and work to maintain it throughout.

For instance, suppose that you are giving a sales talk to a group of potential customers. You can safely assume that they are knowledgeable on your subject matter. They will want to ensure that there is some advantage for them in buying from your company. They will also be alert to potential difficulties in any arrangement they may wish to make with you. Therefore, you can expect them to listen attentively and to ask probing questions when you have finished. They in turn will expect you to know what you are talking about. If you lack confidence or appear to be incompetent their sympathy for you will soon evaporate. Few businesspeople have either the time or the inclination to suffer fools gladly.

Credibility in speaking rests on two foundations – *sound preparation* and *effective delivery*.

Many beginners make the mistake of underestimating the amount of effort that must be put into preparation. Of course, it is possible and sometimes necessary for an experienced speaker to deliver an impromptu address. Such instances include introducing a guest speaker at a conference, congratulating an employee who is getting married or, indeed, any occasion where a brief, complimentary speech is required. But in the majority of cases, speeches and presentations must be carefully researched, planned and rehearsed and the more inexperienced the speaker, the more thorough the preparation should be.

Good delivery is no less important. How often have you heard someone in an audience say of a speaker, 'He's very intelligent, you know, but he just doesn't seem to be able to get his ideas across.' Many a well-prepared speech has been spoiled by dull, insensitive or rambling delivery. Yet competence in presentation is well within the grasp of anyone who pays attention to the basic techniques and who is willing to evaluate his own performance objectively.

PREPARATION

IDENTIFYING YOUR AUDIENCE

A vital first step in preparing a presentation is to find out as much as possible about the audience. Who are they? Are they members of your class, colleagues at work or people you have not met before? How many will be there? What is their age range? How much do they know about the subject? What are their needs and expectations? Are they likely to be sympathetic or resistant to the message?

Finding answers to these questions is relatively straightforward for internal presentations. However, some extra detective work may be needed if you are speaking to an unfamiliar audience. The best source of information is the person organising the presentation, so approach him first. If you are speaking at a conference, the advertising literature often indicates who the event is aimed at, e.g. 'The conference will benefit professional trainers, particularly those working in special needs.' This information, incomplete though it may be, at least gives some indication of the likely attendees.

Keep in mind that the more you find out about the audience the more confident you can be of **meeting their needs** and **speaking to them in terms they will understand**.

DEFINING OBJECTIVES

The next step is to think carefully about the presentation's purpose and objectives. The overall **purpose** will affect length, content, style of delivery and so on. For example, if you are speaking on a social occasion you will need to be brief, congratulatory and perhaps humorous. If supplying information or giving instructions you will need to present your material clearly and coherently. In presentations designed to persuade or promote a new line of action the qualities of enthusiasm and conviction become important.

Objectives are more specific guidelines for structuring and developing the talk. It is usually better to state them in terms of audience outcomes rather than your own aims. For example, suppose you are talking to sales staff on the theme of 'putting the customer first'. What do you want the audience to believe or do when you have finished the presentation? Perhaps, you might want them to:

- *know* what 'putting the customer first' means
- *understand* the benefits in this approach
- *develop* a positive attitude towards the customer
- *change* their behaviour when dealing with customers.

Notice how objectives such as these give a broad shape and direction to the presentation. They also keep the focus clearly on the needs and interests of the audience rather than the presenter.

FILLING IN THE BACKGROUND

Other factors that will influence your handling of the presentation are the venue, the time you have to speak and the context in which the presentation is being given.

- **Venue**

  If you are speaking in an unfamiliar place you should check it out in advance. It is particularly important to do this if you plan to use audio-visual aids. Do not assume that the room is suitable or the equipment is available for what you want to do. Many a presenter with material carefully prepared has turned up at the venue to find that essential equipment such as a projector or video player is missing or not working. The presentation then has to be hastily changed and there is frustration all round.

  Other aspects of the venue may cause difficulties. For example, there may be a lot of background noise, poor ventilation, uncomfortable seating, etc. Obstructions such as pillars may make it difficult for some parts of the audience to see. While there may be little you can do to remedy these problems, you can at least anticipate them and plan your presentation accordingly.

- **Time**

  Few things antagonise an audience more than a speaker who rambles on far beyond the time allocated for his presentation, so find out how long you are expected to speak for and then aim to finish within the time limit. At conferences and similar events quite strict time limits are applied and the chairperson – tactfully or otherwise – will ask you to conclude if you overrun.

  In some cases, the amount of time allowed is very short, perhaps only a few minutes, e.g. when proposing or supporting a motion at a meeting. You may need to practise getting one or two points across concisely and persuasively.

> **'Be sincere, be brief, be seated.'**
>
> Franklin D. Roosevelt had a six-word formula for speeches: 'Be sincere, be brief, be seated.' You cannot imagine how much better a sixty-minute speech sounds if it only takes thirty minutes to deliver – or how grateful your audience will be towards you if you are the one who can pull off this achievement.
>
> If you have any doubt about leaving a point in or taking it out, choose the latter.
>
> Source: McCormack, 1996

- **Context**

  It is helpful to know as much as you can about the context in which your presentation is being made. Are you the only presenter? If there are others, who are they, what are they going to talk about and will they speak before or after you? Are you involved in a group presentation? If so, what is your part and how do you link with the rest of the team? When are you scheduled to speak? Remember that the audience's energy level may be low immediately after lunch or late in the afternoon. A good presenter takes all these factors into account when planning what to say and how to say it.

RESEARCH

Once you have armed yourself with an audience profile and a statement of your objectives, the next step is to gather information about the subject. The need to be thoroughly briefed before giving a business presentation cannot be emphasised too strongly. You must know your subject and be able to give well-informed answers to all questions that are likely to be asked. If it appears that you have neglected important areas you will immediately lose credibility, so your research must be efficient and comprehensive. Here are some suggestions.

1. Randomly jot down your initial thoughts on the subject. There is no need to worry about logical connections at this stage.
2. Decide on additional sources of information. These may include personal knowledge and experience, books, reports, articles, etc.
3. Carry out your research and collect your material methodically. Look for up-to-date and topical information as this will appeal to your audience.
4. When you have collected as much information as you need, make an outline plan containing the main areas you hope to cover.
5. Select the most relevant points and begin to shape them into a persuasive message.

WRITING UP

You will now have to decide whether to speak from a script or from notes. Inexperienced presenters often feel they need the support of a fully written out script. However, this has its drawbacks. A presentation should always have something of the informality and spontaneity of a conversation. It usually lacks both qualities when it is written down word for word and read out.

Speaking from notes, on the other hand, has several advantages:
- the presentation sounds more natural and convincing
- language tends to be more informal and conversational
- it is easier to maintain eye contact with the audience
- you have more freedom to respond and adapt to the audience as the presentation proceeds.

Setting the script to one side may be a daunting prospect, particularly for beginners. People often worry about drying up or losing their train of thought if there is no script to refer to. Such fears are understandable and sometimes difficult to overcome. Nevertheless, you should always consider speaking from notes because the advantages are so significant.

The following tips will help you to set out your presentation in a professional way and deliver it with confidence.

From a script
- Write out what you want to say using simple, clear language. Keep sentences short and do not be too concerned with grammatical correctness. Remember that you are writing to be heard, not read!
- Aim to cover a maximum of four or five main areas only. Audiences cannot cope with too much detail.
- Signpost each main area with a heading. Highlight these in the script. This allows you to glance down and immediately see how far your talk has progressed.
- Indicate clearly where you intend to use presentation aids such as slides or transparencies.
- Write legibly or use a clear, easy-to-read typeface.

From notes
- Condense your talk into a series of key points.
- Write up these points on notepaper or cue cards. Many people prefer cards because they are small and unobtrusive.
- Each card should contain one key point only. A small number of subpoints may be listed underneath. Cues for presentation aids, anecdotes, etc. should

also be marked. See Exhibit 13.1 for an example.

- Keep points short – a word or phrase is usually sufficient to trigger memory. Write down the full text only if you need to remind yourself of precise details, e.g. a quotation, a set of figures.
- Make sure your notes are clearly printed with plenty of white space between one point and the next.
- If you have to use more than one card or page, number each at the top. Write on one side only.

Exhibit 13.1   Cue card

```
                        4.
        The Problem of Litter (Slide 2)
        1.  Are we Europe's 'litter louts'?
        2.  What tourists think
        3.  The litter laws
        4.  Persuading people to clean up
            Tell story about O'Connell St
```

REHEARSING

You have your notes ready, your visuals prepared and are now ready to give the performance of your life! Good, but before you go in front of your audience there is one further important step to take. You really need to polish up the presentation by having at least one full rehearsal.

There are several ways in which rehearsing can be done. Some people simply **read through their notes** and check that all their slides etc. are in order. However, while this may be sufficient for experienced presenters who are familiar with their material it is certainly not sufficient for beginners. An alternative is to speak into an **audio-tape recorder**. This will tell you how you sound and allow you to check on time, pacing, voice quality, etc. Better still is to rehearse in front of a **sympathetic audience** such as friends or family members. This will give you valuable practice in delivery techniques and should elicit some constructive comments. Making a **video recording** is another way of getting useful feedback, particularly on your posture and other aspects of body language.

The benefit of rehearsing is that you can fine-tune the presentation before delivering the real thing. You will probably find that some changes are necessary. A common discovery, for example, is that the presentation is considerably longer than expected. The solution may be to prune back on content or change the tempo. Either way it is better to solve the problem now than to be surprised and disconcerted 'on the night'.

DRESS

The final stage in preparation is deciding how to dress for the occasion. As a general rule, clothes should be neat, comfortable and well fitting. The occasion will usually determine what is appropriate to wear. Jeans and a pullover might be quite acceptable if you are giving a talk to your local youth group. However, fairly formal dress such as a suit is always expected at a business presentation.

If you have to give presentations as part of your coursework, always take care with appearance. Remember – appearances count. Dressing up for the occasion will not only impress the class and your tutor but give you added confidence as well.

THE STRUCTURE OF A PRESENTATION

A good presentation is like a good story – it catches the audience's attention at the outset, it holds their interest while the 'plot' develops and it builds towards a climax at the end. Let us now look at how to structure a presentation so that it is easy to follow and has real impact.

INTRODUCTION

Research shows that an audience's attention peaks soon after the beginning of a presentation and then gradually declines before picking up again near the end. A good presenter exploits this by trying to get off to a strong, confident start. Here is a simple but effective way to begin.

- Introduce yourself and your organisation (if the chairperson has not already done so).
- Introduce your topic ('I will be talking about . . . ').
- Give an outline ('We will be looking at the following issues . . . ').
- State your main objective ('I hope to persuade you that . . . ').
- Put your subject in context/highlight its importance ('As you know, this topic is now of major concern to Irish business . . . ').
- Show the benefits ('Putting these ideas into practice can lead to large cost savings . . . ').

There are also various devices that can be used at the outset to enliven the

presentation and get the audience involved. For example, you could begin with:
- a rhetorical question
- a startling or thought-provoking fact
- a personal anecdote
- a humorous story.

These are all proven and effective methods of gaining audience attention. However, they are not always necessary. Genuine, infectious enthusiasm for your subject is often all that is needed to make the audience sit up and take notice.

Something different

At a 'New Business Ideas' competition, one of the entrants was a small business specialising in a unique range of children's clothes. Before beginning her presentation, the owner of the business asked the audience to look towards the door at the rear of the auditorium. There was a blast of lively background music and then a stream of young models wearing bright, colourful garments came through the door and paraded up the aisle.

Hardly a word had been said, yet the presenter had already won over her audience.

A student who was interested in martial arts decided to make this the topic of his presentation. But he didn't just talk about it. He wore the robe and brought in the fearsome-looking weapons associated with the sport. Then with the help of some of the group he demonstrated a variety of kicks and blocks. This bit of imagination and courage helped him to give a memorable presentation.

MAIN BODY

Presentations can take so many forms that it is difficult to give precise guidelines for the middle part. Nevertheless, there are some generalisations that can be made. It is important to remember that the audience is listening to the message, not reading it. If they lose track of what you are saying they cannot go back and relisten. Therefore, you should do everything in your power to ensure that the talk can be followed without too much difficulty. So with this in mind:
- Set out the points you wish to make in clear, coherent order ('First I will deal with . . . next . . . finally . . . ').
- Use linking devices when moving from one area to another ('Let's now consider . . . ' or 'An alternative view is . . . ').
- Choose a language pitched at the right level for your audience. Avoid technical terms, jargon and pompous words.

- Use some repetition to help your audience grasp crucial ideas.
- In a long presentation give short interim summaries of points already made.
- Avoid too much detail, particularly lists of figures or statistics. If you have to refer to statistics, try to identify the main trends and show these in graphic form, e.g. in pie diagrams, bar graphs, etc.

CONCLUSION

A strong conclusion is no less important than a lively introduction. Inexperienced speakers often make the mistake of ending lamely. They make their final point, perhaps sooner than anticipated, shuffle their papers uncertainly and then murmur, 'Well . . . that's really all I have to say.' Such a lack of inspiration at the end can undermine even the most forceful presentation.

There are several ways in which you can bring your talk to a vigorous and rounded conclusion. You can:
- briefly summarise the main points
- repeat and stress the key message
- propose a course of action
- invite questions
- thank the audience for their attention.

Finishing with an anecdote or joke can be a good idea – it can please the audience and help you conclude on a cheerful note. Be careful, however – it would be a pity to spoil a successful presentation with some ill-judged story at the very end.

BEING PERSUASIVE

While good presentations are entertaining they usually have a more serious underlying purpose. This often involves persuading the audience in some way – to accept your proposal, buy your products or accept your argument.

Some commonly used techniques of persuasion include the following.
- *Beginning with ideas that you know the audience will support*. This will increase their confidence in what you have to say.
- *Giving both sides of the argument*. The audience will appreciate this as it indicates even-handedness and objectivity.
- *Supporting the points you make with well-chosen examples, illustrations or statistics*. This makes your argument more convincing.
- *Appealing to the audience's needs and wishes*. They will respond positively if they feel they have something to gain.

However, there is a thin line between persuasion and manipulation. It is legitimate to present your arguments in the best possible light when you believe in their value. It is not legitimate to manipulate or mislead. Never put at risk the relationship of trust that should exist between you and your listeners.

KEEPING THE AUDIENCE INVOLVED

In a long presentation there is the additional problem of keeping the audience's attention throughout. The efficiency with which an audience listens diminishes steadily after the first few minutes, and even a good listener will have difficulty in concentrating for long periods on what you have to say.

To counteract the problem of wandering attention you should plan to break the routine of your talk as it progresses. For example, you could pause occasionally to tell a joke or a 'human interest' story, you could break off to introduce an exhibit or show a slide or you could allow time for questions. More adventurous things to do would be to introduce role-plays or exercises that involve some physical movement.

Remember that the longer you talk the harder it is for listeners to fight against tiredness, extraneous noise and all the other distractions that crowd in on them. By varying your presentation you make life for your audience that little bit easier.

DELIVERY

OVERCOMING STAGE FRIGHT

Some anxiety at the start of delivery is inevitable. The physical symptoms of nervousness – increased heartbeat, sweaty palms, quicker breathing or a tremulous voice – are undoubtedly uncomfortable but they need not detract from your performance. Indeed, they will hardly be noticed by the audience at all.

Nervousness is a sign that you are charged with energy and ready for a dynamic performance. In this respect, giving a presentation is no different from having a central role in any public event. For example, footballers always feel keyed up before an important match and the moment of greatest tension is just before they run onto the pitch. However, once the match starts, their nervousness usually drains away and is replaced with an intense involvement in the game itself.

Similarly, the worst moment of a presentation is waiting for it to start. There are some simple ways of controlling nerves at this stage. For example, you could try taking slow, deep breaths or tensing and relaxing your muscles, e.g. tightly squeezing your fists under the table and then releasing them. Then launch into your presentation with a few well-rehearsed sentences.

Remember that most audiences are sympathetic and that the first positive response in the way of smiles or nods you get from them will give you all the confidence you need. Once your initial self-consciousness has disappeared you can then begin to exploit with growing assurance the great potential of this form of oral communication.

In the course of your presentation you should try to make good use of the following.

Voice

As we saw in Chapter 12, the voice is a marvellously flexible and versatile medium of communication. By using its qualities effectively you can both hold your audience's attention and enhance their understanding of what you are saying.

- **Clarity**

  Speak clearly and out to your audience. Do not mumble into your chest. Articulate words with extra care.

- **Volume**

  Speak loudly enough to be heard by everyone. After that, you can vary volume for emphasis or dramatic effect. You can always hammer home a point by raising your voice – but remember that a quietly uttered sentence can be just as powerful in its impact.

- **Pace**

  Many beginners speak far more quickly than they need to – usually a sign of nerves. Try to speak a little more slowly than you would in ordinary conversation. Remember also that you can vary pace to highlight particular points. Deliberately slowing the speed at which you speak can give added emphasis. Quickening the pace can convey interest and excitement.

- **Pauses**

  Do not be afraid of brief pauses. They give your audience time to assimilate your preceding remarks and give you an opportunity to glance at your notes and decide what you want to say next. However, remember to pause in the right places, that is, between one thought and another or before you move on to a new aspect of your presentation. This gives a natural fluency to your speech and sets up a sense of expectation in your listeners.

- **Tone**

  Vary tone to suit your subject and the effect you wish to have on your audience. The choice at your disposal is considerable – you can be serious, light-hearted, mocking, cheerful and so on. However, you must be careful not to adopt a tone that your audience might consider inappropriate. For instance, it is never a good idea to be sarcastic, patronising or to treat a serious subject in a flippant manner.

- **Accent**

  Many people worry unnecessarily about their accent. A strong accent causes a problem only when your audience has difficulty in following what you are saying. The answer is to speak a little more slowly and clearly; attempting to disguise your natural voice will only make your talk sound contrived. In fact, a distinctive accent should always be regarded as an asset. So long as it does not obscure meaning it can be one of the most interesting and delightful features of the voice.

- **Using a microphone**

  For large audiences a microphone is a necessity. Its disadvantages are that it distorts the voice, is often awkward to adjust and, when fixed, limits the speaker's movements. Do not use it unless you have to.

EYE CONTACT

Eye contact is an important element in effective presentations for two main reasons.

First, it enables you to build and maintain a rapport with your listeners. Humans use eye contact naturally to regulate and enhance conversation, so the audience will expect you to look at them. If you have good eye contact you will appear assured and in control of the presentation. In contrast, if you continually look away or down at your notes you will come across as shy, uncertain or even shifty.

Second, eye contact provides you with valuable feedback. If the audience is attentive and appreciative then you can go on with increasing confidence. On the other hand, you may need to take remedial steps if you notice signs of boredom, incomprehension or disagreement. For example, you may decide to introduce a visual aid, tell a joke, re-explain a point or otherwise alter your delivery in some way that meets audience needs.

As we know, facing an audience for the first time can be a daunting experience. Nevertheless, the following tips should help you to use eye contact effectively.

- Make eye contact before speaking. This indicates you have something significant to say and gets the audience's attention.
- Look down briefly at your notes and gather your thoughts.
- Re-establish eye contact and begin speaking.
- Do not allow your eyes to wander restlessly across the room. Focus briefly on individual members of the audience.
- Be careful not to look exclusively at one part of the audience or to stare at individuals. This is intimidating for those who get excessive attention and upsetting for those who are ignored.

Body language

Facial expressions, gestures, mannerisms, etc. are also a significant component in presentations. A good speaker controls those that are likely to irritate an audience, e.g. compulsive mannerisms such as scratching one's head or constantly clicking a pen, and consciously uses those that add colour and interest to delivery.

The most sensible rule in presentations is to be as natural and relaxed as possible. Speak with confidence and your body language will take care of itself.

Humour

Jokes can be told at any point in a presentation to keep audience attention and provide light relief. Indeed, speakers with a natural sense of humour and the ability to make their listeners laugh spontaneously have a great gift so long as they use it sparingly. However, inexperienced presenters need to treat humour with some caution. Sometimes a joke seems forced or stilted and falls flat. In such a case the speaker has no alternative but to keep his composure and move on briskly. At other times, attempts at humour, particularly when a serious subject is being discussed, are inappropriate or in bad taste and should be avoided. And, of course, a presenter should never be tempted into telling a vulgar, sexist or ethnically offensive story. Someone in the audience is bound to object – and object strongly.

Presentation aids

The appropriate use of presentation aids can greatly enliven delivery. Their use is discussed in Chapter 14.

Spotlight on Irish Business – IDA Ireland

'People make decisions'

IDA Ireland is the Irish government agency with responsibility for securing new investment from overseas in manufacturing and internationally traded sectors. It also encourages existing investors to expand and develop their businesses.

According to international media manager Brendan Halpin, the IDA is essentially a marketing organisation and its success depends on good communications. The aim is to build relationships with investors. After all, people, not corporations, make decisions. In order for people to make competent decisions, they need to have the relevant information.

Brendan says it's his job to communicate this information in many forms, each of which can be called a presentation, e.g. verbal, written, one to one, seminars and speaking platforms. Whether speaking or using visual aids the objective is the same: for the audience to understand what the presenter is saying.

Firstly, one must know one's audience. An executive in San José who has not been to Ireland will need a different presentation to one who has been to Ireland many times. Also, a presentation should not be overelaborate – it should be kept simple. Speak slowly and clearly and avoid language that tries to create an impression of sophistication. Language should create understanding, e.g. 'the man crossed the road', not 'the human being proceeded across the thoroughfare'.

Presentations are about content. The messages should be relevant and interesting to the extent that the audience cannot help but listen. It should also be memorable so that 'key value points' can be recalled. An audience has the ability to clearly recall only four or five key points, so tell them what you are going to tell them, tell them and tell them again.

Presentations should be enlivened with examples and images – a picture is worth a thousand words. For example, a photograph of Intel's campus in Leixlip clearly shows the level of technology that exists in Ireland. Visual aids should not be cluttered with information, as the audience won't take it in and they won't hear what you are saying! Hard copies of the relevant information can be provided later.

The amount of information required by potential clients to make an investment decision is vast. 'We need to be careful that we don't try to cram it in,' Brendan stresses. 'Decisions can take months and sometimes years. Each presentation, starting from the first one in San José to the final one to the board of directors, will be different and each one has to add value.'

Over the past fifteen years, Brendan has made hundreds of presentations. While they may differ in style, color, slides, video, etc. he always tries to remember the following points:

- know the audience
- keep it simple
- use clear language
- remember that content is what is important
- have four to five 'key value points'
- avoid humor – what's funny to you may be the opposite to a person from another country.

Finally, it must be remembered that *people* make decisions, and it is the presenter's job to ensure they have the information they need. A measure of the IDA's success in informing overseas investors is that there are now over 1,100 multinational companies in Ireland.

DEALING WITH QUESTIONS

Quite frequently time is given over at the end of a business presentation for questions from the audience. This is a demanding part of a presentation and one that needs some forethought and preparation. It gives the presenter an opportunity to display his grasp of the subject matter and to relate directly to individual listeners, but it can also work to the presenter's disadvantage. Many otherwise excellent presentations are undermined when the presenter becomes flustered or tongue-tied on being asked questions he did not expect.

The response to a question should be determined in some way by the questioner's intentions. Most people ask questions because they genuinely want information. There may, however, be other motives at work. For example, the questioner may want to gain attention for himself, display his greater knowledge of the subject or discredit your ideas and proposals. In all circumstances, however, you should remain calm and treat the questioner with courtesy.

Below are some guidelines for coping with the problems and opportunities that can arise during question-and-answer sessions.

- Listen carefully and with an open mind until the questioner has finished.
- Many speakers make brief notes as the question is being asked. This is particularly helpful when dealing with multiple questions.
- When a question is unclear because it is poorly expressed ask the questioner to restate it. Alternatively, paraphrase the question yourself and check with the questioner that you have made the right interpretation, e.g. 'Are you saying that . . . ?' Be as diplomatic as you can.
- Tactfully interrupt someone who is asking a long, rambling question by saying something like, 'Can I just respond to the first issue you raised . . . ?'
- Pause before answering a question even if you know what you want to say. This may protect you from a hasty or unguarded comment.
- Make eye contact with the questioner. If you need to give a long answer look around the audience but re-establish eye contact with the questioner as you conclude.
- If you do not know the answer to a question, say so, but suggest where an answer can be found. Speakers who have prepared thoroughly should seldom find themselves in this predicament.
- Do not become evasive or defensive if the question pinpoints weaknesses in your presentation. Indicate that you are open to ideas and are prepared to think about what the questioner is saying.
- Keep cool if you think the questioner has a hidden agenda or wants to undermine you. Sometimes, a mildly facetious response can take the sting out of the question, e.g. 'Well, we all know what you think about this, Tom . . .'.

- Finally, if you invite questions and none are forthcoming, do not allow an uncomfortable silence to develop. Quite often the chairperson will step in with a question. If not, you can always raise and answer a question yourself: 'Something I'm often asked is . . .'. This will usually be sufficient to get the session going.

IN CONCLUSION

Like all other skills discussed in this book, presentation skills can be acquired only through practise, so if you are a beginner do not shy away from practise. Of course, the first time you address an audience you may come away feeling you have made rather a mess of it, but do not be discouraged.

Start with 'saying a few words' and then gradually move on to longer and more demanding presentations. Try something new each time, like speaking from notes instead of a script or using a visual aid. Actively look for feedback from your audience. If possible record some of your presentations on video – this is one of the best ways to improve presentation skills.

With careful preparation and a willingness to learn from your mistakes you will soon gain in confidence and ability. The reward is well worth the effort, for with persistence, you will eventually have an accomplishment that can prove a valuable asset in business and also give you great personal satisfaction.

ASSIGNMENTS

REVISION

1. Why is it necessary to consider the audience when preparing a presentation? List some audience characteristics that could be important.
2. Presenters are advised to find out about (or visit) an unfamiliar venue before giving a presentation. Why is this?
3. Comment on the importance of *time* in public speaking.
4. Why is it nearly always better to speak from notes than from a script?
5. Set out some guidelines for preparing cue cards.
6. Four methods of rehearsing a speech are suggested. What are these methods?
7. What kind of information can you give in the introduction to a presentation?
8. How can you bring a speech to a rounded conclusion?
9. Describe techniques that can be used to keep the audience involved.
10. What qualities of the voice can be exploited by an effective speaker?
11. Why is eye contact with the audience such an important feature of presentations?
12. What problems can arise during a question-and-answer session? How can these be overcome?

ACTIVITIES AND DISCUSSION POINTS

1. Record a television discussion and watch it as a group. Which speakers made the biggest impression? Try to analyse why they were effective. Was it something about their voice or body language? Was it because they had prepared their material? Were they able to use good examples to support their point of view? Consider those who were less effective. Why did they fail to make an impact?

2. Talk about some well-known television presenters. Which do you like and why? Which do you dislike? Can you make a distinction between the presenter's personality and his or her communication skills?

3. The following are some comments made by people learning presentation skills. Do you agree with them?

    *   'I just hate speaking in front of other people. There's no way you are going to persuade me to do this.'
    *   'I feel really nervous when I speak. I'm sure everyone else notices as well.'
    *   'Public speaking is easy for teachers. They do it all the time.'
    *   'The best speakers are those with a really good sense of humour.'
    *   'The reason I write everything down is because I'm afraid of forgetting what I want to say.'
    *   'I'd much rather give a presentation to complete strangers than in front of my friends.'
    *   'I don't see the point of this. I'm going to get a job where I never have to give presentations.'

EXERCISES

1. Interview the person beside you. Where are they from? What hobbies or interests do they have? What music do they like? What are their favourite films? Then, take two to three minutes to introduce the person to the rest of the group. (A good ice-breaker in a new class!)

2. Imagine that a well-known personality (film star, politician, sports star) is about to give a talk to the class. Find out some biographical information first, then prepare a short address (two to three minutes) introducing and welcoming the speaker.

3. Imagine one of your friends in class is leaving to take up a job. Decide what job would suit, then make a short, humorous speech praising your friend and wishing him or her success.

4. Choose any issue that is being debated in the press or on television or about which you feel very strongly. Prepare and deliver a five-minute talk in which you give your view on the matter.

5. Select any product recently launched on the market, e.g. a new camera, personal computer, video game, bicycle, motorbike. Obtain further information from the manufacturer or retailer and deliver a five-minute sales talk.

6. Talk about your hobby or interest (five to ten minutes). If possible bring in and demonstrate the equipment or materials you use. (The range of interests – and talents – in a group can be surprising!)

7. Are you a good instructor? Give a short talk on *how to do something*, e.g. put on make-up, sail a boat, arrange flowers, tie different knots, make up fishing flies, etc.

8. Each member of the class is invited to pick a card containing a one- or two-word 'trigger', e.g. tattoos, Star Trek, hairstyles, *Coronation Street*, the Gaeltacht, Christmas, etc. Then talk on the subject for one or two minutes *without preparation*.

9. Test your narrative skills. Tell a story about:
    *   the paranormal
    *   a good film you saw recently
    *   last night's match on television
    *   an accident you witnessed or were involved in
    *   the worst thing you ever did at school
    *   your holiday last summer, etc.

10. Research a company under headings such as organisation structure, mission, products and markets, future plans, etc. Present your findings to the class in a fifteen- to twenty-minute presentation using visual aids. (You may consider a group presentation for this.)

14 Visual Communication

In this chapter visual communication is taken to mean the transmission of information by means of visual aids. The chapter is divided into three parts. The first section discusses the role of visual aids in enhancing spoken presentations and sets out general guidelines. The second describes some types of graphic illustrations that are commonly used to display statistical and other information. The third considers in more detail the uses, advantages and disadvantages of different kinds of audio-visual equipment.

VISUAL AIDS

A visual aid may be defined as any device which wholly or mainly uses vision to convey information and which supports the spoken or written word. Some of the methods most commonly employed in spoken presentations are listed in Exhibit 14.1.

Exhibit 14.1 Presentation aids

Chalkboard / whiteboard	Video
Flipchart	Film
Overhead projection	Display / exhibit
Slides	Demonstration
Multimedia projection	Drama / role-play

There is little doubt that the appropriate use of visual aids can enhance a presentation's effectiveness. It is estimated that when speech alone is used the audience misunderstands or forgets as much as seventy-five per cent of what is said. Visual aids can significantly increase both the persuasiveness of the presentation and the amount of information the audience retains afterwards.

Broadly speaking, visual images are used for two main purposes. They impart information that cannot be adequately conveyed by words alone. In addition, they attract attention, create interest, give variety and help to imprint the message on the receiver's memory. Put more succinctly, they may be said to have both **informational** and **motivational** functions (see Exhibit 14.2).

Exhibit 14.2   When to use visuals

For information

Consider using visual aids when you want to:

Outline	Give an outline of the topics you intend to cover in the presentation.
Support	Support verbal communication by providing visual examples and illustrations.
Show	Show the actual appearance of things and, in particular, of parts that are normally invisible or difficult to see, e.g. exploded or cutaway diagrams of machines.
Scale up/ down	Scale up very small objects or scale down very large ones, make visible very fast or very slow actions, e.g. slow motion or freeze-frame on video.
Clarify	Make complicated processes, networks or relationships easier to understand by showing them in schematic form, e.g. wiring diagram, map of London Underground.
Simplify	Present visual models of highly abstract processes and ideas, e.g. model of communication, managerial grid.
Highlight	Show statistical information and, in particular, highlight proportions and trends, e.g. pie diagrams, bar charts, line graphs.
Simulate	Show real-life situations, e.g. video or television programmes.

For motivation

Use visual aids when you want to:

Attract	Attract or retain your audience's attention.
Enliven	Enliven the message and give it greater impact.
Vary	Change the pace and focus of the presentation, particularly if you have to speak for a long time.
Lighten	Provide humorous contrast and interpretations by using cartoons, for example.
Reinforce	Reinforce learning and help the audience to retain information.
Persuade	Get the audience emotionally involved, e.g. by showing emotive pictures of war or famine.

CHOOSING THE RIGHT AID

In recent years there have been remarkable advances in the range and power of audio-visual equipment. The more sophisticated aids such as multimedia projectors enable quite spectacular visual displays to be shown. At major business presentations nowadays it is not uncommon to find inputs from PC or laptops, CD-ROM, video and film seamlessly integrated into a dazzling display of images.

However, it would be wrong to assume that technical wizardry should be the determining factor when deciding which aid to use. Often the simplest of aids – board and marker, for example – can be the most effective. A technically superb presentation may leave the audience feeling that there is more style than substance. By contrast, very simple aids can help to create a more intimate atmosphere and get the audience involved. The key is to select the aid which is most appropriate to the information you wish to convey and to the context in which the presentation is taking place.

The following are some of the factors that should be considered when deciding which aid to use.

- **Content and objectives**

  Different aids suit different purposes and different kinds of information. Flipcharts are ideal for quick, on-the-spot work such as recording ideas and suggestions from the audience. Slides and transparencies are good for bullet points, graphs, charts, maps – indeed, any information that can be displayed in two-dimensional, static form. Photographs can be used to create a mood or show what something looks like. Film and video give a more or less faithful representation of people and things in action. Multimedia technology can be used to give dynamism and excitement to a presentation.

- **Circumstances**

  The physical arrangements at the meeting may permit or preclude certain aids. You may need to consider room size, lighting, the positioning of power points or the moveability or otherwise of furniture before making a decision. The cost and availability of equipment may also have to be taken into account, as well as the time available to prepare material.

- **The audience**

  Audience size is an obvious consideration. In addition, you may have to keep in mind the audience's expectations and previous experience. For example, a group of senior managers will not be too impressed if you use a training video clearly aimed at beginners.

- **Your own expertise**

  It is important to feel at ease with the aids you use. However, this should not be an excuse for following the same routine every time. When there is not too much at stake you should be prepared to experiment with unfamiliar methods. Indeed, it is essential nowadays for business presenters to master the widest possible range of presentation techniques.

DESIGNING VISUALS

Once you have chosen the best aid for your purpose the next step is to ensure that visuals are designed to the highest standard compatible with your resources. Some basic principles for designing *still* visuals, e.g. transparencies, slides, flipchart work, are set out in the box below. You can apply these whether you are using material supplied by someone else, preparing it yourself in advance or producing it on the spot in front of your audience.

Most presenters now use computer graphics when making slides and transparencies. A package like *PowerPoint* provides dozens of different design templates, any one of which will enable you to produce material to a high standard. If you need a really slick professional finish you may consider employing an audio-visual production company. However, this is an expensive option.

Tips for good design

Planning

- Decide the key points of the presentation and what information is best conveyed visually.

- Keep your work simple. Restrict each display to one main idea and try to eliminate irrelevant detail.

- Remember that you are using a *visual* medium. Keep words to a minimum and always try to build in some visual element, e.g. shape, colour, diagram, cartoon.

Layout

- Decide whether to use *portrait* or *landscape* format.

- Fill up the available space in the most effective way possible.

- Don't cram with information – let important points stand out.

Text

- Put a heading at the top of each display in CAPITALS.

- The remaining text should be in lower case with *initial* capitals.

- Make sure all lettering is large and legible enough to be seen over distance.
- Use the same *style* of lettering across a series of slides or transparencies.
- Leave plenty of space *between* lines.
- Don't overload with words – a useful rule of thumb is to have not more than six lines of text on each slide.

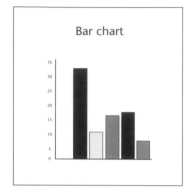

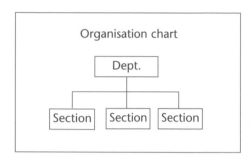

Graphics

- Keep all diagrams, graphs, etc. as simple as possible. Try to cut out distracting details even if this means less realism.
- Lines should be bold and clear – thin lines tend to break up over distance.
- If a graphic is the main focus of the display, keep annotation to a minimum.

Colour

- Use colour for coding, emphasis and liveliness.
- There should be sufficient contrast to give clear definition. As a general rule, background colours should be *lighter* to make text and graphics stand out. In PowerPoint, however, light text against a darker background works better.
- Make sure 'fussy' colours do not reduce legibility or detract from the message.

TABLES, GRAPHS AND CHARTS

In almost all business presentations nowadays (and in many written reports as well) you will find that diagrams are used extensively. The most common types include tables, graphs, charts and maps. These can package information very concisely. They also help to arouse interest and make the message more memorable. With the aid of computer graphics they can be superbly produced – in glowing colour, three-dimensional form, etc. However, they should always be used for a reason, not just to make the presentation or report 'look nicer'.

Tables

Strictly speaking, a table is not a graphic representation, but it is included here because it can be an invaluable method of displaying data for comparison and contrast. The great advantage of a table is that it reduces the need for words to a minimum and so enables numbers in particular to be set out in a clear, concise way.

Exhibit 14.3 illustrates good practice in designing tables. Here are some specific points to note.

- As far as possible keep tables simple and uncluttered. This is essential when they are to be shown on a screen or board.
- Give each table a title.
- Use space rather than lines to separate items. However, horizontal lines may be used to set out column headings.
- Align numbers around the decimal point.
- Consider rounding up numbers when great accuracy is not required.
- A final point! Do **not** copy tables from reports straight onto slides. As a general rule, report tables are far too detailed to be used in spoken presentations and nearly always have to be adapted and simplified. An audience will not thank you if they have to struggle with a mass of figures which they can barely decipher, never mind understand.

Exhibit 14.3 Table

How Overseas Tourists Spent Money in Ireland (2002)					
Breakdown of Spend in Ireland (%)	Total	Britain	Mainland Europe	North America	Rest of World
Bed & Board	31	33	39	29	26
Other Food & Drink	36	39	40	27	33
Sightseeing/ Entertainment	3	2	3	4	4
Internal Transport	9	7	8	13	8
Shopping	17	14	15	29	25
Miscellaneous	4	4	3	7	5

Source: Central Statistics Office

PIE CHARTS

A pie chart is a visually appealing method of showing the parts or proportions that make up a total. It consists of a circle or 'pie' divided into a small number of segments – not more than five is recommended. The segments can be distinguished by colour or shading, and for ease of comparison they can be arranged in order of size. Titles can be written outside the circle and joined to the appropriate segments by lines or they can be written inside the circle if the segments are large enough. Percentages or other values for the various segments should be written in as well. A typical example of this form of illustration is shown in Exhibit 14.4.

Exhibit 14.4 Pie chart

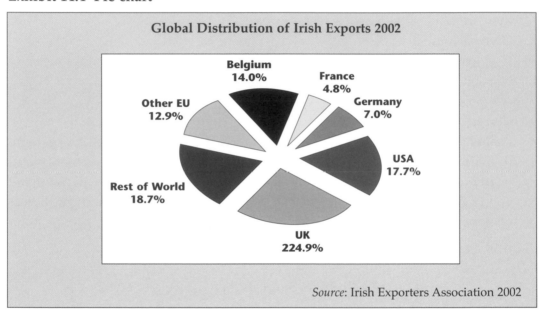

Global Distribution of Irish Exports 2002

Belgium 14.0%
France 4.8%
Other EU 12.9%
Germany 7.0%
USA 17.7%
Rest of World 18.7%
UK 224.9%

Source: Irish Exporters Association 2002

LINE GRAPHS

In the line graph (see Exhibit 14.5) a dependent variable on the vertical axis is plotted against an independent variable on the horizontal axis. In business presentations the dependent variable is often a quantity (sales, exports, revenue) and the independent variable is time (months, quarters, years). Sometimes more than one dependent variable can be plotted on the same graph to allow comparison. When this is done the lines have to be distinguished from each other by colour, variation in thickness or some other device.

Line graphs are particularly useful for focusing attention on rising or falling trends.

Exhibit 14.5 Line graph

Annual Percentage Change in Consumer Prices and Retail Sales for Ireland (1995–2002)

CONSUMER PRICES

RETAIL SALES

Source: IBEC Economic Trends, February 2003

BAR CHARTS

The bar chart is an effective method of presenting data when you want to emphasise differences in quantity. It consists of a series of bars or long rectangles, drawn to a common scale and varying in length depending on the quantities represented.

The bars may be drawn vertically or horizontally (see Exhibits 14.6 and 14.7). They may be separated by a short distance or they may touch, partially overlap or completely overlap. The last of these, however, can be confusing. Grouped bars can be distinguished from each other by colour, cross-hatching or shading. If a more dramatic effect is required bars can be given a three-dimensional appearance. Once this was a job for the professional designer but it can now be done in seconds on a computer.

Exhibit 14.6 Vertical bar chart

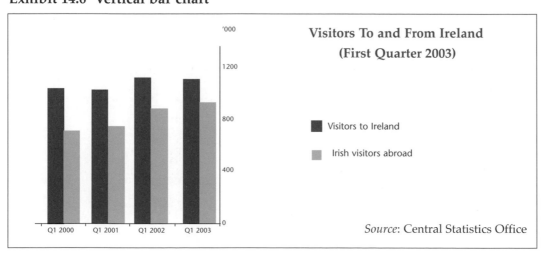

'000

**Visitors To and From Ireland
(First Quarter 2003)**

■ Visitors to Ireland

■ Irish visitors abroad

Source: Central Statistics Office

Exhibit 14.7 Horizontal bar chart

Real GDP Growth 2001

GERMANY	0.7
USA	1.1
BELGIUM	1.1
NETHERLANDS	1.4
ITALY	1.8
PORTUGAL	1.9
FRANCE	2.0
UK	2.3
SPAIN	2.7
IRELAND	5.0

Source: OECD Economic Outlook, December 2001

PICTOGRAMS AND PICTOGRAM CHARTS

Pictograms are simplified pictorial representations of ideas or things. We are familiar with them from road traffic signs, washing instructions on clothes, handling instructions on packages and so on. They are invaluable as a means of conveying simple messages that have to cross language barriers or that have to be understood instantly, even by those who cannot read.

Pictogram charts, in which quantities are represented by pictograms, are sometimes used to display numerical information in business. They are not very accurate, however, as pictograms are difficult to subdivide. Such charts are most effective when the assimilation of figures can be helped by lively or amusing presentation. Thus, they are mainly found in advertisements, magazine articles, staff booklets or any material aimed at the general public.

OTHER TYPES OF DIAGRAMS

Not all illustrations used in business presentations are concerned with displaying numerical data. Among other types you will come across are the following.
- **Organisation charts**: These show how companies and organisations are structured and how the different levels relate to each other.
- **Flow charts**: These are used to trace the logical series of steps involved in performing a task, working through a process or solving a problem.
- **Maps**: Maps are employed when such questions as 'Where is this located?', 'How are these linked geographically?', 'How does this region compare with that?' have to be answered. For instance, you would use a map to:
  ▸ indicate the location of retail outlets

- ‣ chart communication, transport or energy networks, as in Exhibit 14.9
- ‣ show the geographical distribution of different forms of energy or agriculture.

Exhibit 14.9   Irish rail network

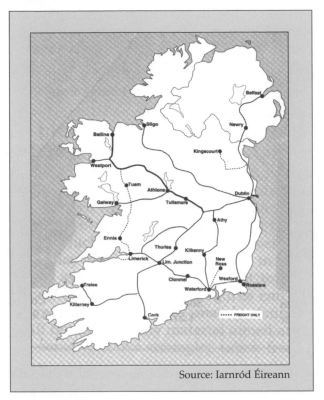

Source: Iarnród Éireann

- • **Drawings:** Some drawings, e.g. exploded or cutaway drawings of machines, are used solely for training and instruction. Others, such as sketches and cartoons, may be used to catch the audience's attention or add interest and variety to a message.

AUDIO-VISUAL EQUIPMENT

We now come to the final component in using visual aids effectively, that is, the skilful and professional operation of audio-visual equipment. This is largely a matter of practice. Most visual aids are easy to operate in a technical sense and can be mastered quite quickly. However, the more sophisticated machines take time to set up and can cause great embarrassment when they fail to work as you expect. If you intend to use an unfamiliar aid it pays to rehearse over and over again until you know the controls inside out and can operate them almost without thinking. The aids most commonly used in business presentations are described below.

These range from the simple and traditional (whiteboard, flipchart) to the exotic (multimedia projector). First, however, there are some general tips that should help you to use all visual aids in a confident and professional manner.

Using audio-visual equipment

1. Always check equipment in advance to make sure it is available and in working order. This is particularly important with projectors, computers and video.

2. Always have at least one run-through to check that you have slides in the right sequence, etc.

3. Check that the board or screen can be seen from all parts of the room.

4. Be careful not to obscure visuals. This might seem like an obvious point, but it is surprising how often a presenter will stand in front of a board or chart, hiding it from the audience's view.

5. Give the audience time to absorb what you are showing them. Pause while they look at the information or note it down. It is unfair to your audience to expect them to look, listen and take notes simultaneously.

6. Resume talking only when you have re-established eye contact with the audience. If necessary, make brief comments on what is being shown.

7. Immediately after you have finished with a visual, remove it. Left on view it ceases to be an aid and becomes a distraction, so wipe the board, turn the chart to a blank page or switch off the overhead projector. This will redirect the audience's attention from the visual to you.

8. Overall, try to blend visuals and speech into a smooth, uninterrupted flow. Your audience should not have to wait in silence while you write paragraphs on the board or fumble with the controls of a machine.

9. Always remember the unwritten law of visual presentations: if something can go wrong, it will. Be prepared for breakdowns and have back-up material ready. Make sure you know who to ask for technical assistance should you need it.

THE WHITEBOARD

The whiteboard is one of the simplest of all visual aids to use. It has a hard, white surface usually made of laminate or enamelled steel. In the office or training centre it may be wall mounted or free standing. It is written on with special markers, some makes of which are refillable. Usually, it can be dry wiped with a cloth or sponge.

Advantages

The great advantage of the whiteboard is that it is a 'live' medium and writing or drawing is done in real time. This means that the presenter can build up points or diagrams in stages and explain as she goes along. The board is ideal for quick, on-the-spot work. It has a smooth surface that is easy to write on and can be cleaned quickly. All colours, except yellow, show up well.

Disadvantages

Information is difficult to capture and it has to be removed once the board is full. The board itself can become permanently marked or discoloured if the wrong marker is used. The cloth used for wiping can get very dirty. Markers are expensive and may run out in the middle of the presentation.

Hints

- Use for bullets and simple diagrams that can be done quickly.
- Try to write in horizontal lines.
- If your handwriting is poor, write in print or block capitals for extra clarity.
- When work is no longer relevant, clear the board.
- Always use proper whiteboard markers and keep spares readily available.

THE FLIPCHART

This is a simple, economical and flexible aid. It consists of a pad of large, inexpensive paper (A1 size) which is usually mounted on an easel. The pages can be torn off or flipped over the top as the presentation proceeds – hence the name 'flipchart'. The writing instruments most commonly used are broad, felt-tipped pens.

Nowadays, the equipment is very light and portable. Easels can be made of strong but lightweight steel tubing and can have retractable legs that can be neatly folded. The whole kit (pad, easel and markers) can often be packed into a compact carrying case.

Advantages

The versatility of the flipchart makes it a popular aid in the training or conference centre. Material can be prepared in advance and then revealed as required. Alternatively, the flipchart can be used for on-the-spot work in the same way as the whiteboard. It is an excellent tool for facilitating audience participation. For example, in a small group discussion, pages can be torn off and given to the group to record information. Some facilitators then display the pages by pinning them on a bulletin board or posting them on walls with bluetack.

Disadvantages

The flipchart is limited to small audiences as writing cannot be seen at long distances. The pages have limited space and tend to deteriorate with regular use. Once written up, information is difficult to alter.

Hints

* Write or draw in simple, bold strokes.
* Use colour for variety, emphasis, etc.
* Use neutral pages, i.e. blank or displaying the company logo, to cover material you do not wish to reveal immediately.
* Stand to one side when displaying and turning the pages.
* If you need to find a particular page quickly, mark it with a folded corner, a paper clip or similar device.
* Use a light yellow pencil to prepare 'invisible' drawings – then you will astonish the audience with your artistic ability when you fill in the lines during your presentation.
* When finished roll up the chart topside out to help keep it flat.

THE OVERHEAD PROJECTOR (OHP)

The overhead projector is extensively used in presentations because it is easy to operate and can provide attractive images.

It consists of a compact light box that projects an image onto a viewing screen. Mechanically, the system includes a lamp, projection stage and lens, on-off switch, small cooling fan and a projector head suspended above the stage by a short post (projection arm).

There are four commonly used methods of producing OHP visuals:

* drawing or writing directly onto a transparency, i.e. A4-size sheet of transparent film, with special OHP markers
* producing the visual on ordinary white paper and then using a photocopier to transfer it to the transparency
* producing the visual on a computer and printing it directly onto a transparency
* producing the image on a computer and displaying it by means of an LCD (liquid crystal display) panel placed on top of the projector.

As a general rule, computer-generated images give the highest quality. Indeed, hand-drawn or photocopied images are now rarely seen in business presentations.

Advantages

The flexibility and convenience of the overhead projector makes it a popular visual aid. Because it has a 'short throw' it can be placed at the front of the room and operated by the presenter herself. It can be used in ordinary light, although a dark background gives a clearer image. Some models are portable – they have a flat projection stage and fit neatly into a small carrying case. When linked to a computer, the OHP can display lively, colourful images.

Disadvantages

The 'keystone effect' presents the main technical difficulty. This is a keystone-shaped distortion to the image caused when it is projected onto the screen at an acute angle. However, most modern screens can be tilted forward at the top to eliminate this. It can also be difficult to place the projector so that it does not block some of the screen from view. Many presenters tend to use too many transparencies or to overcrowd them with information. Once produced, the transparencies are difficult to alter.

Hints

- Try to ensure that everyone can see the screen.
- If using transparencies, leave space on both sides of the projector. This means you can pick up the transparencies on one side and set them down on the other.
- Line up your first transparency and make sure it is properly focused. Then SWITCH OFF.
- When ready to display the transparency SWITCH ON.
- Give the audience time to read and understand the image.
- Use a pointer to highlight key items if you wish – but try to avoid the 'wandering pointer', which can be a distraction.
- When finished with an image SWITCH OFF AGAIN – otherwise it becomes a distraction.
- Do not move the projector while it is still hot. Movement can damage the lamp.

Video

Video enables moving images to be recorded and stored on tape or disc. The two most common ways of playing video tapes are by using a monitor (similar to a TV) or a video projector (the unit you see hanging from the ceiling in many pubs). In addition, video can now be integrated into multimedia presentations using a multimedia projector or a computer monitor linked to a CD-ROM player.

Advantages

The great advantage of video is that it makes moving pictures and complex animated graphics readily accessible to the presenter. Video monitors in particular are easy to set up and give good picture quality in ordinary light. There is an enormous amount of material available. Even if you cannot afford to buy in video programmes (training videos, for example, can be quite expensive) you may be able to produce material yourself with a camcorder.

Disadvantages

Once you start to play video you surrender some control over the presentation. The normal interaction that occurs between presenter and audience ceases and the moving images on the screen become the centre of attention. Besides, many people associate video with entertainment and may see the video session as an opportunity to relax. If the video is in any way dull or poorly produced they may compare it unfavourably with television and lose interest.

Hints

- Check bought-in video before showing it to make sure that it is of good quality and meets your communication objectives.
- Think carefully about how you will integrate video into the presentation. Consider showing only short segments at a time.
- Give the audience something to look for when introducing each video clip. This will encourage them to view with more energy and attention.
- Consider following each clip with a short discussion and analysis.

MULTIMEDIA PROJECTION AND POWERPOINT

Essentially, multimedia is a technology that enables different audio and visual inputs to be combined in a single presentation or learning package. The **multimedia projector** can display images directly from a computer or use graphics, animation and video from any number of sources, including video recorders and CD-ROMs. The presenter can switch smoothly from one source to another at the touch of a button. The machine itself is lightweight and can be carried easily from one location to another. Alternatively, it can be incorporated into a fixed system and ceiling mounted if necessary. The compactness and versatility of this projector makes it an extremely useful presentation aid.

The most common use of multimedia projection is to display PowerPoint slides. PowerPoint, a graphics program developed by Microsoft, has largely replaced the traditional 35 mm slide show and is now widely used in business presentations. It has many advantages in comparison with other visual aids, which no doubt helps to explain its popularity.

- PowerPoint makes it possible to produce slides of high standard without much effort. The user can select from a range of design and colour templates, any one of which will give a professional result.
- The content of slides can be easily edited – there is great flexibility in adding and updating information.
- Because the slides are saved on computer they can be used repeatedly without any deterioration in quality.
- Charts, graphs, cartoons and photographs are easily included. These can be pasted in from ClipArt, image banks and elsewhere.
- Graphics and text can be animated. This makes it possible, for example, to 'fly in' one bullet point at a time.
- The presentation can be printed and photocopied, then distributed to the audience for reference and note-taking. Alternatively, it can be saved as web pages for viewing over the Internet.
- A final advantage of PowerPoint is that sound tracks, video clips, background music or voice narration can be added if you want to give a virtuoso performance.

Yet despite all these attractions, there has been some criticism of PowerPoint. This is partly a case of familiarity breeding contempt as a once-exciting visual aid loses its novelty value. It is also true that PowerPoint has inherent limitations. Even when animation is used, it remains an oddly static medium. Each slide presents information in much the same way as the next, usually in bullet-point form. There is little scope for invention or spur-of-the-moment innovation. Moreover, the image dominates, drawing attention away from the presenter who often seems to do little more than click on a button and talk to the screen. Because of this, opportunities to engage the audience at a personal level are reduced and audience participation can be deadened.

The solution is to learn to use PowerPoint skilfully, confidently and with an awareness of its limits.

- Use PowerPoint to support and reinforce your presentation, not as an end in itself.
- Choose a design and colour that looks good and suits your topic.
- Keep the number of slides to a minimum. You don't need to display every single point of information on screen.
- Avoid text-heavy slides. Keep to short bullet points and use graphics whenever possible.
- Animation and other devices can enliven the presentation, but use them sparingly.

- PowerPoint is an aid, not a prop. Don't repeat word for word what the audience can already see.
- Avoid mechanical, passive delivery. Break the routine by leaving a blank slide on the screen while you speak directly to the audience or engage them in discussion.
- Once you have become proficient with PowerPoint, take the risk of **not** using it. Shut down the computer and encourage the audience to look in **your** direction. Hold their attention with enthusiastic delivery. If you really need a visual aid, use a board or flipchart. Far from being dismayed, your audience will probably be delighted to experience a different approach.

ASSIGNMENTS

REVISION

1. Give six distinct reasons for using visual aids to support a presentation.
2. Elaborate on the main factors that help determine the choice of visual aid.
3. What are the advantages of using tables to display information?
4. Give examples of where you might use a (a) line graph (b) bar chart (c) pie chart (d) map.
5. Pictogram charts are commonly used in staff reports, publicity material and newspaper articles. Why is this?
6. Set out general guidelines for using audio-visual equipment.
7. Describe the advantages and disadvantages of using any three of the following types of AV equipment:
   - whiteboard
   - flipchart
   - overhead projector
   - video.
8. Outline some of the advantages and disadvantages of PowerPoint presentations.

FOR DISCUSSION

1. How could the use of visual aids be improved in the classes or lectures you attend?
2. From your own experience, do you think PowerPoint enhances or weakens presentations?
3. Learning in future may be much more self-directed and technology based while less dependent on classroom delivery by tutors. Do you think this is a positive development?

ACTIVITIES

1. Conduct a survey of daily newspaper readership among your group or class. Perhaps you could find out how frequently members of the group read a daily newspaper and which newspaper(s) they buy. You might also survey which newspapers are best for coverage of news and current affairs, women's issues, music and fashion, business, sport, etc.

    Decide what information you want and design a questionnaire for distribution to the group. Present your findings using suitable charts and graphs.
2. Divide into groups and conduct a brainstorm on any of the following topics. (Add to the list if you wish.)
    * How to improve our college/student services/students' union.
    * How to attract more tourists to Ireland.
    * How to reduce litter.
    * How to make a better bike.
    * How to reduce traffic in city centres.
    * How to improve men's dress sense.

    Record the results of the brainstorm on a flipchart.
3. Give a short talk on any topic that interests you. The qualification is that you should use a short video excerpt to illustrate or support some of the points you are making.
4. Make a video of your group enacting a short role-play of a breakdown in communication or dramatising a short scene from a play.
5. Use the *Golden Pages* to find out what Irish companies sell or hire training videos on communication. Ask them to send you their catalogue. Find out from your school or college whether it is possible to buy or hire videos that may be useful to your course.
6. What are the most recent developments in multimedia? Carry out research and present your findings to the group.

EXERCISES

1. Holiday visitors to Northern Ireland this year are in the following proportions (approximate percentage in brackets):
    * Republic of Ireland: 210,000 (46%)
    * Britain: 112,000 (24%)
    * Europe: 57,000 (12%)
    * N. America: 60,000 (13%)
    * Other: 23,000 (5%)

    Design a pie chart to display this information clearly.

2. Between 1998 and 2002 passenger numbers travelling through Dublin, Shannon and Cork airports increased as follows:
   - 1998: 14.8 million
   - 1999: 16.5 million
   - 2000: 17.9 million
   - 2001: 18.5 million
   - 2002: 19.3 million.

   Show this information on a horizontal bar chart.
3. International Bank Group has made the following advances to its customers this year (percentage of total shown in brackets):
   - Republic of Ireland: €9 billion (45%)
   - Northern Ireland: €4 billion (20%)
   - Britain: €5 billion (25%)
   - United States: €1.5 billion (7.5%)
   - Other: €0.5 billion (2.5%)

   Design a pie chart to show this information clearly.
4. In a survey conducted over three years a representative group of Irish companies was asked about their plans to open a website in the near future. The following responses were given.
   - 1999: Yes, very likely 38%; Yes, possibly 27%; No 32%; Don't know 3%.
   - 2000: Yes, very likely 55%; Yes, possibly 11%; No 27%; Don't know 6%.
   - 2001: Yes, very likely 33%; Yes, possibly 29%; No 38%; Don't know 0%.

   Show this information on a vertical bar chart.
5. According to figures from the CSO, the destination of Irish exports in March 2003 was as follows:
   - United Kingdom: 19%
   - Other EU states: 40%
   - US and Canada: 19%
   - Rest of world: 22%

   Display this information using a pie chart.
6. EuroFerries operates through three Irish ferry ports: Larne, Dublin and Rosslare. This year its passenger numbers for the three ports are as follows: Larne (2.2 million), Dublin (3.5 million), Rosslare (1.1 million). Draw a pictogram chart to represent this information.
7. Draw an organisation chart showing the reporting relationships within your school or faculty.

PART 5

Communication at Work

15 Groups and Teams

ABOUT GROUPS

What is a group?

A group is a collection of two or more people who are affiliated to each other in some way. The members of a group must interact frequently and have a sense of group identity. They must depend on each other to some extent and have shared norms, values and goals. Some groups, such as the family and friendship groups, come into existence organically while others, such as project teams at work, are created artificially to meet a specific purpose. Collections of people that come together for only a short time or who have little sense of affiliation are not normally considered to be groups. For example, people waiting for a bus do not constitute a group.

The structure of groups

Groups have a number of characteristic features that enable them to maintain stability and cohesion. These include **norms**, **roles** and **status differentiation**.

- **Norms**

  Norms are rule-like prescriptions that identify the attitudes and behaviour the group regards as acceptable. However, norms and formal rules are not synonymous, and sometimes they may be in conflict. For example, a group may have a rule that it meets at 8:00 pm but the norm may be closer to 8:15 pm.

  Norms are often enforced by sanctions that require or persuade the members to conform. A person who fails to conform may gain unwelcome attention or be held up to ridicule. Some mockery may seem good natured but its underlying purpose is to bring the individual back into line.

  Norms give groups their identity and cohesiveness. They make it easier for members to know 'the right thing to do' and they can be a useful frame of reference in new or strange situations. When a new recruit has found out the norms of his work group he can settle in and adapt more easily to an unfamiliar work environment.

- **Roles**

  The emergence of group norms requires the members to behave in a co-ordinated and predictable way. However, even within the standardised pattern of a group a range of different behaviours may be necessary for the group to achieve its goals. For example, in a discussion group some members will need to lead while others support, offer ideas, listen, etc., so a division of labour begins to develop with individuals allocated certain tasks and functions. Over time these become institutionalised as group roles.

  A role, then, is characteristic or expected behaviour of a person when in a particular situation or doing a particular job. The role of a team captain is to co-ordinate and motivate the other members of the squad. The role of a meeting chairperson is to manage the meeting, initiate discussion, clarify procedural points, sum up and so on. The advantage of role differentiation is that it enables group members to perform specialised tasks for which they have an aptitude. In this way it reduces the workload for individual members and enables responsibility to be shared.

- **Status Differentiation**

  Even ostensibly egalitarian groups have some status divisions. Different positions in the group acquire different values. In general, the person with higher status is the one who leads, initiates ideas and influences others more than she is influenced herself. A person with expertise that is particularly useful to the group will also acquire status even though he is not the leader. As with norms and roles, status differentiation helps to stabilise the group and make the members' behaviour more predictable. Against that, it introduces hierarchical divisions that can reduce mobility in the group and hinder the full development of individuals.

GROUP DEVELOPMENT

Experience shows us that groups change over time. Even long-lasting and highly stable groups such as the family alter as relationships change or children grow up and move away from home. Some groups eventually cease to exist, perhaps because members lose interest or the group's purpose is fulfilled. The literature on group formation suggests that groups typically pass through five stages of development, as follows.

- **Forming**

  The group comes together for the first time (think of your first class meeting in college). At this stage members of the group can be uncertain and apprehensive. They look around for other people who appear to have the same interests as themselves. They depend on the person in a leadership role, e.g. a class tutor, to suggest some ground rules and outline initial goals. In the absence of group norms they may worry about saying or doing something that shows them up in front of everyone else.

- **Storming**

  This is a difficult stage in a group's development. It is the point at which the group tries to set down boundaries, develop norms and establish goals. Arguments arise over the distribution of roles, status, power and influence. More assertive or extroverted members of the group may make a bid for control, while quieter members withdraw into silence or leave altogether.

  The group facilitator can play a crucial role at this stage by offering guidance and support. He should try to avoid jumping in with his own solutions and instead should bring problems into the open and encourage the group to find its own answers. He may need to give explicit support to members who are disillusioned or rein in individuals who are trying to dominate. It may be helpful to remind members about any ground rules that were agreed initially, such as that everyone should be listened to with respect. Overall, it is important that the facilitator does not regard the group's behaviour as a personal affront, but rather sees it as evidence of the group's struggle for autonomy.

- **Norming**

  The group now moves into a positive phase in which it demonstrates more structure and cohesion. Norms are established and members begin to take on more specialised roles. There is less concern with power struggles in the group and more focus on the tasks the group is charged to complete. Stable friendships begin to form, usually in twos and threes, and there is more humour, joking and teasing than in earlier stages.

- **Performing**

  At this stage the group is performing to its highest potential. There is a high level of cohesion and trust and a clear focus on the group objective. In some cases, this is the point at which the group ceases to depend on the facilitator and becomes a self-sufficient unit. It may have a strong sense of its own identity and find it difficult to admit new members in case the equilibrium of the group is disturbed.

- **Ending**

  Most groups come to an end at some point, and this too can be a traumatic time for group members. Often there is an unwillingness to end the group and attempts are made to keep it going in some form or other. If the group has successfully completed a difficult task there can be an intense feeling of euphoria. Equally, there can be feelings of disappointment or regret about 'what might have been' if the group fails to achieve its goals. Think of the contrasting images that follow the end of an important contest in sport – the winners jumping for joy and the losers falling to the ground in despair.

  The facilitator can help the group to reach a realistic appraisal of its achievements and help members plan for further development outside the group. Often there is a ritual ending such as a party or evening in the pub. This marks the transition out of the group in an enjoyable way.

CONFORMITY AND GROUPTHINK

The individual conforms when he or she concurs with the norms, goals and processes of the group as a whole. In order to conform, the individual may have to set aside or compromise on his own beliefs and values.

Group conformity serves a number of purposes. To begin with, the individual satisfies his need for affiliation, that is, his need to belong to and be accepted by the group. Moreover, the effectiveness of the group is enhanced by agreement among its members – at least with respect to basic goals and norms. Finally, people often choose to belong to groups that already reflect their views and attitudes, and this initial commonality of interests may deepen over time.

However, established groups may suffer from a harmful kind of conformity called *groupthink*. This occurs when the group is so concerned with achieving consensus that it ignores important dissenting views. Among the conditions that give rise to groupthink are the following.
- The group is governed by an authoritarian leader who brooks no opposition.
- The group is insulated from outside influences.
- The group is particularly powerful, e.g. a high-level government advisory group, and begins to think it is infallible.
- There is a crisis or time is short and the group is under intense pressure to find a solution.

The consequences of groupthink can be extremely negative. The group may think itself invulnerable and begin to take excessive risks. It may ignore guidelines and disregard the moral consequences of its actions. Conformity may be enforced by ridicule or exclusion. Decisions may be rushed through without regard for countervailing information.

The *Challenger* disaster in 1986 is often taken as an example of the worst effects of groupthink. Seconds after the *Challenger* space shuttle blasted off from the Kennedy Space Center in Florida it exploded, leading to the deaths of seven astronauts. The cause of the explosion was the failure of a rubber seal that allowed hot gases to escape and ignite during the launch. The subsequent investigation revealed that the launch team had been aware there might be a problem with the seal. They knew the component had never been tested at launch temperatures and, if it failed, the consequences were likely to be catastrophic. Engineers had expressed their concern during a teleconference and advised postponing the launch.

Nevertheless, the team decided to proceed as planned. In doing so, they exhibited many of the characteristics of groupthink. The fact that the space programme had never experienced a fatality gave the team the illusion of infallibility. Important counterarguments were dismissed. Individuals who had doubts about the component failed to express them strongly enough or were coerced into silence. There was considerable external pressure to keep to the launch schedule. The investigation concluded that a highly flawed decision-making process had made a critical contribution to the disaster.

Some recommendations to counter groupthink include:

- assigning the role of critical evaluator to some members of the team
- ensuring key decisions are subject to the scrutiny of trusted outsiders
- holding some meetings in which members are encouraged to be open about objections and misgivings
- dividing the team into subgroups so that the influence of one dominant member can be minimised
- listening carefully to minority or dissenting views.

FROM GROUPS TO TEAMS

Some theorists make no distinction between groups and teams. However, it is useful to think of a **team** as a particular type of group in which there are **specific goals** and a **high level of co-ordination**. Sports teams are often taken as the paradigm case. To be successful, a sports team must have a clear objective – perhaps to win a major competition – and be prepared to put in a sustained collective effort over time to achieve it. In contrast, a friendship group cannot be classed as a team because its goals are diffuse and changeable and its activities are often arranged on a hit-and-miss basis. Nevertheless, friendship groups sometimes take on the characteristics of a team, as when they act in a co-ordinated way to plan and organise a party.

When an employee joins a modern business organisation it is almost certain that he or she will be enlisted onto one or more teams. Dynamic, short-lived teams are increasingly common, so employees may move constantly from one task or project group to another. In some cases the employee may report to a team leader, while in others he may have to assume responsibility for leading the team. Thus, the ability to be an effective and flexible team player is now a nearly universal criterion for success at job interviews.

How do we explain the increasing popularity of teamwork in organisations? In the view of some, the use of teams helps solve two key problems that confront managers: how to make the most effective use of the energy and talent of employees and how to bring about their commitment to organisation goals. Teams are successful because they harness employees' collective knowledge and experience and give them a sense of ownership of decisions. Everything else being equal, teams generally perform better than individuals. Teams also encourage creativity and innovation and thus are widely used in high-technology firms that have to operate under rapidly changing market conditions.

Teams work because...

- They tend to make better decisions than individuals.
- They bring a wider range of knowledge and skills to bear on the problem.
- Information and ideas can be shared, questioned and challenged.
- Issues can be explored in greater depth.
- The whole team can compensate for the person who is temporarily off-form.
- Team members can support and help each other.
- Responsibility for outcomes is shared.
- Team members are more highly motivated and committed than when working alone.
- Teams benefit from synergy – the whole of a team is often greater than its parts.

TYPES OF TEAMS

Teams can be categorised under various headings, but common titles include the three following.

- **Top management team**

  The senior management team draws its members from senior staff representing the main functions of the business. Its responsibility is to develop overall strategy and set the direction of the organisation as a whole. Team members should have wide experience, considerable analytical abilities and the capacity to make sound decisions following complex consideration. They act as bridge between the organisation and the outside world and should be well able to identify external factors such as changing market conditions that impact on the business. Top management teams that can think laterally and have a high tolerance for ambiguity and change are most likely to be successful in an increasingly competitive business environment.

- **Project team**

  A project team is usually short lived. It is set up for a specific purpose, e.g. to solve a quality problem, develop a new product or complete a task, and then disbanded or restructured. Such teams are often **cross-functional,** that is, they bring the expertise of different areas of the business to bear on the problem. In new product development, for example, the design, engineering, marketing and finance functions may all need to be represented.

  It has been suggested that a film crew provides the best example of a highly efficient project team in action. Film crews have a diverse membership and a specific short-term task to perform. Although many members of the crew may be unknown to each other at the beginning, they manage to build relationships and achieve a high degree of collaboration in pursuit of a collective goal. It is thought that in organisations of the future, employees may spend as much as seventy-five per cent of their time on project teams that are similar to the film crew model.

- **Self-managing team**

  The essential idea behind a self-managing team (sometimes called an **autonomous work group**) is that lower-level workers are given a degree of responsibility for organising and managing their work and ensuring that the service or product they provide meets an acceptable quality.

  Operatives are typically organised into cells or teams, each of which is given responsibility for the total work on a selected portfolio of products. The teams have access to all resources, oversee products through all stages of production and may even be able to appoint their own leaders. Instead of being responsible for only part of the work, operatives now take ownership of the whole process.

  In general, it is reported that workers who participate in self-managing teams benefit from higher job satisfaction, greater involvement and enhanced self-esteem. Organisations benefit from reduced costs, less bureaucracy and increased productivity. It has been shown that workers are able to manage themselves quite well when power and responsibility are devolved. Moreover, as they have constant shop floor experience they are often able to identify problems and solutions that desk-bound managers miss.

TEAM ROLES

It is obvious that team members will contribute differently to the team depending on their professional competence. One person may be expert in information technology, another in marketing and each will contribute accordingly. However, how individuals interact on the team is also related to personality and ways of thinking. Members adopt different behavioural roles which can have a significant impact on the performance of the team as a whole. One of the best-known classifications of these roles is provided by Belbin and his associates (see Exhibit 15.1). Ideally, a team will have a mix of complementary roles if it is to be fully effective.

Exhibit 15.1   Team roles

Chairman
Extroverted and self-confident in personality and a natural leader. Is able to focus on objectives and co-ordinate the efforts of the group. Can exercise control without being authoritarian and is a good listener as well as speaker.

Shaper
Competitive and sometimes egotistical, the shaper is the driver of the group. Tries to push the group towards decisions and action. Has little patience with wooly thinking or vacillation. Can sometimes come across as arrogant and aggressive.

Plant
The plant is the most imaginative and intellectual person in the group. Often the source of original or radical suggestions. Focuses on fundamental issues and may overlook practical concerns. Can be resentful when his ideas are challenged.

Implementer
Disciplined, methodical and practical. This worker is the person the group turns to when it wants its decisions turned into reality. Has considerable organising ability and common sense. Is good at planning and scheduling. However, may lack flexibility and be disconcerted by sudden change.

Monitor/evaluator

This person's strength lies in his ability to judge proposals carefully and dispassionately. Likes to have time to think and is good at analysing complex information. Sometimes seems to be overcritical and to lack enthusiasm for group goals.

Team worker

Of all the members of the group, the team worker is most concerned with social relationships. Dislikes conflict and tries to maintain harmony. Is good at interpersonal communication, knows people individually and is always loyal to the group. Not very ambitious or competitive.

Resource investigator

Valuable to the group because of his enthusiasm and wide range of social contacts. Good at improvising under pressure. Can lift the group with his positive attitude, but may lose interest when the initial curiosity fades. Needs others' help to follow through ideas effectively.

Completer

Very conscientious and something of a perfectionist. Can help the group by attending to the finer points and making sure projects are completed to the required standard. May become overanxious or obsessed with minor details.

Specialist

The specialist is an expert in a technical or professional area relevant to the team's work. Provides advice and information in very focused areas. May confuse other members of the team by explaining ideas too quickly or using technical jargon.

COMMUNICATION IN TEAMS

As Belbin's classification shows, a team brings together individuals who have different personalities, outlooks and expectations. Clearly, these individuals must communicate well and establish good working relationships if the team is to have any hope of success. While it is not necessary for members to agree all the time, it is essential that they can articulate their own ideas, defend them effectively in discussion and listen with understanding to the views of others. With regard to interpersonal relationships, members need to be open and honest with each other in an atmosphere of mutual respect.

The rules for communicating information in teams are much the same as for business communication in general. Team members should think about the message before sending it, use simple, clear language, avoid vague generalisations and try to make their contributions as engaging as possible. Openness is important – members should be able to express their views and feelings frankly. If it seems that some individuals are being secretive or guarded, the group's morale is likely to suffer.

Effective listening is also critical to the team's success. Because teams solve problems jointly, members need to listen to and build on the ideas of others. Poor listeners are so wrapped up in their own interests that they quickly switch off when someone else is speaking. A good team listener, on the other hand, focuses on the speaker and makes a conscious effort to hear the entire message. He or she will mentally paraphrase key points, take note of the speaker's feelings and ask for clarification when necessary.

Feedback is also an important component of communication in teams. Members may give feedback about the ideas that are being put forward or about the team process itself. Sometimes, particularly when the team is doing less well, it is useful to examine the dynamics within the group and allow for feedback on individual performance. However, this kind of feedback must be given skilfully if it is to have a constructive effect. Helpful feedback is clear and specific, focuses on the individual's behaviour rather than personality and identifies only those behaviours that can be changed. In high-achieving teams, members welcome feedback and are prepared to learn from it.

Finally, it is often useful to examine the pattern of communication in the team. A team is unlikely to be fully productive when a few members dominate discussion or when there is overreliance on the team leader in setting the agenda. In a strong team there will be open communication between all members and no one will feel excluded or undervalued. Relationships between team members are important, too. Members should support each other and be willing to share information freely. Jobs and responsibilities should be evenly distributed. Disruptive behaviours such as back-biting or nit-picking criticism should be disallowed. The team's business should be conducted in an atmosphere of tolerance and respect. One way to help relationships develop in a positive direction is to set up some ground rules in the beginning and then revise them at intervals during the life of the team.

GENDER AND DIVERSITY ISSUES ▬▬▬▬▬▬▬▬▬▬

More and more frequently, work teams are comprised of members from diverse cultural backgrounds, which clearly has implications for communication among team members. In this section, we discuss some of the problems and opportunities that arise from difference in gender and ethnicity.

GENDER COMMUNICATION

In line with international trends, the number of women participating in the labour force has grown steadily in Ireland in recent years. Women are increasingly succeeding in middle management, although the breakthrough into senior management is proving more difficult. This has implications for communication in work teams as research indicates that women and men tend to have somewhat different communication styles. Organisations need to recognise these differences and to value the contribution that both male and female approaches can make to problem solving, decision making and the like.

Some of the characteristics that differentiate male and female communication are given below.

- Women are more indirect than men in putting forward ideas, tending to phrase them as suggestions or questions. Men appear to make more definite and direct proposals. Men may misinterpret women's less assertive style as a sign of weakness or uncertainty. On the other hand, women may assume that the more direct style of their male colleagues indicates inflexibility. Often what appear to be definite assertions by men are not final positions, but rather the opening moves in a negotiation.

   It is important to realise that both communication styles can be valuable in decision making. Women's more tentative style encourages fuller exploration of the issues and problems involved, while men's more assertive style helps push the discussion towards an end result.

- Men tend to be more comfortable with conflict than women. Men seek resolution through argument in a way that is likely to lead to a winners-losers result. Women, however, prefer consensual results that benefit everyone.

   Depending on the context, either of these strategies may be useful for the organisation. The ability to build agreement and consensus is an invaluable skill in teamwork, but workplaces are also competitive and sometimes hard decisions have to be made. Men have much to learn from the more collaborative style of women, while women may need to accept that conflict and individual hurt cannot always be avoided.

- Women make more effort to establish emotional rapport than men. Women are more willing to offer compliments and to soften criticism by inserting emotional buffers such as 'I'm sorry'. Men offer fewer compliments and are more direct with criticism.

  The female approach has obvious advantages in terms of maintaining good relationships. However, 'softening the blow' in this way may sometimes cause the subordinate or co-worker to hear only the good points and dismiss critical remarks as unimportant. In contrast, the male propensity to criticise rather than praise may bring about the desired change but can be damaging to staff morale in the long run.

- Men are less willing than women to admit to mistakes or accept blame. They are anxious to preserve status and tend to call attention to their accomplishments, whereas women are more self-deprecating. Men are notoriously unwilling to ask for directions when lost. This reluctance to admit to error or ignorance can sometimes have dangerous consequences, as major disasters often testify. Yet men's self-belief can give them an advantage in situations where confident self-presentation counts.

- Men speak and interrupt more often than women in meetings, which may give them an unfair advantage. It may benefit the organisation to examine the composition and group dynamics of meetings and try to introduce procedures that help give women and men an equal chance of influencing outcomes.

- Women and men tend to differ in the topics they choose for informal conversation. Women often talk about personal or relationship issues, whereas men talk about sport or politics. Men's conversation is also characterised by one-upmanship, joking and banter. Both styles can enrich the social environment of work.

These remarks about gender communication indicate general tendencies only. Each person has his or her own way of communicating and there is bound to be much overlap. Many men are hesitant and self-deprecating in putting their view across, while many women are assertive and not greatly concerned with building rapport. Nevertheless, researchers have noticed broad differences in approach between the genders and these do have consequences for teamwork communication. Ideally, organisations should recognise the value of both male and female approaches and seek to use them to advantage depending on the communication context. Moreover, misunderstandings between female and male co-workers are likely to be reduced if each understands and respects the characteristic style of the other.

Intercultural communication

Large corporations not only compete for business on a global scale but also increasingly recruit employees from abroad as well as from the home community. The challenge for management is to integrate workers from diverse cultural backgrounds into cohesive and productive teams in which each individual is treated with respect. It helps if managers and employees are aware that people from different countries may communicate differently or have different expectations about how co-workers should behave.

An *ethnic culture* is the set of values, norms, beliefs and attitudes that a person acquires through membership of a particular ethnic group, religious group or nationality. This leads the person to behave in a way characteristic of her culture and to expect others sharing the same culture to behave similarly. Difficulties arise if we assume that co-workers from another country share our cultural perspective or, more ominously, if we think our culture is innately superior to theirs. For effective communication in a diverse workforce we need to develop cultural sensitivity and learn to respect and understand cultural difference.

There are several areas where misunderstandings can occur.

- **Language**
  One of our earliest and most important cultural acquisitions is a spoken and written language. In Ireland, the first language for most of us is a variant of English, which gives us a useful advantage as English is now the international language of commerce. However, co-workers from other countries may have learned English as a second language. Their understanding of the structure of the language may be as good as our own, but they may be unfamiliar with everyday idiomatic expressions we take for granted. For example, would everyone understand what is meant by 'cash on the nail', 'upping the ante' or 'having money to burn'? Moreover, in oral communication differences in voice tone or pronunciation may cause problems. People from other countries may speak more loudly or quietly than we expect. They may have difficulty in pronouncing some English sounds (just as many Irish people have difficulty with the *th* sound).

- **Time**
  Perceptions of time and how it can be divided and used vary across cultures. North Americans and Northern Europeans place a premium on punctuality. Other cultures, however, have a more relaxed attitude and allow you to turn up late without causing inconvenience or embarrassment. The amount of time spent on discussion varies, too. North Americans in particular prefer to use time efficiently and make quick decisions. Those from a non-Western culture, on the other hand, may want to spend several hours in general discussion

before they get to the main topic of business. They make no clear distinction between 'social time' and 'business time', tending to run the two together.

- **Power and status**
  The symbolic representation of power and status varies between cultures. In cultures where there is a wide power difference between superiors and subordinates, the person with lower status may indicate respect by lowering his eyes while speaking, sitting in obedient silence at meetings and so on. He or she has learned to be respectful of authority and to avoid the open expression of ideas and feelings. Such behaviour can cause problems in teams where everyone is treated as an equal and the team leader can be routinely challenged.

- **Negotiation and decision making**
  Different negotiating styles can be found in different cultures. In the West, there is a dislike of protracted negotiation and a tendency to consider short-term consequences and contractual obligations only. Power to make the final decision is usually vested in a single individual. In Eastern cultures, by contrast, negotiations take much longer and the negotiators take a long-term perspective. Building social relationships that involve trust and mutual obligation can be as important as making contractual arrangements. Final agreement is arrived at by group consensus rather than individual decision. This seeming unwillingness to commit can frustrate Western negotiators who are concerned with efficiency above all else.

- **The concept of face**
  The concept of *face* is more important in the East than in the West. Asians are shamed by loss of face and deeply resent any behaviour that diminishes their status or reputation. This has consequences that Westerners often find difficult to understand. For example, a Japanese businessperson will give a noncommittal answer to a question rather than lose face in front of his colleagues by admitting ignorance or lack of power. Instead of saying 'no' to a proposal he may use a more indirect face-saving expression. In this culture, the blunt, no-nonsense approach favoured by American businesspeople in particular can appear unnecessarily rude and aggressive.

- **Nonverbal communication**
  It is a mistake to assume that nonverbal communication has the same universal meaning across all cultures. There are some significant differences that can cause confusion. A few examples illustrate this. In some cultures touching, e.g. patting on the back, is a sign of affection and trust, but in others it is likely to cause deep offence. Ideas of personal space differ, with North

Americans preferring a wider personal space than, say, their colleagues from the Middle East. We assume that a smile indicates pleasure but in the East a person may smile as a matter of social etiquette whether she is happy or not. Eye behaviour differs, too. In some cultures direct eye contact indicates attention and respect, but in others one shows respect by looking down or away.

- **Social behaviour**
  Finally, there are different expectations about how people should behave socially. Gestures of greeting differ – the handshake is widely but not universally accepted and even the style of handshake can vary from one country to another.

  Rules differ about how and when to present business cards. In Japan, for example, a businessman will present his card with both hands so that the other person can read it. Rules also differ about when to give gifts and what kind of gift is appropriate, how to entertain, how much formality is required in forms of address and so on. In many cultures, food has special significance and the host is likely to be affronted if the guest does not sufficiently appreciate what is being offered.

What implications does the existence of cultural differences have for communication between co-workers and team members in a diverse environment? Here are some general guidelines that may be helpful.

- Do not assume that a person from a different background has the same values and expectations as you, or that your values are superior.
- Show empathy. Listen carefully to the other person and try to understand things from his or her perspective.
- Be patient and flexible. Don't overreact when cultural misunderstandings occur.
- Avoid cultural stereotyping. Respect the other person as an individual with unique capabilities.
- Look for similarities. Although the discussion so far has emphasised cultural difference, co-workers in the same organisation are likely to have many interests and concerns in common.
- Make sure the messages you send are clearly expressed but not patronising.
- Be careful with humour, as it can be misunderstood and unwittingly give offence.
- Finally, appreciate the value of working in a cross-cultural environment. Learning from other cultures can open up new possibilities and new ways of thinking.

Spotlight on Irish Business – Intel Ireland

Managing diversity at Intel

Intel Corporation introduced the world's first microprocessor in 1971 and today is one of the preeminent suppliers of chips, boards, software and other 'ingredients' of the computer industry. Its largest site outside the United States is located near Leixlip, Co. Kildare. The Leixlip plant is Intel's manufacturing and technology centre for Europe and the most advanced industrial campus in Ireland.

Intel Ireland recruits widely and there are many different nationalities among its workforce. The company has adopted a proactive approach towards multiculturalism and aims to create an inclusive workplace where unique perspectives and talents are valued.

When new employees from overseas relocate to Intel Ireland they are supported with a comprehensive package that includes assistance with various aspects of moving, finding housing, adjusting to the Irish tax regime and so on. They also benefit from a one-week orientation programme arranged for all new Intel recruits.

A management team develops and reviews initiatives to create a more inclusive workplace in which the unique contribution of each employee is valued. Education initiatives have been put in place for both managers and staff that aim to increase employees' awareness of diversity and the impact of equality legislation. In addition, Intel Ireland encourages feedback on all aspects of the work environment (including diversity issues) by holding regular open forums and having an 'open door' approach to management.

In all its internal communication activities Intel Ireland utilises many different media, including one-to-one meetings, departmental briefings, e-mail and noticeboards. Every Intel employee has twenty-four-hour access to corporate and local news via the company intranet. This site is where employees can obtain information about employee services, policies, procedures and benefits as well as a wide range of other information.

According to Patty Murray, vice-president and director of human resources at Intel Corporation, 'Intel is committed to providing a workplace in which we value diversity, work together to accomplish the company's objectives and listen to and respect each other.' Intel Ireland has taken many positive steps towards achieving this goal.

ASSIGNMENTS

REVISION

1. Give a short definition of a group.
2. Write brief notes on each of the following structural aspects of groups: *norms, roles, status differentiation.*
3. As groups develop they are said to proceed through five different stages (*forming, storming, norming, performing* and *ending*). Describe what happens at each stage.
4. What is *groupthink*? What factors give rise to groupthink and why can it cause problems? What can be done to counter groupthink?
5. How can we distinguish between groups and teams?
6. What benefits do teams bring to modern business organisations?
7. Write brief notes on the nature and function of the following types of teams: (a) top management team (b) project team (c) self-managing team.
8. Belbin and his associates identified *eight* discrete team roles. Name these roles and give a brief description of each.
9. Discuss the importance of effective communication in teams.
10. Research shows that men and women exhibit somewhat different patterns of communication in teams. Describe any *five* ways in which men and women appear to differ in their communication style.
11. Describe some aspects of intercultural difference that may cause misunderstanding in teams.
12. What steps can be taken to improve understanding and reduce tension between team members from different cultural backgrounds?

ACTIVITIES AND DISCUSSION POINTS

1. Working in small groups of three or four compile a list of the benefits you can derive from (a) belonging to a group of friends (b) joining a college club or society.
2. Imagine a new member is joining your project team and you hope he or she will fit in well and make a useful contribution. What characteristics will you look for in this person?

   On your own, rank the following characteristics from one to ten in order of importance. Then, join a small group and agree a group ranking.

Characteristics	Individual	Group
Always turns up on time	————	————
Listens carefully to other views	————	————
Completes assignments	————	————
Shares information	————	————
Has a sense of humour	————	————
Asks lots of questions	————	————
Supports other people	————	————
Always comes prepared	————	————
Challenges other people's views	————	————
Is willing to lead	————	————

3. Discuss how you might solve the following team problems.
   - One person on the team is very assertive and tends to dominate everyone else.
   - Some members of the team are failing to do work assigned to them.
   - The team is divided between those who want a high level of success and those who want modest success.
   - Someone on the team has complained that he or she is being ignored and marginalised.
   - The team has suffered a setback and morale is low.

4. Divide the class into a number of project teams of five to six members. Each team's task is to identify and develop a business plan for a new and innovative product. The plan should address the following questions.
   - What are the product's unique features and benefits?
   - How it is to be manufactured and supplied?
   - How can quality control be assured?
   - How is the product to be marketed and advertised?
   - What price will be charged?
   - Are there competitors?
   - How will you finance your product?
   - What costs will you have? How soon can you break even? How much profit do you hope to generate eventually?

When the work is completed, each team should present its plan to the class in the form of a group presentation and written report.

After finishing this project there should be an opportunity for each team to review its operation and assess its strengths and weaknesses. A whole-class review of the project is also likely to provide useful feedback. (Some banks provide helpful start-up guides for small businesses that teams may find helpful.)

5. Consider the ways in which your male and female friends communicate when they meet or talk to each other on the phone. Do you agree that men and women tend to communicate differently among themselves and with each other? Give examples of any differences you have noticed.

6. Have you travelled or worked abroad? Did you notice any forms of body language or social behaviour in the country you visited that would be unusual in Ireland?

7. Imagine you have responsibility for giving a brief introduction to Irish culture to tourists from overseas. Working in small groups, try to agree a list of cultural activities or sites that seem to be particularly representative of 'how we are' in Ireland. Do you think your visitors would be impressed by everything you mention?

8. If there are students from overseas in your class, consider giving them an opportunity to speak about their own culture and how they have responded to life here.

9. In small groups, consider the benefits of working in a multicultural environment.

10. Find out about the work of the Equality Authority in the Republic of Ireland (www.equality.ie) or the Equality Commission in Northern Ireland (www.equalityni.org). What is the role of these agencies in promoting good intercultural relations in the workplace?

16 Meetings

'Not another meeting!' is often the cry of individuals who consider meetings a waste of time. Yet whether we like it or not, meetings have a profound influence on our daily lives. Nowadays, nearly all important decisions in local or central government, trades unions, business and voluntary associations are made by groups or committees rather than individuals. It is important, therefore, that students and young employees understand how meetings are organised and conducted. It is essential that, through practise, you learn to become an effective and enthusiastic participant.

There are a great many things that can go wrong with meetings. They can be badly planned and ineffectively chaired. Discussion may be unfocused, tempers may become frayed. Those involved may feel that meetings occur too often, last too long or fail to achieve tangible results. J.K. Galbraith's remark that 'meetings are indispensable when you don't want to do anything' sums up the rather jaundiced view that many people take of meetings.

Despite these criticisms, meetings have several advantages and are likely to remain an essential feature of organisational life.

- They help generate ideas because a range of individual talents and experiences can be tapped at the same time.
- They enable proposals to be examined from many different angles and, in consequence, wrong decisions are less likely to be made.
- They can help different functions in the organisation to co-ordinate and arrange their activities.
- They can be instrumental in breaking down barriers and improving understanding between individuals or groups who hold opposing views.
- Last but not least, they can give participants a feeling of being valued and of having some say in the running of the organisation.

In general, when meetings are well organised and efficiently conducted they are a valuable form of communication.

Later in this chapter advice will be given on how to organise, lead and participate effectively in meetings. First, however, it is important to have an overview of the wide diversity of meetings that may be encountered at work.

TYPES OF MEETINGS

FORMAL OR INFORMAL?

A broad distinction can be made between formal and informal meetings, although it is sometimes difficult to determine where one shades into another.

A *formal* meeting is one conducted according to set rules and procedures, some of which are laid down in articles of association, constitutions and standing orders. The meeting will be controlled by a chairperson and there will be a written agenda. Minutes will usually be taken.

An *informal* meeting may have none of these characteristics. There may be no standing orders, no chairperson, no formal agenda and no minutes. However, even the most casual of meetings must have a structure of some sort if it is to be productive. At the very least there must be common agreement on the meeting's objectives and what is to be discussed.

PUBLIC AND PRIVATE MEETINGS

A *public* meeting is one which any interested member of the public may attend. A typical example would be a meeting held to consider the likely impact of a new motorway on local communities. Such meetings are often advertised in the press or by postering.

A *private* meeting is restricted to the members of an organisation or association, although the public may sometimes attend as observers. Almost all meetings that occur in business are private.

GENERAL MEETINGS

An *ordinary general meeting* is the regular weekly, monthly or quarterly meeting of the members of an association or organisation.

An *extraordinary general meeting* (EGM) is called when a crisis arises that must be dealt with before the next ordinary meeting. The only topic on the agenda is the issue that has given rise to the emergency.

An *annual general meeting* (AGM) provides an opportunity for a general review of the organisation's progress during the previous year. The annual statement of accounts is presented, the chairperson gives an annual address, reports are received from other officers such as the secretary or treasurer and, if necessary, new officers or directors are appointed.

COMMITTEES

A committee is made up of a small group of people who are empowered by the parent organisation to act on its behalf. A true committee has decision-making powers but, in practice, the title is also given to many groups that have only an advisory or investigative function (see Exhibit 16.1). Only committee members normally attend committee meetings (although others may be present by invitation), whereas all members of an association are entitled to attend general meetings.

Committees may be described as **ad hoc** or **standing**. An ad hoc committee is so called because it is set up for a specific, short-term purpose and when its work is done it is disbanded. Standing committees, on the other hand, are permanent. In addition, a main committee may set up one or more **subcommittees** to perform certain tasks on its behalf and report back.

Exhibit 16.1 What committees do

Executive committee	A very influential committee, found in many organisations. It has responsibility for the day-to-day running of the organisation and for putting into effect policy decisions made at general meetings.
Advisory committee	Formulates advice, suggestions or recommendations for a higher authority.
Finance committee	Oversees the financial affairs of the organisation, ensures accounts are kept in order, advises on large items of expenditure.
Membership committee	Oversees and controls the membership of the association.
Standing orders committee	Recommends changes in rules and procedures, organises the agenda for annual conferences, etc.

THE PURPOSE OF MEETINGS

Another useful way of classifying meetings is according to the purpose they serve.

GIVING INFORMATION

(Examples: briefings, news conferences, mass meetings.)

As we have seen, many organisations now give regular briefings to employees through meetings. The information given could be about new duty rosters, changes in work practice and so on. Large organisations hold news conferences when something happens that is of great public interest, such as the sudden resignation of a chief executive. Mass meetings may be called by either management or trades unions when matters of concern to the whole staff arise, e.g. proposed industrial action or threatened closure of a plant.

RECEIVING INFORMATION AND ADVICE

(Examples: progress, advisory, consultative, grievance, round-table.)

The purpose of this type of meeting is to gather information from those attending which will assist management in their decision making. The object could be to canvass trades union opinion on new policy proposals, to air employee grievances or to learn about the progress of a new project from research staff. Many organisations now hold regular round-tables with customers to learn how their products or services could be improved.

NEGOTIATING

Negotiations may be between two companies seeking a merger or between management and union representatives over pay, working conditions, etc. Often a series of difficult and protracted meetings takes place before agreement can be reached. Such meetings demand a great deal of skill from the participants and also, it must be said, a certain amount of guile.

SOLVING PROBLEMS

(Examples: project development meetings, brainstorming.)

Meetings of this type are usually informal in order to encourage an open discussion in which fresh ideas can be generated. The main task of the chairperson (or facilitator) is to stimulate the discussion with timely questions, prompts and suggestions.

MAKING DECISIONS OR CONSULTING

Making decisions is a function of some, but by no means all, meetings. Friction can arise in staff/management meetings when staff believe collective decisions can be made while management regard the meetings as consultative only and reserve the right to make the final decisions themselves. To avoid this confusion, the exact powers of staff/management meetings should be made clear from the outset.

MEETING PREPARATION

All meetings, of whatever type, should be carefully planned. Primary responsibility for this lies with the manager, chairperson or secretary, although there is also an onus on the ordinary participant to prepare. The benefits of planning will be seen in more effective use of time, improved decision making and higher morale at meetings. If this in turn leads to fewer and shorter meetings then so much the better.

Let us now look at the practical arrangements that need to be made before a meeting takes place.

IS THE MEETING NECESSARY?

This may seem an obvious question to ask but it is often overlooked. Many meetings take place simply because they are part of a regular schedule or because a manager thinks, 'It's been weeks since the last meeting so we'd better call another one.' Always consider alternatives. For example, if the meeting's purpose is to disseminate information, could this be done more effectively by sending a memo or e-mail message? If you need to consult other staff could you do this by phone or by having a quick word in your office? Meetings should be held only when there are clearly defined objectives which cannot be achieved in a more effective way.

WHO SHOULD ATTEND?

This question arises when a group or committee is being set up for the first time. The manager should try to ensure that, as far as possible, the expertise of the participants matches the task in hand. The following factors will have a bearing on how efficient and productive the group is.

- **Experience**: Members should have relevant knowledge and experience, otherwise the group will flounder. However, one or two less experienced members may be drafted in to 'learn the ropes'.
- **Balance**: All important interests should be represented. For example, a product development meeting will probably require representatives from the marketing and production functions as well as from research and development.
- **Commitment**: The members should have a positive attitude to the group and be committed to its objectives.
- **Number**: The size of the group can have a significant effect on its productivity. It is generally felt that the most efficient number of members is somewhere between five and fifteen. When there are fewer than five, the range of views is likely to be too narrow. On the other hand, when the number exceeds fifteen

the meeting becomes more difficult to control, cliques and subgroups form and it becomes easier for some participants to withdraw into silence.

NOTICE OF MEETING

The notice is one of a range of written documents that are needed to facilitate a committee's work and to ensure that meetings run smoothly. The secretary is usually responsible for preparing these documents and making sure they are ready as and when required.

A notice should be sent out well in advance of the meeting. This is more than just a matter of courtesy. Timely notice gives the participants the opportunity to prepare for the meeting and, if necessary, rearrange their schedule so that they can attend.

Notices should always be in writing and may be sent by memo, letter, e-mail, etc. (see Exhibit 16.2). It may also be useful to leave an oral reminder on voice mail. Before distributing the notice, it is worth double checking that all necessary details have been given.

Exhibit 16.2 Notice of meeting

MEMORANDUM

TO	Petra Killeen
FROM	Martin Markey
REF	
DATE	3 March 20—
SUBJECT	**Meeting of Staff Representative Council**

The next meeting of the Staff Representative Council will be held on Wednesday, 15 March 20— at 5:00 pm in the Boardroom, Harley House. The agenda is attached.

Martin Markey
Secretary

THE AGENDA

The agenda is a list of topics to be considered at a meeting. It is usually a short document but should not be lightly dismissed on that account. It performs two essential functions: first, it gives the participants advance warning of what is to be discussed and second, it determines the running order at the meeting itself. It is usually circulated along with the notice.

The importance of a clear, well-constructed agenda cannot be overemphasised.

Here are three useful tips that will help you avoid the more common pitfalls in agenda design.

1. **Set feasible objectives and keep the agenda short**

    An overloaded agenda can have several undesirable consequences. The meeting may take hours to finish, some items may get superficial attention, hasty decisions may be made or part of the agenda may have to be postponed. Any one of these results is bad for the group's morale. There are few things as disheartening at a meeting as looking at the agenda and thinking, 'We've just spent an hour on Item 4 and there are still five items to be discussed. Why didn't I remember to bring my sandwiches!'

2. **Put agenda items in an effective sequence**

    The best order depends on a number of factors. In formal committee agendas, as shown in Exhibit 16.3, the placing of some items is determined by tradition. Other items may fall into a natural sequence. For example, it probably makes sense for a Sports and Social Committee to try to agree the following year's programme of events before talking about funding and publicity.

    As a general rule, urgent items are placed at or near the top of the agenda. Items that are contentious or require serious discussion are left further down. (However, some meetings prefer to tackle the thorny issues near the beginning when the participants are still fresh.)

3. **Make sure the agenda is clear and unambiguous**

    It is common practice to describe agenda items in one or two words. Sometimes, however, a word or short phrase may be ambiguous. Bear in mind that it may be necessary to spell out items in more detail and perhaps make clear why they are on the agenda.

Exhibit 16.3 Agenda for ordinary committee meeting (with comments)

> **1. Apologies for absence**
> The chairperson notes those members who are unable to attend and who have sent apologies. This and the two following items are the traditional way of opening a routine committee meeting.
>
> **2. Minutes of the last meeting**
> The minutes of the previous meeting are read out if they have not been already circulated. They must now be approved as a correct record by the members and signed by the chairperson.
>
> **3. Matters arising**
> Some issues arising from the minutes may give rise to further comment, discussion or question. For example, the secretary may have undertaken at

the last meeting to obtain estimates for equipment or cost a proposed function or event. Under 'Matters arising' he may report back with this information.

4. **Correspondence**

This item appears if there is regular correspondence between the committee and other bodies. An important letter may be read out or circulated, otherwise the secretary summarises letters received.

5. **Displacement Allowance dispute**

Having dispensed with matters relating to the previous meeting, the agenda now moves on to new business (Items 5 to 7).

6. **Computer training programme**

7. **Staff newsletter**

8. **Any other business (AOB)**

Normally, this item gives members an opportunity to raise minor points that can be dealt with quickly. For example, the secretary could remind members about a forthcoming event or urge them to get their raffle tickets sold.

Sometimes, however, a member may use AOB to raise an important matter that the meeting has ignored. This may be resisted by the other participants who may not wish to prolong the meeting. An astute chairperson will suggest that the matter be put on the agenda for the next meeting.

9. **Date of next meeting**

The final item may be to agree the date and time of the next meeting. If it is difficult to find a time that suits everyone, the decision may be left to the discretion of the secretary.

THE MEETING ENVIRONMENT

Having a pleasant environment is not a luxury – it can contribute significantly to a meeting's success. A group cannot be expected to work efficiently if the participants are shivering in a room that is too cold or if the meeting is constantly being interrupted by visitors to the door.

When organising a meeting room try to choose somewhere that:

- is quiet and private (no telephone, if possible)
- has sufficient space
- has comfortable chairs
- is well lit and well ventilated
- has a pleasant atmosphere.

The seating arrangement can also influence the way a meeting is conducted (see Exhibit 16.4). In formal meetings, a 'boardroom' or 'classroom' arrangement may be used. The officers may sit behind a table or even on a raised platform facing the ordinary members. This lends a certain dignity to the occasion and enhances the officers' authority, but may inhibit discussion. Informal groups work best when the participants are seated in a circle or horseshoe formation. This promotes freer discussion and encourages the chairperson to adopt a more democratic style of leadership.

Exhibit 16.4 Seating plans

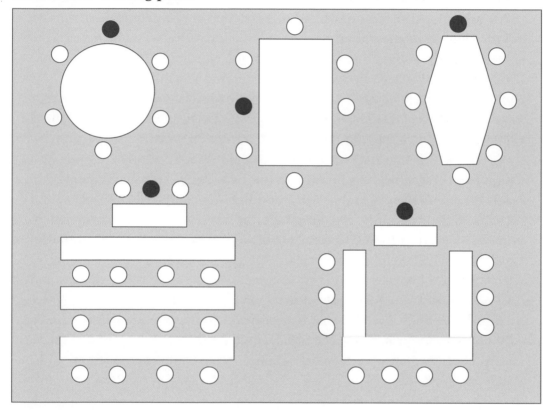

OTHER ARRANGEMENTS

Finally, the organising secretary should take any other steps that will help the meeting run smoothly. These could include:

- preparing a **chairperson's agenda** (an annotated version of the ordinary agenda in which the secretary has added dates, names or other key details that will help the chair to conduct the meeting more efficiently)
- preparing and distributing **agenda papers**, i.e. articles, reports, summaries, etc. which the members need to read before the meeting
- arranging details such as stationery, name cards, refreshments

- setting up and checking presentation aids if these are required
- checking the sound system if microphones are required.

Spotlight on Irish Business – Jurys Doyle Hotel Group

The art of conference management

Capturing the conference and meetings business is an important objective for any company in the highly competitive hotel industry. To achieve this hotels must provide an excellent working environment and state-of-the-art facilities. 'Total operational success on behalf of every one of our clients' is the motto of John Conmee, conference manager with the Jurys Doyle Hotel Group. John is responsible for the conference team at the Burlington Hotel, a popular Dublin venue that has the largest hotel conference centre in the city. He is equally at home whether managing a small business meeting or a major international event. Clients in the recent past have been as diverse as Hilary Clinton, Ronan Keating and the Reuters Group, a top media corporation.

A world-class international conference requires meticulous planning and a high level of technical support. Everything needed for the event must be in place – customised sets, audio-visual and lighting equipment, perfect sound systems and, if required, satellite links for international teleconferencing. With fast broadband (ADSL) connections, a conference presenter located in New York or Philadelphia can speak to delegates on-screen and even interact with the audience by taking questions. When conference notes and documents are needed these can be sent via e-mail or fax.

Small meetings, such as board meetings or seminars, are catered for in specially dedicated suites. Facilities include adaptable modular furniture, multiple phone lines, computer network access and audio-visual aids. Wireless connectivity is available for laptop users. Simple practical aids (pens, paper clips, bluetack) are also provided.

John Conmee stresses the importance of attention to detail in managing conferences and meetings. It is essential, he says, to check in advance that all equipment works and to arrange for back-up in case of breakdown. For example, the failure of an international teleconference link can cause serious problems during a conference, so there is always a second line available.

Today, conference management in Ireland compares with the best in the world. To continue to attract this business, however, the objective must always be to meet and exceed delegates' expectations.

CONDUCTING MEETINGS – THE CHAIRPERSON'S ROLE

The chairperson or group leader has the main responsibility for the conduct of meetings. It is an important responsibility because meetings that are badly conducted leave the participants feeling frustrated and disillusioned.

There is no single style of leadership that is right in all circumstances. A firm, almost autocratic approach might be necessary at a large meeting where there is a full agenda and many participants. On the other hand, a more relaxed, democratic approach would be appropriate when leading a small, informal group. In all cases, however, the chairperson is expected to be efficient, impartial and able to exert authority when necessary.

You should find the following outline of the chairperson's role helpful if you are called on to chair a meeting and are not sure what is expected of you.

OPENING THE MEETING

Your first responsibility will be to get the meeting under way. You should arrive at the meeting place punctually. Check with the secretary that all arrangements necessary for the proper conduct of the meeting have been made. Use this time to introduce yourself to new members and perhaps to take early soundings if a controversial topic is coming up for discussion.

As near as possible to the appointed time, welcome those attending and call the meeting to order. Sometimes, particularly at informal meetings, you may have to explain the purpose of the meeting, discuss procedure or outline the topics to be considered. In regular meetings, however, you simply move on to the first routine items on the agenda. Preliminary matters such as minutes of the previous meeting should be dealt with speedily in order to leave sufficient time for discussion of any major items that arise later.

STARTING DISCUSSION

After a topic has been introduced or a proposal put forward, it is your job to start the discussion. Commonly, this is done by addressing an **overhead question** to the whole group, e.g. 'Well, what do we feel about Carole's suggestion?' Alternatively, you can put a **direct question** to someone who is particularly interested in the topic or who has expert knowledge about it, e.g. 'Liam, I believe you have some experience in this area. What do you think should be done?'

ENCOURAGING PARTICIPATION

Anyone who attends meetings regularly knows that some people participate fully while others say little or nothing. There are various reasons why this may happen.

For example, the silent person:
- may be overawed by more senior or more experienced participants
- may be naturally shy
- may fear rejection
- may not have prepared for the meeting
- may have nothing useful to contribute.

It is not always easy to determine which of these is motivating the person's behaviour. Nevertheless, the purpose of a meeting is to get wide and representative discussion, so you should do what you can to encourage contributions from the quieter participants.

- Look out for signs that the person wants to get involved. Assertive individuals simply begin speaking when someone else has stopped. Shy individuals, on the other hand, may wait to catch the chairperson's eye or give tentative indications of wanting to speak that can be easily overlooked.
- Ask a direct question: 'We haven't heard from you yet, Sean. What do you think of this?'
- Create a participative atmosphere by showing that you appreciate all contributions, even those that are poorly expressed or unenthusiastically received.

Managing the discussion

As the discussion develops, it is the chairperson's responsibility to keep it on track and bring it to a satisfactory conclusion. A well-ordered discussion will often move through the following stages:
- stating the problem (proposal, area of discussion)
- talking around the problem, e.g. looking at the problem from different angles, filling in information gaps, etc.
- establishing priorities
- considering different courses of action
- deciding what to do.

One difficulty that can arise in managing the discussion is 'jumping ahead'. For example, someone suggests a solution before the nature of the problem itself has been fully explored. To prevent this from happening, insist that the discussion moves forward in an orderly way. 'That's a good idea, Stephen, but before we look at it can we just make sure we have all the facts first?'

Another difficulty – and one that causes significant time wasting – is irrelevant discussion. In trying to control this you need to be sensitive to the reason why it occurs. Sometimes, it is a signal that all useful contributions have been made and it is time to sum up and reach a decision. At other times, it indicates that the original proposal has not been properly understood or has been forgotten. If this is so, you will need to restate the proposal and re-explain it.

Deciding when to bring a particular part of the discussion to a close can be a matter of fine judgment. If an agenda item is wrapped up too quickly there may be mutterings about debate being unfairly curtailed. On the other hand, discussion cannot be allowed to continue to the point of inanity. With experience you should develop an instinct for the right moment to finish with one item and move on to the next.

The television presenter's view

'You have to listen with every bit of yourself to what is going on. And watch people, look at reactions, take in all the vibes. You must make connections between what people say. I usually let people confirm what they have said to make sure there is a clear view round the table because there is no point in having half-baked ideas of what has happened. I think you must take charge, you must drive to a conclusion because people get very impatient if they feel nobody is driving a meeting. They lose interest.' (Olivia O'Leary)

Source: O'Connor, 1994: 122

MANAGING PEOPLE

As chairperson, you also have responsibility for managing people at meetings. Most meetings are conducted in a spirit of courtesy and co-operation, but this is not invariably the case. On occasion, sharp conflict can arise, particularly when a controversial topic is being discussed and the participants hold strong and diverse views.

A stormy meeting can be a severe test of the chairperson's ability and temperament. However, you should always try to deal with angry or emotional individuals in a positive way.

- Listen carefully and show a willingness to understand.
- Acknowledge the person's feelings ('I can see that you feel strongly about this').
- Try to clarify the issues involved.
- Look for compromise.
- Stay calm – do not get emotional or upset yourself.

Other problems are posed by people who habitually raise points of order, ask awkward questions or ramble on at great length. Once again, patience is often the best response although you may have to take action against a particularly troublesome individual. If the meeting is severely disrupted you have the option of asking the person to leave or abandoning the meeting. However, do this only as a last resort.

Managing time

The amount of time required will vary from one meeting to the next, but two hours should be the outer limit in most cases. It is often useful for the participants to agree from the outset on a suitable length of time. Then, they will all be aware that they are working to a deadline and the chairperson will be encouraged to move briskly through the agenda. At large meetings, such as annual conferences, it is customary to impose strict time limits both on platform speakers and on speakers from the floor.

Summing up and making decisions

There are a number of mechanisms for reaching decisions at meetings. It is usually desirable to reach a consensus without going through the formality of a vote. However, formal motions and amendments have to be voted on, usually by means of a show of hands or a ballot. In the event of deadlock, you may have a casting vote. However, note that the right to a casting vote is not automatic but must be conferred by the rules of the organisation.

Immediately before a vote is taken, the motion or amendment should be restated. This is done to remind participants what they are voting on and to ensure the minuting secretary has a correct record.

In addition, it is often helpful to summarise the main points of a discussion prior to a decision. This helps both the minuting secretary and anyone who has lost track of the various arguments. Even in meetings that do not involve decision making it is useful to sum up at intervals so that the participants can have a sense of progress.

Concluding the meeting

The meeting should be brought to an end at a reasonable hour. If you consider it necessary you may now reiterate the main decisions made or remind members of work to be done before the next meeting. Or, having dealt with all the items under AOB, you can simply declare the meeting closed. The time at which a formal meeting ends is usually noted and recorded in the minutes.

The secretary's role

Before the meeting:
- make sure the meeting room is available
- draft the agenda in consultation with the chairperson
- send out the notice and agenda on time
- collate correspondence
- gather any other documents etc. needed for the meeting
- make sure room is in order.

During the meeting:
- circulate the attendance book
- distribute copies of the agenda, minutes, etc. to those who may have forgotten them or not received them
- read the minutes of the last meeting
- read (or summarise) and comment on correspondence
- give a 'secretary's report'
- assist the chairperson on points of information
- give advice on procedure
- take notes for the minutes
- generally support the chairperson and look after the members' comfort.

After the meeting:
- write up the minutes
- deal with correspondence
- send out information as agreed at the meeting
- begin the planning cycle for the next meeting.

MINUTES

Minutes are a brief, orderly record of the business of a meeting. The task of writing them up usually falls to the secretary.

TAKING NOTES AND WRITING UP THE MINUTES

While the meeting is in progress the secretary takes notes. These should be accurate and impartial. Not everything said needs to be recorded: indeed, many contributions may be repetitive or peripheral to the discussion and therefore can be ignored. Formal resolutions, however, should be taken down verbatim.

As soon as possible after the meeting the secretary should revise the notes and write the minutes. Important points are likely to be forgotten if there is considerable delay. When the minutes are complete the secretary can get them checked by the chairperson before submitting them to the other members for approval.

Traditionally, minutes were written in longhand into a bound minutes book. Today, they are much more likely to be typed out and stored in a file or loose-leaf binder. The advantages of storing minutes in this way are that they can be readily photocopied for distribution to the members, corrections can be made more easily and other relevant material, such as reports, can be filed in the binder as well.

THE STRUCTURE OF MINUTES

As can be seen from Exhibit 16.5, the pattern of minutes follows almost exactly that of the agenda.

Exhibit 16.5 Minutes

Minutes of the Staff Representative Council meeting held on Wednesday, 15 March 20— at 5:00 pm in the Boardroom, Harley House

Present:

    C. Doherty (Chairman)

    M. Markey (Secretary)

    A. Flanagan (Treasurer)

    P. Killeen

    D. Reade

    M. Redmond

    W. Gardiner

    S. Conlon

Apologies for absence were received from K. O'Sullivan and H. Green.

1. **Minutes of the previous meeting**

   The minutes of the meeting of 11 February were read and approved as a correct record.

2. **Matters arising**

   The chairperson reported that he had conveyed to the catering manager the members' concern about the untidiness of the staff canteen. The problem was due to a temporary shortage of cleaning staff and has since been resolved.

3. **Correspondence**

   (a)   A letter thanking staff for their get well cards and visits was received from Mr J. Buckley.

   (b)   The secretary read a number of quotations for drinks machines. It was agreed that a subcommittee consisting of A. Flanagan, P. Killeen and S. Conlon would consider the quotations and make a recommendation to the catering manager for purchase.

4. Displacement Allowance dispute

The chairperson reported on his meeting with senior management about the Displacement Allowance dispute. Several members felt that the Staff Council should become more actively involved in the dispute. The chairperson pointed out that, as negotiations were between management and the relevant trades unions, it was impossible for the Staff Council to intervene directly.

5. Computer training programme

W. Gardiner informed the meeting that she proposed to run a two-week computer course for beginners. She then gave a brief outline of the course content. Her proposal was warmly welcomed by the members.

6. Staff newsletter

S. Conlon suggested that a regular staff newsletter would help to make the work of the Staff Council better known. Several members had reservations about the cost and time involved in producing a newsletter. It was agreed that the treasurer would enquire into costs and present an estimate at the next meeting.

7. Social Club raffle

M. Redmond reminded members that all tickets for the Social Club raffle should be returned by 24 March.

8.

There being no further business the meeting closed at 6:10 pm and the next meeting was set for 28 April.

Notes

(1) First, the minutes should record the date, place and time of meeting. This information is usually written into the main heading.

(2) Then, the names of those present are listed. However, if the attendance is large only the number is given or an *attendance list* is attached. Apologies for absence may also be noted.

(3) Approval of the minutes of the previous meeting must always be recorded. If necessary, this item is followed by *Matters arising*.

(4) Thereafter, the minutes generally follow the agenda. Items under *Any other business* may be recorded under AOB or under more appropriate headings. The final item is a record of the time of closure.

(5) For ease of reference, minutes should be set out in schematic form, e.g. numbered and headed as above. Note that numbering begins from *Minutes of the previous meeting*.

(6) Minutes should always be written in past tense reported speech (see Appendix III) and in a plain, factual style.

TYPES OF MINUTES

A distinction is commonly made between *resolution, narrative* and *action* minutes. In **resolution minutes** only the decision or resolution is recorded (see Exhibit 16.6). This format is used when extreme brevity is required or when an impression of unanimity needs to be given.

Exhibit 16.6 Resolution minutes

Competition for best sales assistant

It was resolved:

that a competition open to all branches be held to find the best company sales assistant of the year;

that a subcommittee under the direction of Mr P. Dervin be set up to organise and run the competition.

Narrative minutes record not only the decisions made but any discussion leading up to the decisions (see Exhibit 16.7). It is often advantageous to use minutes of this type when recording the proceedings of voluntary associations. Members who freely give up their time to come to meetings like to see their names in print if they have made a contribution.

Writing effective narrative minutes requires considerable skill. The secretary has to accurately summarise what people have said, make sure no worthwhile contribution is overlooked and manage to keep the whole account fairly brief. Indeed, one of the main difficulties with narrative minutes is that they tend to become far too detailed.

Exhibit 16.7 Narrative minutes

Competition for best sales assistant

Mr P. Dervin suggested that the company should organise a competition throughout all the branches to find the best sales assistant of the year. He said that this would encourage sales personnel to give good service to customers. Each branch should nominate a representative and the final could be held at headquarters with a suitable prize for the winner.

Supporting the proposal, Ms S. Linden said that the prize would have to be worthwhile to generate interest. She also pointed out that the competition would have to be well publicised.

> Mr J. O'Keefe said it might be possible to get publicity for the competition in the press, particularly in provincial newspapers. This would help keep the company in the public eye.
>
> The chairperson pointed out that organising the competition would be a major undertaking. He suggested that a subcommittee under the direction of Mr Dervin be set up to examine the proposal and report back. This was agreed unanimously.

Action minutes contain a brief summary of the proceedings and an action column listing the names or initials of those responsible for putting the decisions into effect (see Exhibit 16.8). They are useful in business because they make absolutely clear where the responsibility for action lies.

Exhibit 16.8   Action minutes

> **Competition for best sales assistant**
>
> Mr P. Dervin suggested that the company should organise a competition throughout the branches to find the best sales assistant of the year. After some discussion, it was unanimously agreed that a subcommittee should be set up under Mr Dervin's direction to examine the proposal and report back at the next meeting.
>
> Action by:
> Mr P. Dervin

For most business purposes a fairly succinct account of a meeting is all that is required. Usually this means that the secretary compromises between the brevity of resolution minutes and the comprehensiveness of narrative minutes. Each minute then consists of a short preamble which gives the background to a decision, followed by a record of the decision itself. You should take the minutes in Exhibit 16.5 as a good guide in this respect.

TAKING PART IN MEETINGS

So far this chapter has concentrated on the organising and management side of meetings. Let us now turn to another important aspect of meetings, that is, the role of the ordinary member, for a meeting cannot be productive without the active co-operation of all who are attending.

Knowing how to be an effective participant in meetings is vitally important for people at work. A good performance in a meeting enables you to influence organisational decisions, it gets you noticed as someone who has a useful contribution to make and it enhances your self-esteem and makes you feel you have achieved something worthwhile.

Unfortunately, it is not uncommon for the ordinary participant to come away from a meeting with negative thoughts and feelings. These may be directed at others – the chairperson, perhaps, or the bully who dominated the meeting and antagonised everyone else. But quite often, negative thoughts reflect the person's frustration with his own performance.

Experienced committee members know that there is no magic formula for successful interventions at meetings. However, there are a number of practical steps which, if taken, can help even a novice to speak effectively and have his views heard with respect.

BE PREPARED

Not surprisingly, good preparation is the starting point. The first step is to read the agenda, the minutes and any other documents sent by the secretary. Gather background information from files, reports, etc. that may be helpful at the meeting. As you read, it is a good idea to highlight points that you may need to refer to later on. Write notes in the margins and mark relevant page numbers in some way, e.g. jot them down on your copy of the agenda. The important thing is to be able to find and use references quickly while the meeting is in progress. Then, plan what to say. A useful technique is to prepare **four** or **five** points carefully and aim to make at least one or two of them. Think about how you will get your points across and *write them down in note form*. It is unwise to trust to memory or hope that when the time comes the words will flow!

Breaking the silence barrier!

Some people are confident and relaxed performers at meetings. Others find participation much more difficult. Self-doubt is no respecter of age: the mature person as well as the novice may fear speaking in front of people who are – or seem – more articulate than themselves. The 'silence barrier' can be a formidable problem. Here are some tips on how to break through it.

- Sit where you can be easily seen by the chairperson.
- Signal clearly when you want to speak. Put your hand up before the preceding speaker finishes. Remember: signalling your intention is often the hardest part.
- Speak early. The longer you hesitate, the more confidence ebbs. The discussion will move quickly from one topic to the next and you may miss out if you keep waiting for the right moment.

- Start with a simple comment or question. This may not get much attention from the other members but it breaks the ice – an important consideration from your point of view.
- Volunteer to do something – find information, read a report, draft a document. This really is one of the best ways of getting involved. You can plan carefully what you want to say and the chairperson has to bring you in at the next meeting: 'Andrea, you were to report back on . . . How did you get on?' There is no better way of ensuring that you have the floor to yourself!

COMMUNICATING EFFECTIVELY

Once the initial stage fright is out of the way, it is time to think about making a constructive contribution to the meeting. Essentially, this means being able to communicate your thoughts and ideas in a way that influences others in a positive direction.

Experienced speakers begin by indicating the nature of their intervention. For example:

- A question: 'May I just ask for clarification on . . . ?'
- Useful information: 'Our experience at . . . is very much in line with what you are saying.'
- A suggestion: 'May I propose that . . . '.
- An attempt to change the discussion: 'There's another aspect of this problem we need to think about . . . '.

They then get to the point quickly and support what they say with telling arguments and examples. They speak concisely and bring their remarks to a definite conclusion.

Flexibility is also an important consideration. No single person can control everything that happens at a meeting and the discussion often takes an unexpected course. Be ready to think on your feet and to adapt your remarks in light of changing circumstances.

THE HUMAN SIDE

Meetings are not just about words – they are also about relationships, emotions, attitudes, hidden agendas. Many a sound proposal has been shot down because the proposer has unwittingly hurt or humiliated other members of the group or has failed to appreciate the delicate balance of power among the participants.

Here are some ideas on how to manage the 'human' aspect of meetings.

- Acknowledge other contributions. A simple way to do this is to use phrases such as: 'As Mick said earlier . . .' or 'I'd like to take up a point made by Siobhán . . .'.

- Build alliances by supporting good ideas. Nod in agreement when the other person is speaking. Follow up their contribution with a positive remark that adds something of your own: 'I think that's a great idea, and may I also suggest . . .'.

- Use eye contact. Look most at the person who is most influential or who needs most persuasion, but look at everyone else as well. Each member of the group is a potential ally, so why antagonise people by appearing to ignore them?

- Think carefully before you disagree with someone. Nothing hurts so much as loss of face, so choose words that will not undermine or diminish the other person. An example of a face-saving intervention might be: 'I think we should certainly consider Mary's suggestion for the future, but I wonder if we have the resources at present . . .'.

- Do not get disheartened if your own idea is criticised or rejected. You must be prepared to lose sometimes in the cut and thrust of a meeting, so accept defeat gracefully. On reflection, you will probably find that your proposal deserved its fate anyway.

LOOKING AND LISTENING

Try to watch and listen all the time, even when the meeting moves to a topic in which you have little interest.

Watching can give you a valuable insight into the power relations in the group. Who is speaking most? Whose ideas are having the most influence? What does the body language of the other participants tell you? Is gaze being directed at a particular individual other than the chairperson? Are some people being isolated?

Listening can help you sense the mood of the meeting and perhaps keep clear of pitfalls. For example, you may decide that that brilliant but costly idea you wanted to talk about is best left for another day if everyone else is talking about cost savings and retrenchment.

From careful observation you can learn what other people are good at and how they structure their comments. Some may be good at theory. Others always think of the practicalities. One person may have all the bright ideas while another may be good at drawing the strands of the discussion together. This may help you to recognise and develop your own strengths as a communicator.

GOOD MANNERS

There is one final aspect of participation in meetings that deserves brief comment. One of the best, and easiest, ways to earn respect at a meeting is by being good mannered and courteous towards others. Specifically, this means:

- arriving at the meeting punctually
- listening attentively to others (not interrupting rudely)
- recognising the chairperson's authority
- abiding by rules and procedures
- lastly, accepting the democratic decisions of the meeting, including those you have spoken against.

ASSIGNMENTS

REVISION

1. What are the advantages of meetings as a medium of communication?
2. Distinguish between the following pairs.

formal meeting	public meeting	general meeting
informal meeting	private meeting	committee meeting

3. What is the purpose of the following types of meetings: (a) management briefing (b) customer round-table (c) press conference (d) brainstorm?
4. What factors might a manager take into account when choosing the members of a committee?
5. What suggestions would you make for ensuring that the agenda is an effective document?
6. Briefly describe the purpose of the following items on an agenda: (a) apologies for absence (b) minutes of the previous meeting (c) matters arising (d) any other business.
7. Give an account of the chairperson's role in the course of a meeting.
8. What steps can the chairperson take to: (a) encourage the quieter participants (b) control the more difficult participants?
9. Outline the role of the secretary (a) before (b) during (c) after a meeting.
10. What is the purpose of minutes?
11. Distinguish between (a) narrative (b) resolution (c) action minutes.
12. 'Knowing how to be an effective participant in meetings is vitally important for people at work.' What advice would you give to a committee member who is shy and inexperienced but wants to make a useful contribution?

ACTIVITIES

1. Invite a representative of a college club to give a brief talk on the club's activities. Then hold a brainstorming session in which members of the group put forward suggestions for improving the club. You could consider such questions as:

- How can the club get more publicity?
- How can membership be increased?
- How can funds be raised?
- What extra activities could the club undertake?

Afterwards, review the session and decide what ideas are worth pursuing. Submit your findings to the club secretary in the form of a letter or memorandum.

2. Obtain permission to attend a meeting of a local voluntary or professional association. Among the activities you could then undertake are the following.
   - Propose a vote of thanks to the chairperson for allowing you to attend.
   - Observe how the meeting is conducted and report back to the class on anything you have learned.
   - Take notes during the meeting and afterwards write up the minutes. If possible, obtain a copy of the actual minutes and compare them with your own.

3. Organise a seminar on a topic related to your course in which you have one or two invited speakers. Among other arrangements you will need to decide the theme of the seminar, draw up a programme and publicise the event. Afterwards, hold a postmortem on what happened.

   NOTE Do not undertake this assignment unless you are prepared to be thorough in your preparation.

4. Find out about the work of the Convention Bureau of Ireland. Report back to the group on the result of your investigation.

EXERCISES

1. Jack Straw is chairperson of the Southern Chapter of the Institute of Personnel Practitioners in Ireland (IPPI).

   The following are the notes he has made for his address to the Institute's twenty-first annual general meeting.

   Delighted to address members on such an auspicious occasion – difficult to believe the Chapter is twenty-one years young – a tribute to the small group who started the Chapter many years ago in Cork City.

   This year a great success – membership up by ten per cent – Chapter successfully hosted the annual conference in the Great Southern – remarkable job by organising committee – event highly praised.

   Significant progress on educational front – new IPPI diploma courses up and running in Cork and Waterford colleges – very satisfied with numbers applying – first group of students will be conferred next year.

Many challenges in year ahead – cannot rest on our laurels – new membership drive needed – need to review our Code of Practice – EU directive on industrial democracy will have to be taken on board – perhaps a seminar on it next year?

Finally, wish to thank officers and members for their support. Has been a very busy but rewarding year.

Write a *narrative* minute of this speech under the heading 'Chairperson's Report'. Begin 'The chairperson said . . . ' and remember to write in **past tense reported speech**.

2. You are secretary of the Staff Association Executive Committee at Intertel plc. The most recent meeting of the committee was held on Wednesday, 6 October at 5:30 pm in the boardroom.

The following was the agenda for the meeting (with notes for the chairperson appended).

1. Apologies for absence
   P. O'Connor sends apologies – going to conference in Waterford.
2. Minutes of the previous meeting.
3. Matters arising
   C. Maxwell to report on arrangements for Christmas party.
4. Progress on new Sports and Social Centre
   I have letter from CEO on this. Plans now agreed with architects. M. McKenna wants to raise matter of squash court – he thinks one won't be enough. Also, why no gym?
5. Problem with office heating
   Lots of concern about this. Offices in Block B now really cold in the morning. Expect a few people will want to get in on this one.
6. Staff magazine
   P. Harris wants to raise this again. It's a good idea but she should be talking to management, not us.
7. Any other business.

Write minutes for this meeting in **past tense reported speech**. Add in any extra information you think necessary.

3. Ballybeagh is a small town with a population of just over 6,000 people. At present, it has a girls' secondary school which caters for 250 girls. All boys and some girls have to travel to schools in nearby towns, and for many of these this involves a round trip of forty miles each day. An action group from the local community has been actively lobbying local politicians to do something to improve the situation.

A meeting has now been called and is being held in the local parish hall. The purpose of this meeting is to discuss the issue and, if possible, arrive at some consensus on what should be done.

Simulate the meeting using the role-briefs below or inventing others if you wish.

Local councillor: Chairperson – wants to keep everyone happy (local elections next year) – is looking for a 'middle-of-the-road' decision.

Parish priest: Wants new school – wants to be represented on the board of management – anxious to keep all parishioners happy – anxious to keep parish contribution to a minimum.

Department of Education official: Task is to listen carefully and give useful information on building costs, government grants, etc.

Principal of girls' school: Wants present school to be extended into a co-educational community school – wants Department to fund as much of the building costs as possible.

Parent 1: Wants new co-educational community school without church involvement – will try to keep church representation on the board of management to a minimum.

Parent 2: Has four boys, all of whom are good at technical subjects – wants all-boys' technical college – will settle for community school with a well-equipped science and technology block.

Parent 3: Irish-speaking and wants Gaelscoil for the town – alternatively, wants minibus to transport local Irish-speaking children to Scoil Lorcan, which is twenty miles away.

Parent 4: Boys are happy at their present school, so doesn't think a new school is necessary – thinks the drain on parish funds is too much already – wants the school transport system improved.

Parent 5: Is strongly opposed to co-educational schools but will settle for a community school with church control over the board of management.

Members of the group not involved in the role-play should act as observers. Here are some points they could report on – can you think of others?

- Did the chairperson handle the meeting well?
- What problems arose during the meeting?
- Could these have been avoided?
- Was a fair decision made in the end?

Consider recording the meeting on tape or video if possible.

4. A bypass is to be built around the town of Lisheen, which lies on a busy national road. Plans for the bypass have been on display in the County Council

offices and now a meeting is to be held to gauge the reaction from interested parties.

Among the delegates at this meeting you could have representatives of the town's shopkeepers, the local farming community, the road-planning department, an environmental pressure group, a 'Save our Children' action committee, a landowner who hopes to get substantial compensation, etc.

Discuss the kinds of issues that might arise, then allocate roles and simulate the meeting. Note that this is an information-gathering meeting, so no final decision about the bypass need be made.

Afterwards, discuss how the meeting was chaired and whether it was effective.

17 The Employment Interview

In general terms, an interview may be described as a structured conversation in which one party (the interviewer) exchanges information with another (the interviewee). The type of interview which we probably know best is the television interview in its various manifestations. We are all familiar with the news journalist snatching a few comments from a busy politician, or a chat-show host talking to a well-known guest under the glare of the studio lights. By comparison the interviews that are encountered at work – job, counselling, appraisal, etc. – may seem mundane. Nevertheless, they are an important part of the individual's working life.

This chapter focuses on the employment interview, a form of meeting that you will encounter many times in your career. You may have to attend several interviews before you get your first job. Then, each time you look for promotion within your own organisation or seek to move elsewhere, you will be faced with interviews again. At some stage you yourself may have to interview others for posts at a lower level than your own. You will find that the role of interviewer is no less difficult and demanding than that of interviewee.

The interview will be considered from two perspectives – that of the employer and that of the job seeker. The first two sections below attempt to answer questions about the value and nature of the job interview. The third describes the skills involved in conducting the interview. The final two sections give guidance to the job seeker and interviewee, respectively.

WHY INTERVIEW?

The primary purpose of the job interview is to assist the employer in choosing the best person for a particular job. It remains a standard method of selection despite the fact that there is now a wide range of alternatives available. Almost every employer uses the interview at some stage in the selection process and there are several reasons why it is likely to remain a universally popular device.

- It gives the employer and the candidate an opportunity to meet and exchange views.

- It enables the employer to elicit more information about the candidate's abilities and experience than may be provided on the application form or *curriculum vitae*.
- It gives the candidate an opportunity to find out about the organisation and decide whether she wants the job.
- Face-to-face interaction helps the employer judge whether the candidate will fit in with existing staff and the organisation's culture.
- By conducting the interview fairly and proficiently, the employer can present a positive image of the organisation and its selection procedures.

Yet perhaps the most compelling reason of all for holding the interview is that it fulfils the employer's psychological need to see and hear a candidate before entering into a contract of employment.

It would be a mistake to assume from this, however, that the interview gives a precise measure of the candidate's abilities. Indeed, much of the evidence points in the other direction. A myriad of research studies have revealed defects and biases in the interview which diminish its predictive value. The evidence suggests that unstructured interviews in particular give relatively poor results (see Exhibit 17.1). However, more recent research indicates that the interview's value can be significantly enhanced when it is carefully planned and based on an effective analysis of the job.

Exhibit 17.1 Predictive accuracy of various selection methods

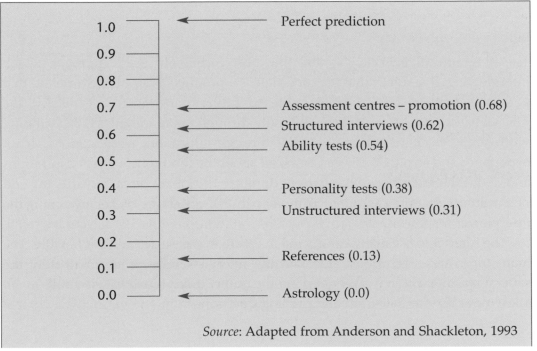

1.0	← Perfect prediction
0.9	
0.8	
0.7	← Assessment centres – promotion (0.68)
0.6	← Structured interviews (0.62)
	← Ability tests (0.54)
0.5	
0.4	← Personality tests (0.38)
0.3	← Unstructured interviews (0.31)
0.2	
0.1	← References (0.13)
0.0	← Astrology (0.0)

Source: Adapted from Anderson and Shackleton, 1993

Glossary:
1. *Assessment centres*: A form of assessment in which a number of different techniques are used in an integrated way. Methods may include simulations, interviews, in-tray exercises, group discussions and so on.
2. *Structured interview*: A type of interview which is carefully planned and highly standardised.
3. *Ability tests*: These measure either existing knowledge and skills (achievement tests) or the candidate's potential to develop such skills and abilities in the future (aptitude tests).
4. *Unstructured interview*: A type of interview that is largely unplanned and undirected.
5. *Personality tests*: These may indicate whether the candidate has key personality aspects required for the job.

TYPES OF INTERVIEWS

Before interviews take place, decisions have to be made about the type of interview to be used, the number of interviewers and so on. The approach chosen is determined by such factors as time constraints, custom and practice within the organisation and the nature of the job. While the overall objective of finding the best candidate remains the same, different approaches will elicit different kinds of information. Some of the main alternatives are discussed below.

BIOGRAPHICAL INTERVIEWS

The biographical interview is still the most commonly used approach to job interviewing. It assumes that the candidate is a product of her life history and that past achievement is a reliable guide to future performance. Typically, the interviewer works her way chronologically through the candidate's CV, beginning with family background and moving through education, qualifications, work experience and so on. Questions are asked about the candidate's career aspirations and about the relevance of her current duties to the job on offer. Towards the end of the interview, the candidate is invited to ask questions of her own and the interviewer responds.

The interview is usually conducted in a way that is structured yet flexible. The main topic areas are preplanned and the interview follows approximately the same pattern for each candidate. At the same time, flexibility is built in by allowing scope for follow-on and probing questions.

STRUCTURED INTERVIEWS

In structured interviews the interaction is not only preplanned but standardised as much as possible. All candidates are asked the same questions in the same order. Questions are based on a job analysis that has identified and ranked the key skills, knowledge and abilities needed to perform the job effectively. The candidates' responses are noted and rated on a rating form (see Exhibit 17.2). Ideally, at least three interviewers should be present: one to ask questions, one to observe and one to record information. Highly structured interviews, although rather inflexible, have been shown to be good predictors of the candidate's future performance.

Exhibit 17.2   Excerpt from structured interview rating form

Candidate: _____			
Criterion Ability to work effectively with others in a team Etc.	**Question** Tell us about any group project you were involved in. What was your contribution?	**Rating**	**Comments**

BEHAVIOURAL INTERVIEWS

In this approach the first step is to define and list the competencies for the job. Candidates are then asked to demonstrate that they have acquired the relevant skills by referring to specific events in their experience. For example, a typical 'behavioural' question might be: 'Could you tell us about an occasion when you took on a leadership role in a team?' Depending on the nature of the response, the interview can probe further to find out what the candidate thought at the time and how she dealt with opportunities or problems that arose. Note that the candidate is not asked directly if she has leadership abilities. Instead, her competence (or lack of it) is judged on the basis of her actual behaviour.

Although behavioural interviewing is still not commonly practised, there is evidence that it improves the selection process (Barclay, 2001). Candidates are less able to make exaggerated or misleading claims because they must provide evidence of performance. Many candidates prefer this approach as they are more relaxed when talking about past experience. However, it is claimed that behavioural interviews may disadvantage candidates who find it difficult to recall the detail of past events, or those such as students who have limited work experience.

One-to-one or panel?

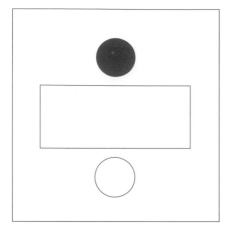

A question that has to be decided in all interviews is whether to have one interviewer or a panel. The one-to-one format is widely used despite the danger that interviewer subjectivity will distort the results. One way of compensating for this is to supplement the interview with objective tests. Another way is to hold a series of one-to-one interviews with a different interviewer in each case. A problem with the latter method, however, is that the candidate may have to give the same information over and over again.

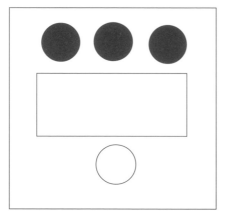

Panel interviews reduce the risk of interviewer bias but are more difficult to control. It is essential for the panel members to meet in advance of the interview and to agree how the interview will be conducted. Each panellist should know the criteria for assessment, how the interview will be structured, what particular area she will cover and how a decision will be made. This preparation should not be left until five minutes before the first interview starts!

CONDUCTING A JOB INTERVIEW

The previous section has outlined some, but by no means all, of the approaches that may be found in job interviewing. Despite these variations, however, there is a common core of skills which all good interviewers use. The importance of developing and refining these skills should not be underestimated. The value of job interviews is greatly increased when they are carried out by trained and competent interviewers. In this section, therefore, we look at the process of conducting the interview and identify the key interviewing skills involved. As you will see, most of these skills are social and communicative in nature.

Preparing to Interview

Let us assume that you are the interviewer and that a number of candidates have now been shortlisted for interview. Your first responsibility is to be well prepared, which means taking the following specific steps.

- Read the job analysis documents carefully to familiarise yourself with the job requirements and the criteria for assessment.
- Read the applications and note any areas that need special attention.
- Take into account any other information that is available about the candidates, e.g. aptitude or personality tests results.
- Have an interview plan that will enable you to obtain relevant and comprehensive information from each candidate.
- Ensure that all preliminary arrangements for smoothly running the interviews have been made. For example, make sure the waiting room is satisfactory and that the receptionist knows where to direct the interviewees when they arrive.

The interview environment

You should pay considerable attention to environmental details such as room, seating, etc. to ensure that candidates are as comfortable as possible during the interview. The physical arrangements in the interview room should be conducive to a fairly relaxed exchange of information. The majority of interviewers prefer to sit behind a desk or table, although you may dispense with this if you wish to create a more informal setting. Remember, however, that many candidates expect the interview to be formal and are uneasy if there is no barrier between themselves and the interviewer. Chairs should be fairly comfortable – but not too plush! The room itself should be quiet and protected from unwanted visitors. The telephone should be disengaged.

Establishing and developing rapport

When the interview begins your first task is to welcome the interviewee and try to put her at ease. The aim at this early stage should be to establish a relationship of trust that will encourage the candidate to talk openly. Introduce yourself and anyone else who is on the interview panel. Shake hands with the interviewee if you think it appropriate and indicate where to sit. If the candidate is carrying an overcoat or portfolio suggest where it may be put.

Your first few questions or remarks should be designed to give the interviewee time to adjust to unfamiliar surroundings and the sound of your voice. For example, you could make a comment about the weather, or if the candidate has travelled a long distance, enquire about the journey. You could also outline the structure of the interview and perhaps encourage the interviewee to ask questions about the job and the organisation as the interview proceeds.

All of these opening moves have a common objective: that of easing the candidate into the interview and creating a helpful, nonthreatening environment. However, even at this early stage you will be learning a great deal from the interviewee's appearance, manner and initial responses. Of course, you must be alert to the problem of first impressions and any judgment made at this stage should be very tentative.

QUESTIONING

Once the preliminaries are over the serious business of interviewing begins. As you have only a limited time in which to obtain the information you need, it is important to ask questions in a clear and efficient manner. There are a number of effective questioning strategies and some strategies that are best avoided.

Types of questions

▶ **Open questions**
These encourage the interviewee to reply freely and at length. They are a particularly valuable interviewing technique and can be asked at any stage in the interview. For example:

- *'I see that you gave up a course in electronic engineering and did computer science instead. Why did you make that decision?'*
- *'You say in your CV that you did some part-time work last summer. Tell us what the job involved.'*
- *'How do you see your career developing over the next few years?'*
- *'What are your greatest personal strengths?'*

▶ **Closed questions**
These require a simple 'Yes/No' or one-word answer, for instance:

- *'Do you speak a foreign language?'*
- *'Was your grade in Maths at pass or honours level?'*

They can sometimes be useful if you need to fill in factual gaps in the interviewee's application. Otherwise, they should be avoided.

▶ **Probing questions**
Probing (or focusing) questions are used when you want to enquire more deeply into something the interviewee has said. For example:

- *'You mentioned earlier that you feel you are not sufficiently challenged by your current job. Could you elaborate on this?'*

▶ **Situational questions**

In this type of question you describe a hypothetical situation that might arise in the job and ask the interviewee how she would respond.

- *'You appreciate that part of your responsibility will be overseeing security in the shop. Suppose you see a customer putting an article of clothing into a bag and suspect that the customer is shoplifting. How would you deal with this?'*

The kinds of questions to avoid are:

- leading questions
- discriminatory questions.

▶ **Leading questions**

These suggest the desired response to the interviewee and therefore give little useful information. For example:

- *'In this job you will have to deal with some difficult clients. Do you think you can cope with this?'*

The interviewee is unlikely to give a negative answer to this question!

▶ **Discriminatory questions**

Any questions which may disadvantage the candidate on grounds of gender, colour, etc. are discriminatory and should not be asked. For example, it is wrong to ask interviewees about their political beliefs or marital plans. Job applicants are now protected by quite stringent equal opportunities legislation and employers need to be aware of this.

All questions should be clearly phrased and carefully articulated. You should not have to repeat a question because you have worded it badly, mumbled or inadvertently asked three questions in one. Some interviewers deliberately ask multiple questions to see how the interviewee will react, but there is no real justification for using this tactic.

Furthermore, you should aim to cover the same ground in roughly the same order with each candidate. It is unsettling for candidates when questions hop from one topic to another without any apparent reason. As was seen above, a common approach in interviewing is to use a biographical sequence. For example, when interviewing a young school leaver, you could deal with the following areas in the order indicated: home circumstances, school and examination results, part-time work experience, perception of the job, ambitions, initiative, social activities and interests, health.

At the same time there should be a degree of flexibility. No two interviews follow exactly the same course, so you should be prepared to alter the pattern of each interview to suit the individual case. Important leads should be followed up even if it means that other areas have to be given less attention. For example, if it appears from the interviewee's application form that she has had several jobs over a short period of time, then obviously you must find out the reason why. This issue would not arise at all, however, in the case of an interviewee who has had only one job since leaving school.

LISTENING AND RECORDING

Clearly, good listening skills are an essential component of the interviewer's repertoire. First, it is important to give the interviewee an opportunity to think about her answers. As there are no obvious answers to open-ended questions, a candidate will need time to marshal her thoughts and decide what to say. An inexperienced interviewer who is embarrassed by silence may be tempted to jump in with a rephrased question when an immediate reply is not forthcoming.

When the answer comes you should listen to it with care. Look interested in what the interviewee is telling you and give encouragement to continue by nodding, smiling, etc. Be alert for remarks that require further elucidation. For instance, if an interviewee tells you that she has little opportunity for social activities because of having to care for a dependant you may want to find out how this responsibility will affect the candidate's job performance. Look out also for interviewees who give you false or inconsistent information or who waffle to disguise weaknesses in their application.

It is essential to take some notes even though it may be difficult to do this unobtrusively. Wait for the appropriate moment and then make a brief record of any point you wish to remember. Avoid scribbling frantically while the interviewee is speaking or immediately after an awkward or embarrassing episode has taken place.

MANAGING THE INTERVIEW

Since candidates need to be on their best behaviour the job of managing an interview can be relatively easy. Nevertheless, some candidates can cause problems, either deliberately or inadvertently. They may tend to talk too much, for example, or attempt to take over the interview. In these situations, the interviewer needs to exercise control in a skilled and diplomatic way.

If an interviewee wanders off the point or talks at too great a length on one subject, do not interrupt rudely. Instead, draw the person back to the other area you want to discuss by introductory phrases such as, *'Perhaps we could return to . . .'*, *'I was very interested in your remark about . . .'*, or *'Good . . . now, I wonder if we could move on to . . .'*.

Do not be tempted to argue with interviewees who hold opinions opposed to your own. By all means, challenge anyone who is expressing superficial opinions or using unsound argument. Test a good candidate by putting forward counterarguments or illustrations to see how she can defend her position, but do not use the interview as a vehicle for converting interviewees who appear to you to be misled on certain issues.

Do not be tempted, either, into criticising interviewees who are obviously weak. A remark such as *'Don't you think you should have found out a bit more about the job before coming to see us?'* can turn a stumbling interviewee into a sullen and unresponsive one. Some interviewers – no doubt with the best intentions – try to give poor candidates advice either on interview technique or on their choice of career. This is almost always a mistake. The interviewee immediately perceives that she failed the interview and, with the disappointment that follows that realisation, is unlikely to pay much attention to the interviewer's advice anyway. Besides, interview skills training and career guidance lie outside the interviewer's proper sphere of competence. You are there for no other purpose than to judge the suitability of applicants for a particular job.

BRINGING THE INTERVIEW TO A CLOSE

Towards the end of the interview give interviewees a chance to ask questions of their own or give you any further information they think is relevant. Normally they will ask about the company or the nature of the job and you should answer honestly. Finally, tell them anything else they need to know – for instance, how many candidates have been shortlisted, when they will be told the results of the interview and so on. Do not make any comment on an individual's performance, however. You cannot know whether she has been successful until you have seen all the other candidates.

Try to end each interview within the allotted time. If you spend an inordinate amount of time with one candidate you may have to give others less attention than they deserve. When the interviewee has left the room fill in the assessment form and write up your report immediately. If there are other panellists a short discussion of the candidate's merits should follow. (Time for this should always be allowed in the interview schedule.)

After all the candidates have been interviewed your final task is to weigh up the merits and demerits of each as objectively as you can and decide who is most suitable for the job. An offer of the job, subject to the usual medical examination and satisfactory references, can then be made to the successful person.

APPLYING FOR JOBS

So far we have considered the selection process from the employer's point of view; let us now consider the process from the job seeker's perspective. Jobs do not come easily. In fact, getting a job requires a great deal of planning and effort, even in areas of employment where demand exceeds supply. In this section we look at the first steps in job hunting: finding out about jobs and putting in applications.

INFORMATION ABOUT JOBS

Employers use many different methods of recruitment (the particular choice depends on the nature of the job, the size of the firm, whether the job is temporary or permanent, etc.), so be prepared to look in different places for the job you want.

- **Press advertisements**

  The press, which includes national newspapers, local newspapers and specialist magazines, carries thousands of job ads every day.

- **Personal contact**

  Many employers recruit locally by 'word of mouth'. Knowing someone who works in the industry is often the best way to find out about a job.

- **Employment Services Offices**

  FÁS, the Irish Training and Employment Authority, runs a country-wide network of Employment Services Offices. These centres provide a range of services for job seekers, including up-to-date lists of job vacancies. (FÁS also publishes an online job bank on its website at www.fas.ie.)

- **Employment agencies**

  Employment agencies are private businesses which engage in recruitment for client companies. They are often used when the company wants to fill temporary positions or to 'headhunt' for senior posts.

- **Internet-based recruitment**

  Increasingly, large companies use their websites to advertise job vacancies and invite candidates to apply online. Some systems ask applicants to send their CVs via e-mail, while others provide a standardised online application form. Vacancies may also be found on the growing number of websites that specialise in recruitment.

- **Career officers**

  Many schools and colleges, or college departments, provide a career advice service.

- **Unsolicited applications**

  It can be worthwhile making contact with organisations where you would like to work and sending them your CV 'on spec'. Employers do actually check unsolicited applications when they have vacancies.

The job advertisement

If you are attracted by a job advertisement it is important to analyse the ad carefully for clues about the job and the type of candidate required. As a general rule, small classified ads are used for recruiting junior staff. Notice how the ad below gives much precise information in under thirty words.

Exhibit 17.3   Job advertisement (small classified)

> **Secretary** required, 1–2 years' experience, excellent computer and dictaphone skills essential, legal background desirable. Reply with CV to Barret & Lowe, Solrs, 4 Lagan Crescent, Cork.

Display advertisements (Exhibit 17.4) are used when managerial, professional or senior secretarial positions have to be filled. Such advertisements are aimed not only at those who are actively seeking jobs but at those who are successful in their present positions and who may not yet have made a conscious decision to move.

Exhibit 17.4   Job advertisement (display)

> ### SECRETARY/PERSONAL ASSISTANT
>
> Alpha Computers Ltd, an Irish-owned computer software company with an outstanding record of growth since its formation in 1990, invites applications for the post of secretary/PA to the marketing manager.
>
> Applicants should be Chartered Secretaries with at least five years' experience in the commercial sector.
>
> This is a senior appointment and the successful candidate will be expected to carry out a wide range of professional duties with a minimum of supervision.
>
> Excellent communication skills and qualities of drive and enthusiasm will be essential requirements.
>
> An attractive salary and benefits package will be offered to the right person.
>
> Apply with full curriculum vitae to the
> **Marketing Manager, Alpha Computers Ltd, Shannon, Co. Clare.**

You can gather a great deal about the job from a close reading of this advertisement. The company sees itself as a dynamic, forward-looking organisation and will look for candidates who reflect this. The job requires experience so the company will not be interested in someone straight out of school or college. As well as being qualified, candidates will need to give evidence of flexibility, enthusiasm and the ability to take responsibility on their own. They will be expected to demonstrate excellent communication skills.

If you read a job advertisement (carefully!), feel you meet the criteria the recruiter has set and are interested in applying, the next step is to produce an effective CV and covering letter.

Curriculum vitae (CV)

The curriculum vitae is a summary of your personal details, education, work experience, interests and achievements. It should have a neat, attractive layout and give information in a clear, logical sequence. An example is given in Exhibit 17.5 below.

Take time with your CV – it is your introduction to a potential employer. Remember the importance of first impressions!

Tips for the CV writer

- Write a rough draft first and revise it thoroughly before deciding what to put in your final draft.
- Use good-quality paper for your final copy. It should be standard A4 size. White is the most common colour although some applicants prefer off-white or a light pastel shade.
- All CVs are typed or printed. Remember – letter quality, not draft. Do not make the document fussy by using several different fonts.
- A CV is a structured document so make effective use of headings and subheadings. Headings of equal value should be set out in the same style.
- Try to begin each page with a new section – the document looks neater as a result.
- Write in a concise, brisk style. Avoid long narrative sections. Try instead to put information in point form.
- Make your CV as verb intensive as possible and avoid the personal pronoun 'I'.
- When describing work experience, highlight the skills and accomplishments you have developed.
- Make the most of your nonwork interests and activities. It is important to show that your horizons are wider than your college courses.

- Avoid exaggeration. As a student you are still relatively young and unproven, so grandiose claims fool no one.
- When you have finished your CV read it carefully for mistakes. Send it off only when you are satisfied that it is absolutely correct.
- Opinions differ on the value of putting covers on CVs. A cover can give the CV a neat appearance, but loose pages are easier to file.

Exhibit 17.5 Curriculum vitae

CURRICULUM VITAE

Personal Details

Name:	Martin Thomas Nugent
Date of birth	14 June 1981
Address	14A Weston Terrace
	Rathmines
	Dublin 6
Telephone	01-123-4567
Mobile	086-765-4321
E-mail	martin.nugent@opal.ie

Education and Qualifications

	B.Sc. (Management), 2000–2004, Dublin Business Institute
Final year subjects	Corporate Finance, Strategic Management, Management Accounting, Economics, Marketing
Dissertation topic	'Developing brand awareness in the retail sector'
Degree classification	Upper second class honours
	Leaving Certificate, 1994–2000, St Joseph's Presentation College, Navan, Co. Meath
Higher level	Mathematics (B2), English (B2), Business Organisation (B1), Accounting (C1), Geography (C2)
Lower level	Irish (B1), Physics (C1)

Work Experience

Summer 2004	Sales Supervisor, Sports Dept, Arnolds plc, Dublin 1 Responsible for customer service, stock control and supervising junior staff.
Summer 2003	Call Centre Assistant, Eircom, Dublin Giving technical assistance via telephone, leading a small technical support team.
Summer 2002	Sales Assistant, Lifesports, Dublin 6

Achievements and Interests

College	Captain of DIT Gaelic football team. Secretary of college branch of AIESEC, the international association for business studies students. Attended AIESEC conventions in Sweden (2002) and Spain (2003).
School	School prefect (1998–1999). Played in Leinster Schools Cup in Gaelic football.
Other interests	Keen swimmer, holder of Red Cross First Aid Certificate, completed European Computer Driving Licence (ECDL).
Skills profile	*Teamworking*: Acquired through work experience and group projects in college. *Leadership*: Responsible for supervising small groups of staff and leading sports teams. *Communication*: Have given presentations in college and spoken at AIESEC conventions.

Referees

Ms Aoife Lennon, Head of Business Studies, Dublin Business Institute, Ashfield Place, Dublin 2.

Mr Michael McKee, Principal, St Joseph's Presentation College, Navan, Co. Meath.

THE COVERING LETTER

You should always include a covering letter with your CV (see Exhibit 17.6). Everything else being equal it is the covering letter that may tilt the balance in your favour. This letter should be set out with the same care and professionalism as any other form of business correspondence. Normally, it consists of three parts:

- the introduction expresses an interest in the post
- the middle section highlights aspects of your education or experience that you think will appeal to the employer – this is where you get a chance to sell yourself
- the conclusion states that your CV is enclosed and expresses the hope that you will be called for interview.

A covering letter should always be tailored to the particular job you have in mind. Address the letter to a specific individual and make clear why working for the company appeals to you. Highlight your strengths and match them to the job on offer. Show how you would be a valuable addition to the team.

Finally, keep the letter concise (not more than one page) and make sure it is free of errors.

Exhibit 17.6   Covering letter

> 14A Weston Terrace
> Rathmines
> Dublin 6
>
> 5 September 2004
>
> Ms Jean Harman
> Head of Human Resources
> Acton Stores Ltd
> Cabinteely
> Dublin 18
>
> Dear Ms Harman,
>
> I wish to apply for the post of trainee manager as advertised in the *Sunday Journal* of 1 September 2004. My ambition is to pursue a career in retail management and I believe that my academic and other experience has enabled me to develop skills and abilities of particular value to your company.
>
> In June of this year I successfully completed the course leading to the B.Sc. (Management) degree at the Dublin Business Institute, graduating with upper second class honours. This course is practical in orientation and gives an excellent grounding in all business subjects. My particular interest was in the field of marketing and I examined the subject of retailer brands in my final year dissertation.

While at college I had ample opportunity to develop good teamwork, communication and leadership skills. As well as captaining the college Gaelic football team, I was an active member of AIESEC, the international association for business studies students. These interests enabled me to travel abroad and become involved in many promotional and organisational activities.

My work experience has given me a good insight into supervisory management and customer relations. I particularly enjoyed my most recent part-time work in Arnold's department store, as this introduced me to a busy city-centre retail environment.

I would like to be considered for the post on offer and enclose a copy of my curriculum vitae as you requested. I am available for interview at any suitable time and look forward to hearing from you.

Yours sincerely,
Martin Nugent

The 'standout' candidate

Mark McCormack has been credited with inventing the field of sport management. Here is what he has to say about covering letters.

'In my experience, the cover letter that accompanies the résumé (CV) is a far more revealing document, and a better indicator of a candidate's worthiness. Résumés, by definition, are generic. They adhere to a rigid format, and after so much massaging and polishing, they totally lack any personality. They could belong to anyone.

'Cover letters, on the other hand, require some ingenuity. That's where the standout candidates actually stand out.'

Source: McCormack, 1996: 148

APPLICATION FORMS

Sometimes you will be required to fill in an application form instead of sending a CV. This, too, should be approached with care. The information given should be accurate, complete and well presented. An application form spoiled by mistakes or crossing out creates a bad impression and may cause the application to be rejected. The tips below should help you to avoid mistakes.

- Make one or two copies of the application form and fill these in first before copying the information onto the form itself.
- Information can be either handwritten or typewritten. Always write in black – never in red or in pencil. Make sure handwriting is neat and legible.

- Look out for sections that have to be completed in BLOCK capitals.
- Fill in all sections. If a particular section does not apply to you write the words 'Not applicable'.
- Write in straight lines. Placing a lined page under the form can act as a simple but effective guide. Do not overrun the spaces provided.
- Outline your most recent experience at college or work first, as it is most relevant.
- Usually there is space provided at the end for 'Additional information'. Use this to highlight 'selling points' not already covered in the other sections.
- When you have completed the form, check it thoroughly for mistakes in spelling and expression.
- It is a good idea to include a short covering letter as you would with a CV.

FACING THE INTERVIEW

Let us assume that you have submitted your application and have recently received a letter calling you for interview. You probably feel apprehensive. There is nothing unusual about this since most interviewees, even those with considerable experience, regard interviews as an ordeal. You can still do yourself justice if you approach the interview in the right way. Here are some suggestions on how to proceed.

BEFORE THE INTERVIEW

- Reread the advertisement and any other information about the job that the company has sent you.
- Find out as much as you can about the company and the nature of the job from other sources. You may be able to obtain information from the company's website or promotional literature, your career guidance officer, your local library, etc. If possible, speak to someone who either works in the company or does similar work elsewhere.
- Keep yourself well informed about recent developments in the area of business concerned by reading the relevant specialist magazines and newsletters, e.g. *Irish Computer*, *Accountancy Ireland*, *Business and Finance*, *Banking Ireland*, etc. In addition, read at least one of the national newspapers regularly to keep yourself up to date with current affairs.
- Organise any documents you wish to take to the interview. If you want to show projects etc. as evidence of your ability, make sure the material is of good standard and well presented. A shabby folder containing a few scraps of dog-eared paper will not improve your chances of success.

- Think about possible questions. Be prepared, at least, for 'old reliables' such as 'Why have you applied for this post?' or 'What do you think you have to offer this company?'
- Think up questions of your own. Asking the interviewer about opportunities for training or promotion will make a favourable impression.
- Make your travel plans with the aim of arriving at the place of interview in good time.

On the day of the interview

- Take care with your appearance. In particular, make sure that you have tidy hair, clean fingernails, neat clothes and shoes that are not in need of repair.
- Set out for the interview with time to spare and arrive punctually.
- Try to relax if you have to wait some time before the interview begins. Do not be overawed by other interviewees who appear to be knowledgeable and self-assured. Underneath their show of bravado they are probably just as nervous as you.

During the interview

- The interviewer will be assessing you as soon as you enter the interview room, so from the outset give an impression of good manners and quiet confidence. Greet the interviewer with a smile and a firm handshake. Move to the chair that has been placed for you and sit in a comfortable but alert position.
- Listen carefully to each question as it is put to you. As we have seen, skilled interviewers usually ask open questions, so be prepared to answer at length. If a question is difficult, take time to think out what you want to say.
- Speak as clearly as you can. Avoid slangy expressions and fillers such as 'you know', 'well', 'um', 'ah'.
- Emphasise the positive aspects of your career but do not be afraid to discuss mistakes you have made in the past. Usually, there is no advantage in trying to cover weaknesses by telling lies.
- Do not become agitated or defensive if the interviewer is more aggressive in her questioning than you had anticipated. She may be anxious to probe further into areas of your career or aspects of your personality that are still puzzling or want to see how you react under pressure. Perhaps the interviewer is simply morose by nature. Whatever the motives, you should stay calm and respond thoughtfully and politely.
- Equally, do not relax too much if the interviewer appears to be friendly and sympathetic. This may be a deliberate tactic to get you off your guard.

- Convey enthusiasm for the work on offer in everything you say. An employer will not be interested in you if your commitment is only half hearted.
- At the end of the interview thank the interviewer for having seen you.

AFTER THE INTERVIEW

Look back and try to make an honest appraisal of your performance. Were there any stages in the interview when you felt you made the wrong impression? Were there questions you had difficulty in answering? Did the interviewer show up weaknesses in your preparation that you need to work on before the next interview? Could you perhaps strengthen your curriculum vitae by obtaining an additional qualification or by making better use of the opportunities in your present job?

If you fail the interview you will inevitably feel disappointed and suffer some loss of confidence, but do not be too despondent. You can turn this setback to advantage if you are willing to learn from experience.

If you succeed – congratulations!

Spotlight on Irish Business – KPMG

Assessing candidates for graduate recruitment

KPMG is a leading provider of business advisory services to national and international clients operating in all sectors of the Irish economy. Every year the company recruits over 150 graduates to join them as trainee accountants, the majority of whom pursue the Association of Chartered Accountants (ACA) qualification. KPMG places a great deal of resources behind ensuring that trainees succeed in their professional exams and develop broader business skills.

The key goal of the selection process at KPMG is to establish how well candidates match the roles for which they have applied. Each candidate is assessed against a graduate competency framework, which values:

- **Personal effectiveness**: Are you committed and motivated to achieving challenging goals?
- **Teamwork**: Can you co-operate with others and contribute to a team atmosphere?
- **Communication**: Can you express your ideas clearly, convincingly and effectively?
- **Client relationships**: Do you respond promptly and professionally to client requests?

- **Business awareness:** Can you demonstrate a broad understanding of business issues?
- **Leadership:** Are you prepared to take the lead?
- **Problem solving and innovation:** Do you consider all relevant factors when making decisions?
- **Task management:** Do you plan, prioritise and prepare?
- **Career motivation:** Have you considered your own personal career goals in depth?

Candidates have the opportunity to demonstrate their competencies in these areas across four assessment stages: application form, first interview, selection exercise and second interview.

Application form

All graduate candidates are required to complete an application form. This form explores the candidate's educational and vocational background, career motivation and leadership/business skills.

First interview

The first interview focuses on the assessment of personal attributes and is conducted by a manager in the firm. The broad purpose of this interview is to establish rapport with the candidate and explore the information on the application form. The interviewer will identify areas for further exploration at the second interview and promote KPMG as an employer.

Selection exercise

Graduates are also asked to undertake a selection exercise designed to measure more accurately and objectively the following competencies:

- task management
- business awareness
- thinking skills
- communication skills.

It is important to KPMG that candidates find this exercise stimulating, interesting and fun. The style and tone of the exercise sends key messages about KPMG and the roles for which the candidates are applying.

Second interview

The second interview is conducted by a partner or senior director with the firm. The interview provides an opportunity for personal contact and rapport-building between the candidate and a senior member of staff. At the interview, the selection exercise is assessed and areas of concern raised at the first interview are explored in more depth.

KPMG offers the following advice on the interview process.

Tips on application form
- Make sure to meet the submission deadline.
- Ensure the form is written neatly and legibly (or type the form online where possible).
- Give all answers equal attention.
- Keep a copy of the form.

Tips on CV preparation
- Keep the CV to two pages in length.
- Use correct spelling and punctuation.
- Be consistent, e.g. use the same style for dates and headings.
- Use good-quality paper.
- Keep it simple. There is no need for presentation folders or fancy binding – a staple is fine.
- If posting, use correct postage.

Interview tips
- Read up on firm literature (brochure/website).
- Reread your application form/CV.
- Prepare some questions.
- Speak to acquaintances within the firm.
- Enjoy it! The interview process is not a test – it is as much about you getting to know the firm as it is about the firm getting to know you.

ASSIGNMENTS

REVISION

1. Give reasons for the popularity of the interview as a selection device.
2. Write short accounts of the following types of job interviews: (a) biographical interview (b) structured interview (c) behavioural interview.
3. What preparations should the interviewer make prior to conducting the interview?
4. Describe simple steps that can be taken to build rapport with the candidate and ease him or her into the interview.

5. Define and give examples of the following types of questions: (a) open question (b) closed question (c) probing question (d) situational question.
6. 'The interview should be structured, yet flexible.' Elaborate on this comment.
7. Why are listening and note-taking skills important in an interview?
8. What advice would you give on *managing* the interview?
9. List five sources of information about jobs.
10. Why is it important to read the job advertisement carefully?
11. Set out guidelines for either (a) writing a curriculum vitae or (b) filling in an application form.
12. What are the main functions of a covering letter?
13. How should an interviewee prepare for a job interview?
14. You have a friend who is shortly to go for her first interview before a selection board. She is anxious to make a good impression. What advice would you give her?

FOR DISCUSSION

1. Share your experiences of job interviews. How was the interview organised? What kind of questions were asked? Was there anything unusual about the way the interview was conducted?
2. What criticisms would you make of the interview as a selection method? Can you think of any methods not mentioned in this chapter that might be more effective?
3. One-to-one or panel interviews: which do you favour and why?
4. 'You should always tell the truth in an interview.' Do you agree?
5. 'Interviews always favour the extroverted and articulate candidate at the expense of the quieter candidate.' Do you think this is true?
6. 'It's the unusual application that stands out and gets you noticed.' What is your view of this?

EXERCISES AND ACTIVITIES

1. Find out about the services offered for young job seekers by your local FÁS office. Report back to the group.
2. Assume that you are applying for the job advertised below *with your current experience*. Write the covering letter that will accompany your application.

NATIONAL BANK

Junior Bank Official – Frontline Customer Services

National Bank is a leading provider of financial services in Ireland. We are committed to providing the highest level of customer service and are looking for confident individuals who can excel in a customer-oriented work environment.

National Bank offers a rewarding career in which there will be opportunity for continuous learning and development within the organisation.

The ideal candidate for the above position will have the following characteristics:

▶ confidence and enthusiasm
▶ good teamwork skills
▶ the ability to work to deadlines
▶ good communication and interpersonal skills
▶ strong PC skills.

Please submit your application to Ms Sandra Baker, Personnel Office, National Bank, Grand Canal Street, Dublin 4 to arrive *not later than 5:00 pm, Friday 24 March.*

3. Consider holding mock interviews based on the above advertisement or on an advertisement you have chosen from a newspaper. First, draw up an interview plan. For example, decide how the interview should be conducted, how long it should last, what questions should be asked. Then role-play the interviews with some members of the group playing the interviewer(s) and some the interviewees.

4. Invite businesspeople or professionals from outside the school or college to conduct mock interviews. Participants should apply and attend the interview as if dealing with a real job. If possible, video the interviews for discussion and analysis.

5. Organise a careers seminar at which you invite potential employers in the local community or in a particular industrial sector to speak about job opportunities, industry requirements and so on. You will need the active support of your school or college if you wish to undertake this project.

6. Organise a trip to a local factory or plant to gain an insight into the work environment.

A NOTE ON THE APPENDICES

As we saw in Chapter 7, written communication may fail because the writer has chosen the wrong style. However, there may be a more fundamental reason why the writing is poor. The writer may simply be ignorant of or uncertain about the basic elements of punctuation and grammar. The aim of Appendices I, II and III is to help those who are weak in these areas.

These appendices are intended as a reference which you can dip into from time to time. For example, suppose you are unsure about using the apostrophe. You will find rules for the apostrophe in Appendix I on p. 330. You can try the practice pieces and then apply what you have learned in your next essay or assignment. Gradual improvement is better than trying to achieve everything at once.

WHY IS CORRECT USAGE IMPORTANT?

- One practical reason is that you may lose marks in examinations if your basic writing skills are poor. Examiners in English and Communication often deduct marks directly for mistakes in grammar, punctuation, etc. In other subjects, marks may be lost indirectly because the examiner is unable to make complete sense of what you have written. Examiners have to correct many scripts, often under quite severe time pressure. They would be superhuman if they were not influenced to some degree by the fluency (or lack of it) displayed in your writing.

- Poor English can seriously undermine the quality of projects and theses. A very high standard is required in these and mistakes will be noticed. In any case, *printed* mistakes always seem to jump off the page.

- Job applications must be mistake free, otherwise you may be rejected out of hand. An employer may assume that if you are careless in the way you write you will be careless in other things as well. Equally, a flawless application may get you an interview. Businessman Mark McCormack once called an applicant for interview simply because she had taken the trouble to type the correct accents on the word *résumé*.

- Writing at work also has to be mistake free. The kinds of 'howlers' and 'clangers' that amuse and infuriate examiners are just not accepted in business writing.

Remember – it really is worth your while making the effort to improve your English. If you are motivated enough, this is your opportunity to master some or *all* of those mistakes which may have bedevilled your work in the past.

Appendix I: Punctuation

When we speak we can use pauses, intonation, stress, etc. to help convey meaning. These are absent in writing; instead we rely on punctuation, space and other visual devices such as bold or italics.

Twelve punctuation marks are used in English, if we include capitals. Some, such as commas and full stops, are used frequently. Others, such as the colon and semicolon, are needed less often. If you are uncertain about the use of a particular mark, the rules below should help you out. Most of the rules are straightforward and should become second nature if you apply them consistently. You can also try the practice pieces for reinforcement (answers on p. 336).

Full stop (.)

There are three main uses of the full stop (or period).

1. The most important function of the full stop is to mark the end of a sentence (as here).
2. Full stops are also used to mark abbreviations, such as *e.g.*, *i.e.*, *Co.*, *Nov.* However, they are usually left out in abbreviations that begin and end with the same letters as the original words (*Dr*, *Ms*, *Mr*).

   There is also a tendency to leave out full stops in the names of organisations formed from initials (*RTÉ*, *BBC*, *DIT*, *UCD*, *EU*).
3. A series of three full stops indicates that material is being omitted. For instance:

   The consumer . . . needs to be able to make his or her purchases both quickly and economically.

Capital letters

Capital letters mark:

1. The beginning of sentences or passages of direct speech.

   She asked, 'Have you seen this report?'

2.   Proper nouns.

> the Cranberries
>
> Shannon Airport
>
> Co. Laois

3.   The personal pronoun 'I'.
4.   The names of days and months.

> Tuesday, June, September

5.   Titles of newspapers, magazines, books, plays, films, etc. Note, however, that the 'minor' words in titles (prepositions and articles) are capitalised only when they appear at the beginning.

> *Pride and Prejudice*
> *The Catcher in the Rye*
> *Of Mice and Men*

Hint

If you find it difficult to distinguish between proper and common nouns, remember that a proper noun refers to a *specific* person, place or thing. You do not use capital letters when a *general* meaning is intended. For example:

The role of the marketing manager today is a complex one.

Traffic through Irish airports is expected to increase by six per cent next year.

Practice 1

Rewrite the following passages, putting in full stops and capitals as appropriate.

1.   mr and mrs murphy walked slowly away from their house in dorset street.
2.   i am in my mother's room it is i who live there now i don't know how i got there perhaps in an ambulance certainly a vehicle of some kind i was helped i'd never have got there alone
3.   kerry beat a well-regarded cork side in the munster final however this particular laois side has never lost at croke park furthermore these sides met three times in challenges laois won one match in killarney easily the other two were drawn
4.   oasis have landed at a time when there are many more distractions then it was just rock 'n' roll and movies now it is mtv, cd-rom, the world wide web and whatever you are having yourself the brilliance of oasis is that they managed to get to the top despite that

COMMA (,)

Commas are used:

1. To separate items in a list.

    For the meeting we will need pens, notepaper, name cards and some light refreshments.

    He introduced himself, made a brief statement, answered a few questions and then left.

2. To mark off a word or phrase that is inserted into a sentence to give additional information. Such a phrase is said to be *in parenthesis*. It can be removed without destroying the grammatical completeness of the sentence.

    I am afraid that, due to circumstances beyond our control, the festival will have to be cancelled.

    No one, I feel sure, could have done better.

    'I believe,' said the county manager, 'that we have now reached a decision.'

    The offer, nevertheless, should be accepted.

3. To follow initial words and phrases such as *however* (in the sense of 'nevertheless'), *in fact, first, next, of course*, etc.

    In fact, these figures are quite misleading.

    Next, let us consider the importance of body language.

    National sales have fallen; however, the overseas market has continued to grow this year.

    But However promising this seems, the company cannot afford to be complacent.

4. To mark off thousands in large numbers.

    €15,000
    €3,500
    13,000-mile border

PRACTICE 2

Insert commas where appropriate in the following sentences.

1. To gain access to the Internet you need a PC a telephone a modem and an account with a service provider.

2. There is strong evidence that an exploding star a supernova provided the material from which the Earth is made.
3. The third question which is the most searching one by far will take a little longer to answer.
4. Paul said that all being well he would visit the following week.
5. Nevertheless we managed to make a profit of €35400.

And finally a more difficult one:

6. Down the Pacific coastline in Mountain View California James Barksdale president of Netscape was bracing for another day of standing in Bill Gates's way. Barksdale slipped into a suit grabbed a quick breakfast and pointed his Mercedes towards Netscape's Mountain View headquarters.

APOSTROPHE

Few features of writing get so much attention and cause so much trouble as the apostrophe. Letter writers to quality newspapers regularly complain that 'no one knows how to use the apostrophe nowadays'. Indeed, it is not unusual to come across glossy brochures and sales letters, obviously produced at great expense, but spoiled by misuse of this simple punctuation mark.

In fact, the rules governing the apostrophe are fairly straightforward. It has two clear-cut uses.

1. It indicates possession or relationship. In singular nouns the apostrophe is placed before the *s*. In plural nouns, it is placed after the *s*.

   the speaker's notes   a year's supply   (one speaker, one year)
   the speakers' notes   five years' supply   (more than one speaker, year)

   Note that *irregular* plurals are treated as singular: *men, women* and *children* are the most obvious examples.

   the children's toys
   women's magazines

2. It indicates where letters have been omitted in contracted words.

   can't (cannot)
   shouldn't (should not)
   he'll (he will)

Now, some **don'ts**!

1. Possessive pronouns do **not** have apostrophes (mine, yours, his, hers, its, ours, yours, theirs).

Yours sincerely (**not** Your's sincerely)
The company is writing to its shareholders (**not** it's shareholders)

2. Do not confuse the possessive *its* and *whose* with the contractions *it's* (short for it is/has) and *who's* (short for who is/has).

3. Do not use the apostrophe in the plurals of abbreviated words.

New PCs are coming down in price.
Five TDs were absent.

4. Do not insert an apostrophe into names ending in s.

Dickens's novels (**not** Dicken's novels)

Practice 3

A few years ago the Superquinn chain offered a free bottle of wine to every customer who found a misplaced apostrophe on any notice in its stores. Which of the following sentences have an unnecessary apostrophe?

1. You should never judge a book by it's cover. *its*
2. Have you heard the story about Sean's car? *Seans*
3. It's obvious that a mistake has been made.
4. I like your collection of CD's. *CDs*
5. Our leading brand has maintained it's share of the market. *its*
6. The two front runner's are well clear of the rest of the field. *runners*
7. 'The Wild Swans at Coole' is one of my favourite Yeat's poems.
8. You can't beat a good night's sleep.
9. We will have to take account of these new provisions in the Company's Act.
10. *Revolver* is the best of the Beatles' albums. *Beatles't*

Semicolon (;)

The semicolon is a valuable punctuation mark that should be used more often. It represents a stronger pause than a comma, but something less than a full stop. It can be used:

1. In place of a conjunction to join units of thought that are closely connected in meaning.

We are pleased with results this year; there has been a steady rise in production and net profit has more than doubled.

2. To balance ideas in a sentence and often to express a contrast.

You are obviously in favour of this project; we, however, have grave doubts about it.

3. To separate long phrases in a list, particularly where some of the phrases contain commas of their own.

> The spare room is furnished with a settee; two armchairs, one of which is in poor condition; a small table; and a solid pine bookcase.

COLON (:)

The most common use of the colon is to 'flag' that something such as an explanation, a list or a quotation is to follow.

> The reason for the upturn in the economy is obvious: the increase in house prices is restoring consumer confidence.

> We can provide the following services at very reasonable rates: plumbing, tiling, plastering and carpentry.

The colon is also used to counterpoise two sharply contrasting ideas and is often found in short, pithy sayings.

> A quick temper causes strife: a soft answer turns away wrath.

PRACTICE 4

Insert commas, colons and semicolons in the following sentences where appropriate.

1. Remember to take the following a sleeping bag a torch sandwiches and a change of clothing.
2. Man proposes God disposes.
3. I am reminded of the line from Kavanagh 'O commemorate me where there is water . . .'.
4. I can take you only as far as the gate once there you will have to find your own way.
5. There were several reasons for the unofficial strike at the factory first the company did not honour its agreement with the union second the supervisors had received no formal training and were ill equipped to handle the employees third the union members were apathetic and did not attend union meetings and fourth the shop stewards were militant and excessively powerful.

DASH (–)

The dash separates units in a sentence, but does so in a more dramatic way than the comma or semicolon. It often suggests something added to the sentence as an afterthought. It should be used sparingly in formal business writing.

1. Two dashes are used to mark off a phrase that unexpectedly or awkwardly interrupts the flow of a sentence.

   This project – thankfully, we are not involved in it – will cause nothing but trouble.

2. A single dash is used to introduce a summarising remark after a series or list.

   Intelligence, patience, common sense – these are the signs of a good chairperson.

3. A single dash is also used to introduce and highlight a new idea at the end of a sentence.

   Our representatives can call to your home with samples – and all estimates are free!

A roof with a view

The following excerpt taken from Dylan Thomas's *Portrait of the Artist as a Young Dog* shows how the use of dashes, commas and semicolons can help give shape and meaning to a very long sentence. The passage describes four young boys and their first view of the field where they are to spend a camping holiday.

Leading down from the gate, there was a lane to the first beach. It was high tide, and we heard the sea dashing. Four boys on a roof – one tall, dark, regular featured, precise of speech, in a good suit, a boy of the world; one squat, ungainly, red-haired, his red wrists fighting out of short, flayed sleeves; one heavily spectacled, short-paunched, with indoor shoulders and feet in always unlaced boots wanting to go different ways; one small, thin, indecisively active, quick to get dirty, curly – saw their field in front of them, a fortnight's new home that had thick pricking hedges for walls, the sea for a front garden, a green gutter for a lavatory, and a wind-struck tree in the very middle.

Of course, this style is not recommended for business writing. (The long sentence contains 101 words.)

BRACKETS ( )

Brackets are used when you want to interrupt the sentence to explain, define, give an example or translate what has gone before.

Only three sizes (B1, B2 and B3) are now available.

A *bit* (short for *binary digit*) is the basic building block of computer memory.

When buying second-hand, remember the saying *Caveat emptor* (Let the buyer beware).

Note that when a complete sentence is enclosed in brackets the full stop is placed *inside* the brackets. When a sentence ends with a bracketed phrase the full stop is placed *outside* the brackets, as in the last example above.

PRACTICE 5

Where would you use dashes or brackets in the following sentences?
1. To retrieve a file you need an FTP file transfer protocol.
2. I'm told that Jim can you believe this has just taken a year's leave of absence.
3. Jewellery, watches, cash, antiques all these were stolen.
4. *Festina lente* 'Hasten slowly' is good advice.

HYPHEN (-)

The hyphen is shorter than the dash and is used to join rather than separate.
1. The main use of the hyphen is to link the parts of compound words:

> ex-directory
> anti-pollutant
> accident-prone

Over time, many hyphenated words drop the hyphen as they become more established. There is no general rule that will tell you which compound words require hyphens, so it is best to consult a dictionary if you are unsure.
2. A second use of the hyphen is to divide a word at the end of a line. The division should be made where there is a natural break in the word.

> Indent-ure **not** inde-nture

Words of one syllable, no matter how long, cannot be divided, e.g. through, bought.

QUESTION MARK (?)

A question mark follows a direct question only.

> Who called while I was away? (Direct)
> **But** She asked who called while she was away. (Indirect)

Note that the question mark contains a full stop and therefore should nearly always be followed by a capital letter.

Students should be wary of using direct questions in exams. It is all too easy to string together a series of questions without either question marks or capitals. For example:

When writing you should always ask who are my readers? what do they know about the subject, what are their priorities.

Change this to:

When writing you should ask the following: who are my readers? What do they know about the subject? What are their priorities?

EXCLAMATION MARK (!)

The exclamation mark is used to express surprise, alarm, excitement or irony. Like the dash, it should be used sparingly. It is probably most at home in advertising copy.

Kellogg's Golden Crisp . . . the ultimate breakfast experience!
(Well, they would say that, wouldn't they!)

PRACTICE 6

Insert a hyphen, question mark or exclamation mark in each of the following sentences (or sentence groups).
1. In the back street they found a little frequented restaurant
2. Eilis is a happy go lucky person
3. What is mind what is matter how does one influence the other
4. What a lucky break
5. We met many English speaking people in India
6. I can't believe it
7. It's time to switch on the Christmas tree lights
8. Is it a one or two horse race

INVERTED COMMAS (')

Inverted commas, also known as *speech marks* or *quotation marks*, have three main uses.
1. They enclose quotations and direct speech.

Remember the saying, 'A picture is worth a thousand words.'

2. They mark off the titles of articles, poems and short stories. However, the titles of books, plays and other longer works should be displayed using underscoring in type and italics in print.

I particularly like 'The Swing' in Seamus Heaney's collection, *The Spirit Level*.

3. They indicate that a word is being used merely as a word or that it is different

in tone from the rest of the sentence.

'Brown bread' is rhyming slang for 'dead'.

It is now common practice to use single rather than double inverted commas, although there is no hard and fast rule about this. Double inverted commas can be used to mark a quotation within a quotation.

PRACTICE 7

Punctuate the following sentences. Use inverted commas where needed.

1. Have you a copy of Consuelo O Connors book The View From the Chair
2. What exactly does the phrase turned on mean
3. He stated his main theme in the following words this party will not be re-elected until it becomes a united party
4. The doctor told Maria you must rest for a week at least
5. Siobhán asked what did he mean when he said tread softly
6. Did he say I'll be there on Tuesday or I'll be there on Wednesday

PRACTICE 8

Now, some more difficult passages:

1. irish mainport holdings was formed ten years ago the companies in the group provide ship agency services ship booking warehousing road transport and air freight the head office in cork is opposite páirc uí chaoimh the new office in dublin is opposite croke park im very interested in the gaa remarks general manager finbarr roynane

    he is bemused by the hostile reception he has received in dublin its quite funny really he says dublin used to come down to cork and do what we call brass-plating they would have no investment locally when they got work from a shipping company they would bring people down from dublin to do it now they are crying foul when a corkman lands in the market.

2. giving flowers for special occasions has become very popular people are now sending cards for many other occasions besides birthdays anniversaries and mothers day

    because of the expansion in the flower business the flower industry represents a growth industry in employment working in floristry offers plenty of variety a real opportunity to be creative and a chance to meet people from all walks of life

    retail selling is a basic part of the work but some of the other things a fully trained florist might do include the following decorating churches halls and sometimes private houses designing wedding bouquets making flower and plant arrangements for banks and offices and visiting flower growers and markets very high standards and much experience are required to cope successfully with such a wide range of work

3. girls attending notre dame secondary school in churchtown are examining aspects of the political system here as part of a project theyre doing for the council of europe in may along with schoolchildren from fourteen other nations but they have to raise the money to get there themselves so far weve raised about €3000 but we need €7000 altogether says the schools vice principal weve been holding coffee mornings video games and so on besides weve had gifts from individual people and local concerns

ANSWERS

PRACTICE 1

1. Mr and Mrs Murphy walked slowly away from their house in Dorset Street.
2. I am in my mother's room. It is I who live there now. I don't know how I got there. Perhaps in an ambulance, certainly a vehicle of some kind. I was helped. I'd never have got there alone. (The opening lines in Samuel Beckett's novel *Molloy*.)
3. Kerry beat a well-regarded Cork side in the Munster final. However, this particular Laois side has never lost at Croke Park. Furthermore, these sides met three times in challenges. Laois won one match in Killarney easily. The other two were drawn.
4. Oasis have landed at a time when there are many more distractions. Then it was just rock 'n' roll and movies. Now it is MTV, CD-ROM, the World Wide Web and whatever you are having yourself. The brilliance of Oasis is that they managed to get to the top despite that.

PRACTICE 2

1. To gain access to the Internet you need a PC, a telephone, a modem and an account with a service provider.
2. There is strong evidence that an exploding star, a supernova, provided the material from which the Earth is made.
3. The third question, which is the most searching one by far, will take a little longer to answer.
4. Paul said that, all being well, he would visit the following week.
5. Nevertheless, we managed to make a profit of €35,400.
6. Down the Pacific coastline, in Mountain View, California, James Barksdale,

president of Netscape, was bracing for another day of standing in Bill Gates's way. Barksdale slipped into a suit, grabbed a quick breakfast and pointed his Mercedes towards Netscape's Mountain View headquarters.

PRACTICE 3

1. You should never judge a book by its cover.
2. Have you heard the story about Sean's car?
3. It's obvious that a mistake has been made.
4. I like your collection of CDs.
5. Our leading brand has maintained its share of the market.
6. The two front runners are well clear of the rest of the field.
7. 'The Wild Swans at Coole' is one of my favourite Yeats poems.
8. You can't beat a good night's sleep.
9. We will have to take account of these new provisions in the Companies Act.
10. *Revolver* is the best of the Beatles' albums.

PRACTICE 4

1. Remember to take the following: a sleeping bag, a torch, sandwiches and a change of clothing.
2. Man proposes: God disposes.
3. I am reminded of the line from Kavanagh: 'O commemorate me where there is water . . .'.
4. I can take you only as far as the gate; once there, you will have to find your own way.
5. There were several reasons for the unofficial strike at the factory: first, the company did not honour its agreement with the union; second, the supervisors had received no formal training and were ill equipped to handle the employees; third, the union members were apathetic and did not attend union meetings; and fourth, the shop stewards were militant and excessively powerful.

PRACTICE 5

1. To retrieve a file you need an FTP (file transfer protocol).
2. I'm told that Jim – can you believe this – has just taken a year's leave of absence.
3. Jewellery, watches, cash, antiques – all these were stolen.
4. *Festina lente* ('Hasten slowly') is good advice.

Practice 6

1. In the back street they found a little-frequented restaurant.
2. Eilis is a happy-go-lucky person.
3. What is mind? What is matter? How does one influence the other?
4. What a lucky break!
5. We met many English-speaking people in India.
6. I can't believe it!
7. It's time to switch on the Christmas-tree lights.
8. Is it a one- or two-horse race?

Practice 7

1. Have you a copy of Consuelo O'Connor's book, *The View from the Chair*?
2. What exactly does the phrase 'turned on' mean?
3. He stated his main theme in the following words: 'This party will not be re-elected until it becomes a united party.'
4. The doctor told Maria, 'You must rest for a week at least.'
5. Siobhán asked, 'What did he mean when he said "tread softly"?'
6. Did he say, 'I'll be there on Tuesday' or 'I'll be there on Wednesday'?

Practice 8

1. Irish Mainport Holdings was formed ten years ago. The companies in the group provide ship agency services, ship booking, warehousing, road transport and air freight. The head office in Cork is opposite Páirc Uí Chaoimh; the new office in Dublin is opposite Croke Park. 'I'm very interested in the GAA,' remarks general manager Finbarr Roynane.

    He is bemused by the hostile reception he has received in Dublin. 'It's quite funny really,' he says, 'Dublin used to come down to Cork and do what we call "brass-plating". They would have no investment locally. When they got work from a shipping company they would bring people down from Dublin to do it. Now, they are crying "Foul!" when a Corkman lands in the market.

2. Giving flowers for special occasions has become very popular. People are now sending cards for many other occasions besides birthdays, anniversaries and Mother's Day.

    Because of the expansion in the flower business, the flower industry represents a growth industry in employment. Working in floristry offers plenty of variety, a real opportunity to be creative and a chance to meet people from all walks of life.

    Retail selling is a basic part of the work, but some of the other things a fully trained florist might do include the following: decorating churches, halls and, sometimes, private houses; designing wedding bouquets; making flower and plant arrangements for banks and offices; and visiting flower growers and markets. Very high standards and much experience are required to cope successfully with such a wide range of work.

3. Girls attending Notre Dame Secondary School in Churchtown are examining aspects of the political system here as part of a project they're doing for the Council of Europe in May along with schoolchildren from fourteen other nations, but they have to raise the money to get there themselves. 'So far, we've raised about €3,000, but we need €7,000 altogether,' says the school's vice-principal. 'We've been holding coffee mornings, video games and so on. Besides, we've had gifts from individual people and local concerns.'

Appendix II: Grammar

The grammar of a language is the set of rules that govern the way it is used. This set of rules is always in a process of change because language is a living thing. Yet the change is gradual, and on the whole the rules remain remarkably stable. This is because they usually have a sound logical basis and when they are broken, meaning becomes ambiguous or obscure.

Whole books are written on grammar, but all that can be attempted here is to highlight some of the areas where mistakes are commonly made.

SUBJECT AND PREDICATE

To be complete, a sentence must consist of two elements: subject and predicate. The subject is the word (or words) that forms the focus of the sentence. The predicate is what is said about the subject.

Subject	Predicate
The boy	ran away from home.
Mary	has got a place at university.
It	rained all day.
The union	agreed to consider the offer.
(You)	Give this to Mr Smith.
(You)	Stop!

Note that the subject is implied in the last two sentences.

A common mistake is to write a sentence in which one or other of these two elements is missing. Take the following example:

An overhead projector is an excellent visual aid. [1] Being cheap, easy to use and flexible. [2]

Sentence [1] is correct, as it has both subject and predicate. Sentence [2] is incorrect. Can you see why?

Practice 1

Which of the following are complete sentences?

√1. Night fell.
2. Be careful!
3. Getting nowhere fast.
4. Thanking you in anticipation.
√ 5. A quick fix.
√6. Could you do me a favour?
7. All in a day's work.
√8. He said he would come on Tuesday.
√9. It being a bank holiday.
√10. Let's see what's happening.

The rule of agreement

Both subject and verb should agree in number, i.e. singular with singular, plural with plural. The verb tells you what the subject is doing.

> The secretary *writes* the minutes. (singular)
> **But** Secretaries *write* minutes. (plural)

Although the rule of agreement is straightforward, it is not always easy to apply in practice. Here are some problem areas.

- **The 'error of attraction'**
  The following sentence illustrates this mistake.

  > The box of groceries were much appreciated.

  Here, the verb is made plural because of its proximity to *groceries*. It should really agree with the singular subject, *box*.

  > The box of groceries was much appreciated.

- **'The news is . . . '**
  Some nouns, although plural in form, are always treated as singular.

  > The news is good today.
  > Maths is a difficult subject.
  > The United States intends to protest to the UN.

- **Collective nouns**
  A collective noun, i.e. a noun denoting a group, is usually treated as singular.

  > The audience appears to be smaller tonight.

Sometimes, however, the meaning of the sentence makes it necessary to consider the group as a collection of individuals.

Normally, the audience leave their coats in the foyer.

Be careful not to treat a collective noun as both singular and plural in the same sentence. It would be a mistake to write:

Having completed *their* work, the committee *was* disbanded.

- **'Each, every . . . '**
  Pronouns such as *each, either, neither* and compounds of *any, every, some* and *no* are singular.

  Either of the jobs is suitable.
  Everyone is invited to the reception.
  What if nobody turns up?

- **'None'**
  There is some doubt as to whether none should be treated as singular or plural. However, in formal contexts it is usually singular (listen to how it is used on news programmes, for example).

  None of the money has been recovered.
  None of the banks is expected to raise interest rates this week.

- **'Fish and chips'**
  Closely related nouns joined by *and* are sometimes thought of as forming a single item.

  Fish and chips is a nutritious meal.

- **The media**
  There is an increasing tendency to consider plurals such as *media* (sing. *medium*) and *data* (sing. *datum*) as singular collective nouns.

  The media is to be congratulated on its handling of the affair.
  The data in this area is not reliable.

Practice 2

The rule of agreement is broken in each of these sentences. Can you see where the mistake is made?
1. This book is one of the best that has been published this year.
2. When the committee was asked for its opinion, it decided to defer the matter until their next meeting.

3. Everyone should accept *his or her* their responsibility for the dispute.
4. Neither of the rooms *was* were completely comfortable.
5. I think none of these colours *is* are suitable.
6. This is one of the plays which *were* was recommended by the critics.
7. The 'Mona Lisa', with other paintings from the Louvre, *was* were sent on loan to the United States.
8. There *were* was only twenty people at the exhibition.
9. Everyone in the college must give *his or her* their assistance.
10. Many applications *were* was received for the course.
11. The value of the books and letters *is* are considerable.
12. Neither the referee nor the umpire *was* were aware of what was going on.

CONSISTENCY

A fundamental rule of grammar is that the same construction should be used consistently throughout the sentence. At best, lack of consistency creates unnecessary 'noise' by upsetting or jarring the reader's expectations. At worst, it makes the writing illogical and confusing.

Here are some particular cases.

1. When the pronouns *you, one, he* or *she* refer to 'everyone in general' they should be used consistently.

   Wrong: One may forget what you have been told.
   Right: One may forget what one has been told.

2. The auxiliary or 'helping' verbs *may, might, could, would*, etc. should be consistent.

   Wrong: I should be grateful if you will . . .
   Right: I should be grateful if you would . . .

3. Be particularly careful not to mix constructions in 'Not only this but that' sentences.

   Wrong: She was not only ambitious but she worked very hard.
   Right: She was not only ambitious but very hard working.

   In the first sentence, the adjective *ambitious* is incorrectly mirrored by a verb (*worked*). In the second sentence it is correctly mirrored by another adjective (*hard working*).

4. Lists can cause problems – indeed, the longer the list the more likely it is to go wrong. Notice how the following sentence breaks down towards the end.

   An efficient system of communication is needed to keep staff informed about company policy, to stop gossip and it generates a sense of belonging. (**Right**: . . . to generate a sense of belonging)

5. Be careful when using bullet points; these, too, should be consistent. The following list goes astray quite quickly. Can you see where? How would you correct this?

    Before a meeting the secretary has to:
    - send out the notice and agenda
    - draft the chairperson's agenda
    - ~~prepare~~ agenda papers ~~may also have to be prepared~~
    - ~~has to~~ arrange the meeting room
    - name cards, refreshment, etc.

6. Lists of questions can be really troublesome, and you would be well advised to avoid them altogether in exams. For example, notice how the following sentence disintegrates into a mix of direct and indirect questions as it goes along.

    You should find out what size your audience is, what type is it? how long do you have to speak for? and where is the venue.

    The only way to rescue this sentence is to make everything indirect.

    You should find out what size your audience is, what type it is, how long you have to speak for and where the venue is.

PRACTICE 3

Rewrite these sentences so that all parts are consistent.
1. When he telephoned the personnel officer *he* it was answered by the secretary.
2. We have ~~not~~ *neither* succeeded nor failed.
3. No sooner had we started out ~~when~~ *than* it began to rain.
4. The Gardaí were not only concerned with recovering the stolen property but *not only* with catching the persons responsible.
5. I ~~shall~~ *should* be most grateful if you would send me a copy of your most recent catalogue.
6. One should always read a contract carefully before ~~you~~ sign it.
7. Although traffic is dense in this area, it only occurs at peak periods.
8. Walking home yesterday a car, going very quick, passed me, nearly knocking me down and which didn't stop.

'DANGLING' PHRASES AND CLAUSES

'Dangling' or unattached phrases and clauses should be avoided. If they are left 'dangling' the result can sometimes be unintentionally funny.

> The farmer bought the cow wearing a cap and wellies.

> The queue stretched down Grafton Street which was getting longer every minute.

> Entering the stadium, the pitch was in perfect condition.

How would you change these sentences to remove the ambiguity?

PRACTICE 4

Here are some more.
It was a summer
1. Being summer, I spent most of my time at the seaside.
2. Reaching the end of the journey, a warm fire greeted the travellers.
3. Pulling out the drawer its contents fell to the floor.
4. It was decided that, being Christmas, the offices should close until Monday.
5. The chair should be carefully adjusted when typing.
6. Wanted: car seat harness for child with quick-release button.

THE RULE OF PROXIMITY

As a general rule, adverbs and adjectives should be placed as close as possible to the words they modify. Be particularly careful with the words *only, just, not, nearly* and *even*.

Can you see the difference in meaning between the following pairs?

> *Only we* sell this product at a discount.
> We sell *only this* product at a discount.

> The company made *nearly all* its workers redundant.
> The company *nearly made* all its workers redundant.

MORE RULES ABOUT ADJECTIVES AND ADVERBS

1. Adverbs and adjectives should not be confused.

    You seem to write very slowly. (**not** very slow)

2. Use the comparative when comparing two, the superlative when comparing more than two.

    I cannot decide which of the two is better.

Of the two speakers, I thought the second argued more persuasively.
She is the tallest of the four girls.

3. Do not double comparatives and superlatives.

I have never felt happier.
Not I have never felt more happier.

. . . AND FINALLY, SOME TRADITIONAL RULES

1. It is now acceptable to split an infinitive if the meaning demands it. For example, compare:

He completely failed to understand my point.
and He failed to completely understand my point.

2. 'End' or 'postponed' prepositions are also acceptable when it would be too awkward to avoid them. For example, 'Where are you going to?' sounds far more natural than 'To where are you going?'

PRACTICE 5

Correct the following sentences.
1. You could arrange your work neater if you tried.
2. He is by far the taller in the group.
3. She chose the cheapest of the two dresses.
4. Run quick and catch him before he leaves.
5. We are now a more richer society than twenty years ago.

ANSWERS

PRACTICE 1

Complete sentences are marked in bold.
1. **Night fell.**
2. **Be careful!**
3. Getting nowhere fast.
4. Thanking you in anticipation.
5. A quick fix.
6. **Could you do me a favour?**
7. All in a day's work.
8. **He said he would come on Tuesday.**
9. It being a bank holiday.
10. **Let's see what's happening.**

PRACTICE 2

1. This book is one of the best that *have* been published this year.
2. When the committee was asked for its opinion, it decided to defer the matter until *its* next meeting.
3. Everyone should accept *his* or *her* responsibility for the dispute.
4. Neither of the rooms *was* completely comfortable.
5. I think none of these colours *is* suitable.
6. This is one of the plays which *were* recommended by the critics.
7. The 'Mona Lisa', with other paintings from the Louvre, *was* sent on loan to the United States.
8. There *were* only twenty people at the exhibition.
9. Everyone in the college must give *his* or *her* assistance.
10. Many applications *were* received for the course.
11. The value of the books and letters *is* considerable.
12. Neither the referee nor the umpire *was* aware of what was going on.

PRACTICE 3

1. When *he* telephoned the personnel officer *he* was answered by the secretary.
2. We have *neither* succeeded *nor* failed.
3. *No sooner* had we started out *than* it began to rain.
4. The Gardaí were concerned *not only with recovering* the stolen property but *with catching* the persons responsible.
5. I *should* be most grateful if you *would* send me a copy of your most recent catalogue.
6. *One* should always read a contract carefully before *one signs* it.
7. Although traffic is dense in this area, heavy traffic occurs only at peak periods.
8. As I was walking home yesterday, a car, which was going very quickly, passed me and nearly knocked me down. The car didn't stop.

PRACTICE 4

1. As it was summer, I spent most of my time at the seaside.
2. A warm fire greeted the travellers when they reached the end of the journey.
3. As I was pulling out the drawer its contents fell to the floor.
4. It was decided that, as it was Christmas, the offices should close until Monday.
5. The chair should be carefully adjusted when you are typing.
6. Wanted: child's car seat harness with quick-release button.

Practice 5

1. You could arrange your work *more neatly* if you tried.
2. He is by far the *tallest* in the group.
3. She chose the *cheaper* of the two dresses.
4. Run *quickly* and catch him before he leaves.
5. We are now a *more rich* (or *richer*) society than twenty years ago.

Appendix III: Reported Speech

Reported speech is used in many forms of business writing (minutes, reports and summaries in particular). It occurs when you report what someone has said without using their exact words.

The rules for changing from direct to reported speech are relatively simple.

1. You begin with an introductory phrase such as:
   - The chairperson ruled that . . .
   - She said that . . .
   - He maintained that . . .
2. Speech marks and question marks are left out.
3. First and second person pronouns are changed to third person.

   I, me, mine you, yours, we, us, ours

   become

   he, she, him, her, his, hers, they, them, theirs

The repetition of third person pronouns may cause ambiguity, so it is sometimes necessary to name the person intended. For example:

He said that he (Mr Smith) would be the best person to contact.

4. Verb tenses change as follows.

I am writing	**becomes**	He said he was writing
I have written		She said she had written
I was writing		He said he had been writing
I wrote		She said she had written
I shall write		He said he would write
I shall have written		She said she would have written

5. Words denoting time and space become more distant.

now	**becomes**	then
here		there
this		that
today	**becomes**	that day
yesterday		the previous day
tomorrow		the following day

So, for example, the following passage of direct speech:

> 'I think we should make a decision now about the contract and not leave it until tomorrow.'
> **becomes**
> He said he thought they should make a decision *then* about the contract and not leave it until *the following day*.

6. A wide range of verbs can be used to replace 'said' depending on the nature and tone of the direct speech. For example:

agreed	maintained
insisted	urged
suggested	proposed
asserted	argued
replied	advised

Appendix IV:
Useful Internet Addresses

Advertising Standards Authority for Ireland
www.asai.ie

Association of Advertisers in Ireland
www.aai.ie

BUBL Link (academic subjects directory)
www.bubl.ac.uk

Central Bank of Ireland
www.centralbank.ie

Central Statistics Office
www.cso.ie

Department of Enterprise, Trade and Employment
www.entemp.ie

Economic and Soical Research Institute
www.esri.ie

The Economist
www.economist.com

Enterprise Ireland
www.enterprise-ireland.com

European Commission in Ireland
www.euireland.ie

FACTfinder (Irish business database)
www.factfinder.ie

Finfacts (gateway to Irish business information)
www.finfacts.ie

Forás (national advisory board for enterprise)
www.foras.ie

Government of Ireland (Rialtas na hEireann)
www.irlgov.ie

Higher Education Authority
www.hea.ie

HEAnet (higher education research network)
www.heanet.ie

Information Society Commission
www.isc.ie

Industrial Development Authority
www.idaireland.ie

Institute of Advertising Practicioners in Ireland
www.iapi.ie

Institute of Public Relations
www.ipr.org.uk

International Monetary Fund
www.imf.org

The Marketing Institute
www.mii.ie

OECD
www.oecd.org

National Development Plan
www.ndp.ie

Public Relations Institute of Ireland
www.prii.ie

RDN (academic subjects directory)
www.rdn.ac.uk

Small Firms Association
www.sfa.ie

SOSIG (gateway to social sciences and business)
www.sosig.ac.uk

Tourism Ireland
www.tourismireland.ie

University of Maryland (research skills tutorials)
www.umuc.edu/library

The World Bank
www.worldbank.org

World Trade Organization
www.wtc.org

Bibliography

Anderson, N. and V. Shackleton, *Successful Selection Interviewing*, Oxford: Blackwell Publishers 1993.

Barclay, J. M., 'Improving selection interviews with structure: organisations' use of "behavioural" interviews', *Personnel Review*, XXX/1 (2001).

Barrass, R., *Writing at Work: a guide to better writing in administration, business and management*, 2002.

Barrett, D. J., 'Change communication: using strategic employee communication to facilitate major change', *Corporate Communications*, VII/4 (2002), 219–231.

Belbin, R. M., *Team Roles at Work*, Oxford: Butterworth-Honeymoon 1993.

Bentley, T., *Report Writing in Business: the effective communication of information*, 2nd ed., London: Kogan Page 2002.

Corfield, R., *Successful Interview Skills: how to present yourself with confidence*, 3rd ed., London: Kogan Page 2002.

Cram, Carol M., *E-Commerce Concepts*, Boston, MA: Thompson Learning 2001.

Daly, J. and I. Engleberg, *Presentations in Everyday Life: strategies for effective speaking*, Boston: Houghton Mifflin Company 2001.

Fiske, J., *Introduction to Communication Studies*, 2nd ed., London: Routledge 1990.

Forfás, *Report on e-Commerce: the policy requirements*, Dublin: Forfás 2000.

Hargie, O. *et al.*, *Communication in Management*, Aldershot: Gower 1999.

Hargie, O., *The Handbook of Communication Skills*, 2nd ed., London: Routledge 1997.

Harkin, J., *Mobilisation: The growing public interest in mobile technology* (Internet) London: Demos 2003. Available from: www.demos.co.uk.html (accessed 20 June 2003).

Hartley, M., *Body Language at Work*, London: Sheldon 2003.

Information Society Commission, *Information Society Commission Business and General Public Survey* (Internet) Dublin 2003. Available from: www.isc.ie/about/reports.html (accessed 1 July 2003).

Information Society Commission, *Building the Knowledge Society* (Internet) Dublin 2002. Available from: www.isc.ie/about/reports.html (accessed 1 July 2003).

Kreps, G., *Organizational Communication*, New York: Longman 1990.

Lewis, R. G., *The Small Business Guide to the Internet*, Dublin: Oak Tree Press 1999.

McCormack, M., *McCormack on Communicating*, London: Century 1996.

McQuail, D. and S. Windahl, *Communication Models*, Harlow: Longman 1993.

Morris, D., *Peoplewatching*, London: Vintage 2002.

Morris, S., *Perfect E-mail: all you need to get it right first time,* London: Random House Business Books 2000.

Norris, M. and S. West, *eBusiness Essentials,* 2nd ed., Chichester: John Wiley & Sons Ltd 2001.

O'Connor, C., *The View from the Chair*, Ballivor: Zircon Publishing 1994.

Perreault, W. D. *et al., Basic Marketing*, Maidenhead: McGraw-Hill 2000.

The Economist, The Economist Style Guide, 6th ed., London: Profile Books 2000.

Weatherall, A., *Gender, Language and Discourse*, Hove: Routledge 2002.

Trauner, M. *et al., Videoconferencing Cookbook* (Internet) 2002. Available at www.videnet.gatech.edu (accessed 5 July 2003).

INDEX

ADSL (asymmetric digital subscriber line), 61

advertisements for jobs, 313–14

advertising, 39–47
    analysis of advertisement, 40–3
    ethics of, 45–6
    role of agency, 43–5

Aer Rianta, case study, 33–4

agenda for meetings, 280–2

analogue system, 61

annual general meetings, 276

answering machines, 209

apostrophes, 330–1

appearance and dress, 195–6, 224

application forms, 318–19

attribution, 15

audio-visual equipment, 245–52
    flipcharts, 247–8
    multimedia projection, 250–2
    overhead projectors, 248–9
    videos, 249–50
    whiteboards, 246–7

aural communication *see* oral/aural communication

Bank of Ireland, case study, 100–1

bar charts, 243–4

barriers to communication, 10–15
    in organisations, 27–8

bibliographic databases, 82–3

Bluetooth, 62

body language *see* nonverbal communication

books, reference, 77–8

Bose (Ireland), 31

brackets, 333

briefings, 31–2

broadband services, 61

browsers, 56

bulletins, 30–1, 170–2

business correspondence *see* letters

business report *see* reports

capital letters, 327–8

chairperson, role of, 285–9

channels of communication, 8
    in organisations, 21–4

charts, 242–5

circulars *see* memoranda

colons and semicolons, 331–2

commas, 328–30
    inverted, 335

committees, 276–7

communication process, 3–17
    barriers to, 10–15
    context, 9
    decoding message, 8–9
    encoding message, 4–6
    feedback, 9
    intention, 3–4
    medium/channel, 6–8
    noise, 9–10
    principles of, 15–17

community relations, 49

company publications, 32, 33–4

conference management, 284

consumer relations, 49

conversation, 3–4, 188, 201–6

corporate marketing, 57

corporate videos, 35

correspondence *see* letters

cultural diversity, 267–71

curriculum vitae (CV), 314–16

dashes, in punctuation, 332–3

databases, 82–3

decoding, 8–9

diagonal communication, 24

digital system, 61

directories
    in print, 77
    websites, 80–1

downward communication, 22–3
dress and appearance, 195–6, 224

e-commerce, 55–6
e-journals, 81–2
electronic communication, 6, 7, 53–67
    benefits of, 65
    e-commerce, 55–6
    e-mail, 59–60, 172–4
    Internet, 53–4, 62
    in organisations, 29–30
    telephone, 60–3
    teleworking, 65–6
    video conferencing, 63–5
    websites, 56–9, 79–83
e-mail, 59–60
    style and etiquette, 172–4
embargo, 179
employment interviews, 302–25
    accuracy of, 303
    case study, 321–3
    conducting, 306–11
        closing, 311
        environment, 307
        establishing rapport, 307–8
        listening and recording, 310
        managing, 310–11
        preparation, 307
        questioning, 308–10
    facing interview, 319–21
    reasons for, 302–3
    types of, 304–6
encoding, 4–6, 11
ethnicity and communication, 267–71
exclamation marks, 335
extraordinary general meetings, 276
eyes, nonverbal communication, 191, 229

face, concept of, 269
face-to-face communication, 204–6
facial expression, 190
fashion, 196
feedback, 9, 188, 203, 265
flipcharts, 247–8
flow charts, 244

fonts, 98–9
formatting, 98, 160
full stops, 327

gatekeeping, 27
gateways, 80–1
gender issues, 265–7
general meetings, 276
gestures, 189–90
grammar, 340–7
grapevine, 25–6
graphs, 242–3
groups, 256–60
    conformity and groupthink, 259–60
    development stages, 257–9
    structure of, 256–7

health and safety report, 148–50
house magazines, 32, 33–4
hyphens, 334

IDA Ireland, case study, 230–1
induction manuals, 32–3
information see research
information technology see electronic
    communication
Intel Ireland, case study, 270
Internet, 53–4
    gateways and directories, 80–1
    mobile phones, 62
    research using, 79–83
    search engines, 79–80
interviews see employment interviews
intranet, 29–30
intrapersonal communication, 3
ISDN (integrated services digital network),
    61

jargon, 11, 109
job application, 312–19
    advertisements, 313–14
    application forms, 318–19
    covering letters, 316–18
    curriculum vitae (CV), 314–16
    information on vacancies, 312–13

journals
    e-journals, 81–2
    in print, 78–9
Jurys Doyle Hotel Group, case study, 284

kinesics, 189–91
KPMG, case study, 321–3

language *see* oral/aural communication
lateral communication, 24
letters, 120–39
    elements of, 121–4
    formats, 125–6
    guidelines for writing, 137–9
    internal communication, 30
    types of, 126–37
        collection, 134–6
        complaint and adjustment, 132–4
        enquiries, 126–8
        goodwill, 136–7
        job applications, 316–18
        orders, 132
        quotations and estimates, 131
        replies, 128–30
libraries, 75–9
line graphs, 242–3
listening skills, 12, 211–13

management style and communication,
    27–8
maps, 244–5
marketing communication, 39–50
    advertising, 39–47
    public relations, 47–50
    sales letters, 174–7
    websites, 57
mass media, 7, 49–50
m-commerce, 62
media of communication
    in organisations, 29–35
    types of, 6–8
media relations, 49–50
meetings, 275–97
    conducting, 285–9
    internal communication, 31–2, 277–8

minutes, 289–93
preparing for, 278–84
    agenda, 280–2
    attendance, 279
    environment, 282–3
    notice of, 280
purpose of, 277–8
secretary's role, 283, 289
taking part in, 293–7
types of, 276–7
memoranda, 30, 163–70
    content, 164–8
    elements of, 163–4
    layout, 168–9
    style, 169–70
mind maps, 92–3
minutes of meetings, 289–93
    structure, 290–1
    taking notes, 289–90
    types of, 292–3
mobile telephones, 61–3
multimedia projection, 250–2

noise concept, 9–10
nonverbal communication, 186–97
    conflict with verbal signals, 11–12
    cross-cultural, 269
    functions of, 187–9
    kinesics, 189–91
    physical appearance, 195–6
    physical contact, 194–5
    practical tips, 197
    proxemics, 192–4
    when giving talks, 229–30
note-taking, 213–14, 289–90
notices, 30–1, 170–2

online shopping, 55–6
oral/aural communication, 201–14
    cross-cultural, 267–70
    face-to-face, 204–6
    gender issues, 265–7
    listening skills, 211–13
    note-taking, 213–14
    speech, characteristics of, 201–4

telephone, 206–10
oral media, 7
order forms, 132
organisation charts, 244
organisations, communication in, 21–35
    barriers, 27–8
    charter for, 28
    formal/informal, 24–6
    internal channels, 21–4
    internal media, 29–35
orientation, 193–4
overhead projectors, 248–9

paralanguage, 202–3
pay packet inserts, 30
PDAs (personal digital assistants), 62
perception, 12–13
personal space, 192–3
persuasion, 226–7
physical contact, 194–5
pictograms, 244
pie charts, 242
plagiarism, 86
posture, 191
PowerPoint, 250–2
prejudice, 14–15
presentation of documents, 97–9, 159–60
presentations *see* talks and presentations
press releases, 177–80
principles of communication, 15–17
proxemics, 192–4
public meetings, 276
public relations, 47–50
publications, company, 32, 33–4
punctuation, 327–39

Quelle, 55–6
question marks, 334
questions, types of, 308–9
quotations and estimates, 131

recruitment methods, 312–13
reference books, 77–8
reports, 142–60
    format and types of, 142–4

objectives, 144–5, 154
preparation, 153–8
presentation, 159–60
research analysis, 155–8
stages in report writing, 153
structure of, 145–52
writing and revising, 158–9
research, 72–87
    evaluating information, 83–4
    organising and using, 84–7
    planning, 73–6
    resources in print, 76–9
    using the Internet, 79–83
roles in teams, 263–4
Runway magazine, 33–4

sales letters, 174–7
search engines, 79–80
secretary, role of in meetings, 283, 289
    minute-taking, 289–93
self-image, 14
Shannon and Weaver model, 9–10
slang, 11
speech, characteristics of, 201–4
speeches *see* talks and presentations
staff induction manuals, 32–3
staff reports, 32
stage fright, 227–8
stereotyping, 14
style of writing, 105–14, 138, 159
    concise, 111–12
    direct and persuasive, 106–8
    importance of, 105–6
    'loose' writing, 112–14
    plain, 108–10
    sales letters, 175–7
suggestion schemes, 34
Superquinn, case study, 210–11

tables, 241
talks and presentations, 218–33
    dealing with questions, 232–3
    delivery, 227–31
        body language, 230
        eye contact, 229

talks and presentations, *continued*
  humour, 230
  overcoming stage fright, 227–8
  voice, 228–9
  preparation, 219–24
    defining objectives, 219–20
    identifying audience, 219
    rehearsing, 223–4
    research, 221
    scripts and notes, 222–3
    venue and timing, 220
  structure of, 224–7
  see also visual communication aids
tall organisation structure, 28
teams, 260–71
  communication in, 264–5
  gender issues, 265–7
  intercultural diversity, 267–71
  roles, 263–4
  types of, 261–3
teamworking, case studies, 31, 151–2
telemarketing, 60–1
telephones, 60–3
  communication using, 206–10
  landline, 60–1
  mobile, 61–3
  services, 60–1, 206
    high-speed, 61
  voice mail, 209
teleworking, 65–6
territoriality, 193
text messaging, 61, 63
Tourism Ireland, case study, 46–7

upward communication, 23

video conferencing, 63–5
videos, 249–50
  corporate, 35
visual communication aids, 236–52
  audio-visual equipment, 245–52
  tables, graphs and charts, 240–5
  visual aids, 236–40
    choosing, 238–9
    designing visuals, 239–40
visual media, 7
voice mail, 209

WAP (wireless application protocol), 62
websites, 56–9
  design, 57–9
  research, 79–83
whiteboards, 246–7
women and gender issues, 265–7
writing process, 90–101, 326
  background and objectives, 90–2
  presentation, 97–9
  research, 94–5
  revision, 97
  structure, 95–6
  writing, 96–7
  writing plan, 92–5
  see also style of writing
written communication forms
  letters, 120–39
  memoranda, 30, 163–70
  notices, 30–1, 170–2
  press releases, 177–80
  reports, 142–60
  sales letters, 174–7